Juvenile Justice Systems

An International Comparison of Problems and Solutions

JUVENILE JUSTICE SYSTEMS

An International Comparison of Problems and Solutions

Editors:

Nicholas M.C. Bala, *Queen's University*
Joseph P. Hornick, *Canadian Research Institute for Law and the Family*
Howard N. Snyder, *National Center for Juvenile Justice*
Joanne J. Paetsch, *Canadian Research Institute for Law and the Family*

THOMPSON EDUCATIONAL PUBLISHING, INC.
Toronto

Copyright (c) 2002 Thompson Educational Publishing, Inc.

All rights reserved. No part of this publication may be reproduced or transmitted in any form or by any means, electronic or mechanical, including photocopy, recording, or any information storage and retrieval system, without permission in writing from the publisher.

Requests for permission to make copies of any part of the work should be directed to the publisher or, in the case of material reproduced here from elsewhere, to the original copyright holder.

Information on how to obtain copies of this book may be obtained from:

Website: www.thompsonbooks.com
E-mail: publisher@thompsonbooks.com
Telephone: (416) 766-2763
Fax: (416) 766-0398

National Library of Canada Cataloguing in Publication Data

Main entry under title:

   Juvenile justice systems : an international comparison of problems and solutions

Includes bibliographical references.

ISBN 1-55077-127-2

     1. Juvenile justice, Administration of. 2. Criminal justice, Administration of. 3. Juvenile delinquency. I. Bala, Nicholas, 1952-

HV9069.J796 2002   364.36   C2002-900487-X

Interior Design: Danielle Baum
Cover Design: Elan Designs

Every reasonable effort has been made to acquire permission for copyrighted materials used in this book and to acknowledge such permissions accurately. Any errors or omissions called to the publisher's attention will be corrected in future printings.

We acknowledge the support of the Government of Canada through the Book Publishing Industry Development Program for our publishing activities.

Printed in Canada.

1 2 3 4 5   06 05 04 03 02

Table of Contents

List of Contributors   vi
Foreword   vii

1. Introduction: An International Perspective on Youth Justice   1
   Nicholas Bala and Rebecca Jaremko Bromwich

2. Juvenile Crime and Justice in Canada   19
   Lorne D. Bertrand, Joanne J. Paetsch, and Nicholas Bala

3. Juvenile Crime and Justice in the United States of America   43
   Howard N. Snyder

4. Juvenile Crime and Justice in England and Wales   67
   John Graham

5. Juvenile Crime and Justice in Scotland   107
   Maureen Buist and Stewart Asquith

6. Juvenile Crime and Justice in Northern Ireland   135
   David O'Mahony

7. Juvenile Crime and Justice in Ireland   153
   Kieran O'Dwyer

8. Juvenile Crime and Justice in New Zealand   189
   Gabrielle Maxwell and Allison Morris

9. Juvenile Crime and Justice in Australia   221
   Ian O'Connor, Kathleen Daly, and Lyn Hinds

10. Conclusion: Trends in Juvenile Justice   255
    Nicholas Bala, Joseph P. Hornick, and Howard N. Snyder

List of Contributors

Stewart Asquith is Head of the Department of Social Policy and Social Work at University of Glasgow, Scotland.

Nicholas Bala is a Professor of Law at Queen's University in Kingston, Ontario, Canada, who concentrates his research in the area of family and children's law.

Lorne D. Bertrand is the Senior Research Associate with the Canadian Research Institute for Law and the Family, Alberta, Canada.

Rebecca Jaremko Bromwich is an LL.M. Candidate at Queen's University in Kingston, Ontario, Canada.

Maureen Buist is formerly a research fellow with a number of Scottish Universities and is currently working for the newly established Criminal Justice Social Work Development Centre for Scotland at the University of Edinburgh.

Kathleen Daly is with the School of Criminology and Criminal Justice, Griffith University, Brisbane, Queensland, and is also an Associate of the Australian Institute of Criminology, Canberra, Australia.

John Graham is Deputy Director of the Strategic Policy Unit, Home Office, London, England.

Lyn Hinds is with the School of Criminology and Criminal Justice, Griffith University, Brisbane, Queensland, Australia.

Joesph P. Hornick is Executive Director of the Canadian Research Institute for Law and the Family, Alberta, Canada.

Gabrielle Maxwell is the Acting Director of the Crime and Justice Research Centre, Victoria University of Wellington, New Zealand.

Allison Morris is a consultant to the Crime and Justice Research Centre, Victoria University of Wellington, New Zealand.

Ian O'Connor is with the School of Social Work and Policy, University of Queensland, and is an Associate of the Australian Institute of Criminology, Canberra, Australia.

Kieran O'Dwyer is Head of Research, Garda Research Unit, Garda Síochána, Ireland.

David O'Mahony is a Lecturer in Youth Justice, Institute of Criminology and Criminal Justice, School of Law, Queen's University Belfast, Northern Ireland.

Joanne J. Paetsch is the Administrator/Research Associate with the Canadian Research Institute for Law and the Family, Alberta, Canada.

Howard N. Snyder is the Director of Systems Research for the National Center for Juvenile Justice in Pittsburgh, Pennsylvania, USA.

Foreword

Few topics receive more public and media attention in the world's English speaking countries than youth crime and violence. In many countries, there is much commentary and controversy about appropriate legal responses to youth crime. Many argue that there is a need for a "get tough" approach to youth crime, and that a more punitive response is needed to protect society and hold adolescent offenders accountable. Others contend that the younger the offender is, the more lenient and rehabilitative the approach should be.

This volume, *Juvenile Justice Systems: An International Comparison of Problems and Solutions*, is designed to inform debates about the juvenile justice systems in industrialized countries. It presents detailed information on the common themes, problems, strengths, and weaknesses of juvenile justice systems of eight different jurisdictions with the intent of informing the reader about a wide range of responses to youth offending.

This volume is the final product of a number of research activities over several years, made possible by the generous funding of the Donner Canadian Foundation. First, site visits were made to each country, which permitted direct observation of the workings of the various systems, and facilitated the identification of local experts to write the chapters. Next, a common chapter outline was developed and draft chapters were prepared in each jurisdiction. Then, in May 1998, the contributors of the chapters and the editors of this volume met with Canadian policy makers and practitioners who deal with youth offending, at a conference held in Ottawa, Ontario, Canada. Trends, issues, and innovations were discussed. Some of the discussions are reflected in the Introduction and Conclusion of this volume. Finally, the chapters were updated and revised, and appear in this volume.

The editors of this volume and the Canadian Research Institute for Law and the Family would like to acknowledge the generous support of the Donner Canadian Foundation for making this unique project possible, as well as the Department of Justice Canada for co-funding the conference. In addition, we would like to thank Bill Whyte, Director of the Criminal Justice Social Work Development Centre for Scotland, who provided up-to-date information on the review of the Scottish system, and Inspector Chris Graveson, National Co-ordinator of Youth Aid for the New Zealand Police, who provided valuable information on the New Zealand system. Finally, we would like to acknowledge the tireless effort of Ms Linda Bland who produced numerous drafts of this volume. The Canadian Research Institute for Law and the Family is support by a grant from the Alberta Law Foundation.

CHAPTER 1

Introduction: An International Perspective on Youth Justice

Nicholas Bala and Rebecca Jaremko Bromwich

Every legal system recognizes that children and adolescents are different from adults and should not be held accountable for their violations of the criminal law in the same fashion as adults. There are, however, very substantial differences in how different countries give effect to this basic principle and, indeed, in how they legally define such fundamental concepts as "child," "youth," and "adult."

An important and revealing measure of a society is its response to those who are at its margins. Adolescents in conflict with the law are often seen as marginal. They are often excluded from the economic, social, cultural, and racial mainstreams of their societies, in addition to being alienated by virtue of their developmental stage. Understanding how a society responds to young persons who violate its criminal law provides important insights into that society as a whole.

This book offers a comparative study of how the world's major, predominantly English-speaking jurisdictions respond to juveniles who have violated the law. The comparative study of the treatment of young offenders should be of interest to all those who seek to better understand social dynamics and the place of adolescents in their societies, as well as of value to those who want to be better understand how their own society can improve its juvenile justice system.

Nicholas Bala is a Professor of Law at Queen's University in Kingston, Ontario, who concentrates his research in the area of Family and Childrens Law.

Rebecca Jaremko Bromwich is an LL.M. Candidate at Queen's University in Kingston, Ontario, Canada.

The Legal Recognition of Childhood and Adolescence

When children are born, they have very limited physical and social capacity and no capacity to make decisions or control their actions. Although newborn infants have some legal rights (for example, to inherit property) and are entitled to the protection of the law, their legal rights can be exercised only through a legal guardian or other adult. As they mature, children gradually gain in physical strength, intellectual judgment, and social capacity. They slowly develop the ability to make decisions and form moral judgments, and they gradually begin to exercise legal rights and assume legal obligations on their own. When adulthood is reached (in most countries, between the ages of 18 and 21 years), a person is afforded a full range of legal rights and obligations.

By the beginning of adolescence, between the ages of 10 and 13, youths display a growing sexual, social, and moral awareness, as well as increasing physical size and strength, though most continue to mature intellectually, psychologically, physically, and socially until adulthood. While physical growth ends for many adolescents around the age of 15, there is growing evidence that neurological and social development continues into the years of late adolescence, from 16 to 18 years of age, and even into early adulthood. Childhood, which can be defined as the period between birth and the beginning of adolescence, is the formative stage of life, but also a stage of limited capacity, including only a limited capacity to harm others. By adolescence, a youth has at least the potential to cause serious harm to others.

Adolescence is a time of great change and development for most youth, as parents, teachers, and adolescents themselves well know. Sometimes adolescents seem quite childish, but at other times they act like adults, or at least want to be treated as such. Adolescence is a period of growing self-awareness and increasing autonomy, as well as a time to challenge authority figures and test limits. While adolescents have a growing knowledge of the world around them, they often lack judgment and maturity. Frequently, they feel as though they are "invulnerable" and act in an impulsive and irresponsible fashion. Adolescents tend to be more impulsive and concerned about immediate consequences rather than with their long-term well being, and are more susceptible to peer pressure than adults. In far greater numbers than adults, adolescents engage in high-risk activities such as unsafe sex, driving while under the influence of alcohol, and substance abuse.

Adolescence is often characterized by feelings of alienation from parents, teachers, and society as a whole, with a greater willingness to test social norms and conventions as well as to engage in offending behaviour. Adolescence is also a time of life when, for some individuals, feelings of alienation and depression may peak; it is a time when there is a high risk of suicide and self-destructive behaviour. There are substantial differences between countries in types and levels of youth crime and deviant behaviour, but in all modern societies, the rates of delinquent and antisocial behaviour peak somewhere between the ages of 15 and 21, in late adolescence or early adulthood, reflecting the immaturity and lack of judgment of this period of life as well as its energy and search for excitement.

While there is significant variation between countries in terms of legal regimes, in every society there is the recognition of a stage of life when there is no criminal law accountability for wrongful acts — a legal recognition of childhood. And in every country the law recognizes adolescence in some fashion, holding young persons accountable under criminal law, but not to the same extent or in the same manner as adults. While terminology and approaches vary, this recognition of adolescence creates what is referred to as "youth," "children's" or "juvenile" justice systems.

The Value of Comparative Analysis

This book explores the different responses to criminal behaviour on the part of children and adolescents in Australia, Canada, the United Kingdom (with separate treatment of England & Wales, Northern Ireland, and Scotland), Ireland, New Zealand, and the United States.

The nature of the special legal treatment afforded to children and youth has not been constant. In each of these countries, the approaches to youth crime are in flux and there is controversy, often intense, about juvenile justice issues. There is, however, widespread appreciation that children and adolescents have special needs and limited capacities, and hence require distinctive, or at least separate, treatment from adults.

By studying the experiences in different countries, one can discern common problems and themes, as well as better understand the strengths and weaknesses of the approaches in each country. This comparative study of approaches to juvenile justice provides a set of case studies that explore the relationship between political, social, and economic context and legal responses to youth crime. Comparative study can help policy makers and professionals consider a wide range of possible responses to youth offending and help them determine which strategies work most effectively in different contexts. The dissemination of innovation has long been an important feature of juvenile justice. The first juvenile justice regime separate from the adult system was established in the United States at the end of the nineteenth century; this model was highly influential in other countries, which soon after established their own juvenile justice systems — systems that all initially shared a distinctive welfare-oriented focus. More recently the development in New Zealand of "family group conferences," which seek to achieve objectives consistent with restorative justice, has been very influential in the development of diversion and restorative justice mechanisms in other countries.

Comparative study provides an opportunity for countries to continue to learn from each other's experiences. Ultimately, this type of comparative study should help each country to develop better approaches to dealing with the universal problem of youth crime.

At the same time, making international comparisons poses considerable challenges. As many researchers engaging in cross-cultural study have found, concepts do not always translate well across cultural borders. Despite sharing a language and a common legal heritage, the countries in this study have legal systems that differ significantly. While the legal systems of all countries in this study have to a large extent been influenced by the English Common Law, Scotland and Canada are also influenced considerably by the Civil Law system dominant in Continental Europe. Even where legal concepts are shared, differences between the social, economic, and political context of countries give rise to distinct legal cultures that are not always easy to compare. Comparison of terms used in describing juvenile justice provides an important example illustrating the problems in the translation of concepts between cultures.

Countries differ significantly in how they define children and youth. Different terms are often applied to individuals in the same age category. An obvious example of this is that in Canada and South Australia adolescents in conflict with the law are referred to as *young persons* or *youths*, while the term *juveniles* is used in Queensland and in the United States. In Scotland, the term *children* is used.

Conversely, the same terms may be used to refer to different things in different countries. An example of this is the age range of people dealt with by the juvenile justice systems of various countries. Illustratively, persons aged 7-15 inclusive in Scotland are dealt with by the juvenile justice system as *children*, while in South Australia, the juvenile justice system deals with *children* aged up to 18. In Canada, the term *child* is used to refer exclusively to those under the age of 12, who are immune from criminal prosecution.

Different terminology is only the tip of the iceberg of variation between the legal cultures of these countries. Another important dimension of variation in approach is reflected in the different types of statistics that are available for each jurisdiction.

In each country different social phenomena and characteristics are seen as worth counting. For example, in the chapter on Northern Ireland, O'Mahony describes his country as a divided society in which Catholics constitute a prominent religious minority who are marginalized in many respects, but there are no data on representation of Catholic and Protestant adolescents in the juvenile justice system. By way of contrast, in the United States, religion is not an important social variable in assessing juvenile crime, but race is considered an important factor for understanding the juvenile justice system and comprehensive data on visible minority representation in the juvenile system are available.

Differences in terminology, concepts and data mean that international comparisons must be approached carefully, with close attention paid to context.

Juvenile Justice: Evolution and Models

The historical development of the youth justice systems of the countries studied in this book over the past century reflects ideological shifts in the perceptions of the needs, rights, and capacities of children and adolescents.

Separate systems that deal with juvenile justice are a relatively recent phenomenon in human history. In European cultures, prior to the nineteenth century, there was little social or legal recognition of the special needs and particular capacities of children and youth. This is graphically demonstrated in any European museum by the posed portraits of upper-class children standing stiffly, dressed as little adults, and by the sad predicament of working-class children labouring in mines, in factories, and on farms.

Until the nineteenth century, the only recognition of childhood as a distinct period of life for criminal law purposes was the defence of *doli incapax* (Latin for incapacity to do wrong). In English Common Law, children under 7 years of age were immune from prosecution, while between the ages of 7 and 14, there was a presumption of incapacity, which, if not rebutted by the prosecution, meant that they could escape criminal sanction. However, there were no separate juvenile justice systems, and older children and adolescents were subjected to punishments such as hanging or imprisonment in penitentiaries with adults.

Towards the end of the nineteenth century, as part of a broader movement of social reforms that included the enactment of child labour laws and the establishment of the first child welfare agencies, the first reformatories and training schools were established to confine child and adolescent offenders separate from adult criminals. The first juvenile court was established in the United States by the State of Illinois in 1899. In the first few years of the twentieth century, all of the countries in this book enacted legislation to establish juvenile justice systems. Canada's *Juvenile Delinquents Act*, and the *Children Act* of England and Wales were both enacted in 1908.

These original juvenile justice regimes were characterized by an informal and private process and by a philosophy that emphasized the rehabilitation of youthful offenders. The philosophical premise of these regimes was the treatment of "delinquent" juveniles by probation officers and juvenile court judges in the way of a "wise but stern parent," with a focus on the long-term welfare of the child. This was an enormous improvement over treating young offenders in the same way as adults, though in practice, juveniles often faced harsh treatment in juvenile correctional facilities.

These early juvenile justice systems were established on what is now commonly referred to as a "welfare model" of juvenile justice, with the main focus of intervention, at least in theory, being the promotion of the welfare of the child (Corrado et al., 1992). Since the promotion of the child's welfare was the objective, the focus of intervention was to help "wayward youth" rather than to punish them for the offence. This welfare orientation was used to justify minimizing concerns about due process of law. There was also a broad definition of "delinquency" that permitted speedy intervention to "save" the child from a life of crime.

While the term *welfare model* is not used consistently in the juvenile justice literature, it is a helpful theoretical construct that captures the salient features of these early juvenile justice regimes, and can still be used to characterize the juvenile justice systems of countries such as Northern Ireland and Scotland.

The welfare model can be understood as one polarity on a theoretical continuum of possible models of regimes of juvenile justice, though in the real world, no justice system exists in one of the pure forms described by analytical models.

In a welfare model, the focus of juvenile justice is on the offender rather than the offence, and on the welfare of the youth rather than the punishment or accountability for an offence. Characteristics of a welfare model are informality and lack of due process, as well as indeterminate sentencing, since a youth should be kept in custody as long as necessary to effect rehabilitation. Another characteristic of juvenile justice systems operating on a welfare model is the high degree of discretion given to judges, probation officers, and juvenile correctional officials, so that they can do what they consider best for the individual juvenile with whom they are dealing.

The welfare model can be summed up nicely, as Buist and Asquith note with reference to Scotland's current Children's Hearing System, as focusing on the juvenile's "needs, not deeds." Where the focus is on the child's welfare, the lines between justice and child protection are easily blurred and there is only limited recognition of a child's legal rights.

Across national boundaries, the prime rationale for establishing a juvenile justice system separate from the adult system was the belief that youths are more vulnerable than adults as well as more amenable to rehabilitation. Long-term social protection was seen to be best achieved by concentrating resources on their rehabilitation and by protecting them from the glare of public accountability. At the very least, the establishment of separate juvenile justice systems was justified by concerns about the corruption or abuse of children and youth if they were placed in correctional facilities with adult offenders.

While the systems set up by these early welfare regimes were a very significant improvement over former treatment of youthful offenders, they were not without serious problems. By the latter part of the twentieth century, many of these regimes were coming under increasing criticism. A central concern was that focusing on the special needs and rehabilitation of youth did not necessarily translate into "more lenient" treatment.

Critics contended that the welfare model was predicated on "naive arrogance" (Zimring, 2001). A desire to promote rehabilitation formed the basis for a more intrusive approach or a longer period in a youth custody facility than an adult might receive for the same offence, even though the facility was separate from one that was used for adults and had programs with more emphasis on rehabilitation. The rationale for a longer sentence might have been that the youth needed the benefit of a longer period in a rehabilitative environment, or a longer period away from a corrupting living situation. Inconsistencies in the treatment of juveniles from different socioeconomic classes or racial heritages were criticized as a discriminatory consequence of the high level of discretion accorded judges and correctional officials.

As a "rights" culture developed in various countries, the welfare model of juvenile justice was criticized for its paternalism, violation of rights, and potential for discriminatory treatment. Informal proceedings in juvenile courts were highlighted as violative of the presumption of innocence and the right of an accused youth to counsel. The reality of the operation of juvenile courts was criticized as fundamentally divergent from their welfare rhetoric. In *Re Gault* (387 U.S. 1 at 27 [1967]), Justice Fortas of the United States Supreme Court wrote:

> Ultimately ... we confront the reality... of the juvenile court process.... The boy is committed to an institution where he may be restrained of liberty for years. It is of no constitutional consequence — and of limited practical meaning — that the institution to which he is committed is called an Industrial School ... however euphemistic the title.

Worse still, it is now clear that the privacy, discretion, and lack of rights characteristic of the early juvenile justice regimes created an environment with a high potential for exploitation and abuse of juveniles in custody facilities by staff or fellow inmates. It was only towards the end of the 20th century that adult survivors of institutional abuse started to come forward in large numbers to document the institutional abuse that they experienced as children, for example, in Ireland's "reformatories" and Canada's "training schools."[1] The greater emphasis on rights and greater awareness of issues of abuse makes it more difficult for institutional abuse to occur, though it remains a serious concern.

At the same time as these criticisms were being levied, public concern about youth crime was increasing in a number of countries. With this increase in concern about youth offending came a new public focus on public protection and a recognition that not all juvenile offenders are amenable to rehabilitation. There was a growing appreciation that the welfare model might not be well equipped to deal with "persistent offenders." There is not enough knowledge to effectively rehabilitate all youth offenders, or even to know with a high degree of certainty which offenders are likely to be recidivists.

These criticisms and a changing political climate resulted in legislators in a number of countries dramatically changing their juvenile justice regimes in the last years of the twentieth century. While Scotland and Northern Ireland continue to operate under welfare-oriented regimes, other countries radically revamped their juvenile justice regimes. Examples of these new laws include Canada's *Young Offenders Act*, which came into force in 1984, and New Zealand's 1989 *Children, Young Persons and Their Families Act*.

These new legal regimes, particularly those enacted in most of the United States, moved away from a welfare model towards what is referred to as a "justice model" of juvenile justice (Corrado et al., 1992). In a justice model, there is a recognition of the importance of legal rights and, for those convicted, a focus on punishment for specific criminal offences through determinate sentences.

While the newer legislative regimes mark a move away from the welfare model towards regimes that reflect a justice model, in all of the countries studied in this book there continues to be at least a rhetorical commitment to the importance of rehabilitation of juvenile offenders. Although these new regimes acknowledge the importance of legal rights and the need to protect society, the preservation of the rehabilitative ideal remains an important rationale for having a distinct youth justice system.

In most countries discussed in this book, the twentieth century saw two distinct periods in the administration of youth justice. In Canada and the United States, there were clear moves away from the welfare model in the 1980s towards the justice model, while other jurisdictions such as Scotland continue to operate juvenile justice systems that have a strong welfare orientation.

Legal Rights for Adolescents

In the past 50 years there has been a remarkable increase in the recognition of the importance of human and legal rights (Ignatieff, 2000; Abella, 1999). Women, employees, consumers, indigenous peoples, ethnic and racial minorities, the disabled, and others have increasingly demanded rights and have increasingly seen those rights recognized in the courts.

Beginning with the adoption by the United Nations of the Universal Declaration of Human Rights following the Second World War, a rights consciousness began to develop that transcended national boundaries. It included movements to end colonialism in Africa and Asia, and in the 1950s and 1960s, the civil rights movement to end discrimination against the African-American descendants of slaves in the United States. In the 1970s the women's movement began to demand that women have equal opportunity to participate in politics and employment.

Rights consciousness, and specifically the right to substantive equality, soon spread from women and minorities to other equality-seeking groups. Rights rhetoric spread into advocacy for young people, and into the legal realm of juvenile justice. In 1967, in *Re Gault*, the United States Supreme Court held that "due process" rights applied to adolescents in juvenile court proceedings, entitling them to state-provided legal counsel. This seminal declaration that children have due process rights gradually spread to become an international concern by the 1980s.

The countries studied in this book have in important respects become "rights-based societies," and there is greater recognition of the importance of legal rights in most juvenile justice systems than was the case in the past. An example of the link between rights consciousness and changes to juvenile justice is provided by Canada. The rights culture was both reinforced and reflected by the enactment of the *Canadian Charter of Rights and Freedoms* in 1982, the same year the *Young Offenders Act* was enacted, legislation that also recognized the rights of adolescents, for example, by ensuring that they could have access to legal representation. While there is significant variation between countries as to the level of protection for juveniles' due process rights, such as a right to counsel, in all of these countries consciousness of these rights has had some impact.

Although rights rhetoric is an important aspect of the discourse about juvenile justice systems, the concept of "rights" for children and youth remains contentious and in some respects confused. While one can assert that, for example, people of all races are inherently equal and entitled to equal treatment, youth are inherently different from adults. Children and adolescents lack the physical, social, and intellectual capacities of adults and are justifiably denied some of the rights afforded adults, such as the right to vote. In some countries in this study, such as Canada and the United States, there is an emphasis on affording adolescents in conflict with the law "due process" legal rights that are similar to those rights recognized for adults. In other countries there is much less emphasis on "legal rights" for adolescents, though there is still a recognition of the importance of the "social rights" of adolescents, the rights to a priority for the receipt of educational and rehabilitative services.

The different attitudes and approaches to rights for adolescents in the countries in this study marks an interesting dimension of contrast as there is quite a wide variation in approach. Readers may consider the advantages and disadvantages of the differing approaches.

Consciousness of children's rights culminated in the enactment of changes to domestic legislation in several countries and in the signing of comprehensive international agreements setting out standards for the treatment of children and adolescents by the end of the 1980s.

International Standards for Juvenile Justice

Internationally accepted norms and principles for juvenile justice have been gradually evolving over the past century and are now explicitly recognized in the United Nations *Convention on the Rights of the Child.*

It has long been accepted that the general rules of international customary law concerning torture, capital punishment, and humanitarian law apply to juveniles at least as much as to adults. The *Standard Minimum Rules for the Treatment of Prisoners* of 1955, which was itself an endorsement by the United Nations of an earlier League of Nations treaty signed in 1934, required the separation of "young prisoners" from adults in custodial facilities (UNICEF International Child Development Centre, 1998).

In the past two decades greater international attention has turned to specific protection of children's rights. In the 1980s, mounting concern for the rights of children resulted in several child-focused international treaties that set out standards for the treatment of young persons in conflict with the law. Some of these international treaties are declarations, guidelines, and rules that provide standards but offer no formal mechanisms to ensure that the standards that are aspired to are actually achieved. Important examples of these international standards for the treatment of juveniles are the 1985 *Standard Minimum Rules for the Administration of Juvenile Justice* (the Beijing Rules), and the 1990 *Riyadh Guidelines and United Nations Rules for the Protection of Juveniles.*

The *Convention on the Rights of the Child* (CRC) was adopted by the United Nations in 1989. It is the most important international treaty concerning the rights of children and youth, establishing standards for a range of legal, civil, political, economic, social, and cultural rights of children. UNICEF describes the CRC as establishing "non-negotiable minimum standards and obligations" for the treatment of children. The CRC deals with a broad range of issues, including juvenile justice, and establishes provisions for the monitoring of each signatory country's level of compliance.

By 1997, all of the members of the United Nations had ratified the CRC except the United States of America and Somalia. Opposition to the Convention in the United States comes from a number of sources, including those who fear that it might erode the rights of parents or place burdens on the government for the provision of services.

The central principle of the Convention requires that in "all actions concerning children, whether undertaken by public or private social welfare institutions, courts of law, administrative authorities or legislative bodies, the best interests of the child shall be a primary consideration" (Article 3). Article 37 has specific protections for all of those who are under 18 years of age and faced with "deprivation of liberty" and is of direct relevance to the juvenile justice process:

> Art. 37: States Parties shall ensure that:
>
> (a) No child shall be subjected to torture or other cruel, inhuman or degrading treatment or punishment. Neither capital punishment nor life imprisonment without possibility of release shall be imposed for offences committed by persons below eighteen years of age;

(b) No child shall be deprived of his or her liberty unlawfully or arbitrarily. The arrest, detention or imprisonment of a child shall be in conformity with the law and shall be used only as a measure of last resort and for the shortest appropriate period of time;

(c) Every child deprived of liberty shall be treated with humanity and respect for the inherent dignity of the human person and in a manner that takes into account the needs of persons of his or her age. In particular, every child deprived of liberty shall be separated from adults unless it is considered in the child's best interest not to do so and shall have the right to maintain contact with his or her family through correspondence and visits, save in exceptional circumstances;

(d) Every child deprived of his or her liberty shall have the right to prompt access to legal and other appropriate assistance, as well as the right to challenge the legality of the deprivation of his or her liberty before a court or other competent, independent and impartial authority and to a prompt decision on any such action.

Article 40 of the CRC explicitly articulates standards for juvenile justice, recognizing both due process rights for individual juveniles and the obligation of the state to provide a range of rehabilitative services:

Art 40 (1): States Parties recognize the right of every child ... accused of, or recognized as having infringed the penal law to be treated in a manner consistent with the promotion of the child's sense of dignity and worth, which reinforces the child's respect for the human rights and fundamental freedoms of others and which takes into account the child's age and the desirability of promoting the child's reintegration and the child's assuming a constructive role in society.

(2) To this end and having regard to the relevant provisions of international instruments, States Parties shall, in particular, ensure that ...

(b) Every child alleged as or accused of having infringed the penal law has at least the following guarantees:

(i) To be presumed innocent until proven guilty according to law;

(ii) To be informed promptly and directly of the charges against him or her, and, if appropriate, through his or her parents or legal guardians and to have legal or other appropriate assistance in the preparation and presentation of his or her defence;

(iii) To have the matter determined without delay by a competent, independent and impartial authority or judicial body in a fair hearing according to law, in the presence of legal or other appropriate assistance and, unless it is considered not to be in the best interest of the child, in particular, taking into account his or her age or situation, his or her parents or legal guardians;

(iv) Not to be compelled to give testimony or to confess guilt; to examine or have examined adverse witnesses and to obtain the participation and examination of witnesses on his or her behalf under conditions of equality;

(v) If considered to have infringed the penal law, to have this decision and any measures imposed in consequence thereof reviewed by a higher competent, independent and impartial authority or judicial body according to law;

(vi) To have the free assistance of an interpreter if the child cannot understand or speak the language used;

(vii) To have his or her privacy fully respected at all stages of the proceedings.

(3) States Parties shall seek to promote the establishment of laws, procedures, authorities and institutions specifically applicable to children alleged as, accused of, or recognized as having infringed the penal law, and, in particular:

(a) The establishment of a minimum age below which children shall be presumed not to have the capacity to infringe the penal law;

(b) Whenever appropriate and desirable, measures for dealing with such children, without resorting to judicial proceedings, providing that human rights and legal safeguards are fully respected.

(4) A variety of dispositions, such as care, guidance and supervision orders; counselling; probation; foster care; education and vocational training programmes and other alternatives to institutional care shall be available to ensure that children are dealt with in a manner appropriate to their well being and proportionate both to their circumstances and the offence.

The CRC provides for a process of monitoring of implementation in different countries, which is intended to allow for public scrutiny and pressure to ensure compliance. Each country is obliged to present a report to the UN Committee on the Rights of the Child every five years. The primary report for a country is made by the national government, though various nongovernmental advocacy and children's services groups are also involved in reporting. The UN Committee on the Rights of the Child issues a report that comments on the degree of each country's compliance for use by advocates for children and governments. The UN Committee can recommend that actions be taken, but it has no power to direct governments or agencies to act.

UNICEF reports that, despite the rhetoric in the international community about the importance of children's rights, the monitoring of the implementation of the Convention shows that "the rights, norms and principles involved are regularly ignored and seriously violated virtually throughout the world ... on a scale ... unmatched in the field of civil rights implementation" (UNICEF International Child Development Centre, 1998). A consideration of the limitations of the Convention and the constraints on implementation helps to explain the discrepancies between stated commitments to the recognition of the rights of children and their limited implementation in practice.

The nature of international treaties and the constitutional division of powers within nations create formidable obstacles to the implementation of international standards in the treatment of youth who come into conflict with the criminal law. The responsibility for entering into international treaties, such as the Convention, rests with national governments, but in many countries the national government has little or no responsibility for juvenile justice. For example, in Australia, juvenile justice is within the legislative jurisdiction of state governments while the federal government signed the CRC. Even in those countries where youth justice is within the legislative jurisdiction of the national government, the country's constitutional division of powers may pose problems for implementing that legislation. For example, in Canada, while it is the federal government that makes laws concerning youth justice, it is the provinces that implement and administer these laws. Where there are ideological or other conflicts between the different levels of government, attempts to implement the international standards articulated by the Convention may be frustrated.

Another obstacle to implementation of international standards reflects the consensual nature of the international treaty-making process, as countries are permitted to determine that they will not be bound by either the entire treaty or particular provisions of it. In particular, the United States has not ratified the CRC and is in no way bound by it. Further, several countries have filed reservations[2] to particular parts of the CRC, stipulating that they are not bound by some of its provisions. All of the countries in this study, with the exception of the Republic of Ireland, have elected not to be bound by Article 37(c) of the CRC, which requires that children who have committed offences are to be detained separately from adults.[3]

While the Convention provides for an international monitoring process, in most countries there are no mechanisms to allow children or adolescents, or advocates acting on their behalf, to directly assert the rights in the CRC through a legal process. However, the CRC is being cited by courts and policy makers as an important bench-mark against which to assess national policies and programs. In Canada, for example, the CRC is sometimes cited by courts as an aid to help in the interpretation of legislation.[4]

A couple of recent Australian and Canadian decisions demonstrate that at least in some situations advocates may be able to use the CRC to advance the position of those involved in court processes. Both of these decisions involved situations in which parents were facing deportation; the courts held that the failure of immigration authorities to even consider the effect that these decisions would have on the welfare of their children was wrong, citing the Convention as a basis for interpreting and applying domestic laws.[5] Despite these two decisions, in most situations the Convention is more likely to be a tool for political advocacy than directly applicable in the courts.

Political Context and Public Sentiment Towards Juvenile Justice

While there is greater respect for human rights and less deference towards authority than in the past, the 1990s and the start of the new millennium have been politically conservative times. The reasons for this more conservative environment are complex. At least in part this environment is a response to government debt problems, the end of the Cold War, and an increasingly global and competitive economy, as well as to some of the expensive social reform projects of the post-Second World War period that have not produced the desired results.

Governments have become more conservative, particularly with respect to spending on social programs, and in a number of countries have adopted "get tough" rhetoric and policies on youth crime. Negative public responses to youth offending, and towards young people in general, is a recurring theme in this book. There is a strong theme of anti-youth sentiment, which is described aptly as "moral outrage" by Graham in the chapter on England and Wales. This pervasive anti-youth public sentiment has troubling sources and dimensions.

The media has played a role in increasing public concerns about youth crime. An increasingly competitive market for news media has created a more sensationalist approach to reporting, which has often resulted in disproportionate coverage of youth violence. Reports of youth crime are frequently inflammatory. Youth crime, and especially youth violence, attract considerable media attention and contribute to the sense of "moral panic" and demands for government action to "do something" about youth crime.

An obvious and tragic case that illustrates the extent of media reporting of youth violence was the coverage of the murder in England of 2-year-old Jamie Bulgar by two 10-year-old boys. This was certainly a terrible crime, but it was also unique. It received months, actually years, of detailed worldwide media coverage. It was the impetus for dramatic legislative change to English juvenile justice legislation and is often cited in countries such as Canada as a reason for lowering the age of criminal accountability. While this crime was horrific, it did not justify a "toughening" of youth crime laws, especially since there is no evidence that harsher responses to youth crime increase the protection of society.

Like other dramatic news reports, media stories about youth offending "sell" because they are shocking. It is important to recall that they shock us precisely because they are unusual. Somewhat paradoxically, youth crime might be more cause for concern if it stopped being newsworthy.

It is also clear that politicians use the issue of youth crime to advance a particular agenda. Youth crime raises the specter of social decay and the need to "take a stand" to prevent a further decline in values and behaviour. As O'Connor notes with reference to Australia, a "get tough" stance on out-of-control youth is a metaphor for unease with social change. Politicians can use a concern with youth crime and demands for a "get tough" approach relatively easily as a rhetorical tool to rally aging voters with nostalgia for an idealized past. It is clear that a "get tough" agenda serves political interests, not the best interests of young people or community health (U.S. Surgeon General, 2001). The unfortunate irony is that politicians too often promote a "get tough" approach to youth crime, arguing that this is a means of increasing public safety, while at the same time advocating reductions in government spending for health, education, and social services, which will inevitably lead to conditions that will increase youth crime. Unfortunately, "get-tough" strategies do not seem to benefit at-risk youth or society in general. Those youth who are inclined to commit crimes, especially serious and repeat offenders, lack the judgment, foresight, and self-control to be in any way deterred by the prospect of longer sentences.

At least in part the political and media concern with youth crime reflects the fact that populations are aging. Youth seem increasingly distant and alien to the average voter. At its most benign, anti-youth public sentiment may simply reflect the "generation gap." In these times of rapid technological and social change, young people are growing up in a radically different world from that in which their parents and grandparents came to maturity. As societies change more rapidly, it is not surprising that young people start to seem more strange in the eyes of adults. Of course, there has always been a tendency for people, as they grow older, to find teenagers more strange and threatening. What is different now is that the relative size and influence of the older generations is growing. The growing anti-youth sentiment, then, may have its roots, at least to some extent, in demographic change.

More disturbingly, this relationship between population demographics and anti-youth sentiment may also have a subtle racist dimension. Young people in the countries studied in this book are increasingly of ethnic minority or indigenous heritage. Increased immigration of visible minority groups and higher birth rates among some minority and Aboriginal groups make the racial composition of adolescent populations quite different from the adult populations in Australia, Canada, England, New Zealand, and the United States. The change in the ethnic and racial composition of youth means that young people do not seem strange simply by reason of their behaviour, music, and appearance or other reflections of a distinctive youth subculture. As young people are increasingly not just members of a different generation, but also of a cultural, ethnic, racial, or linguistic minority, these adolescents may be resented at least in part because they may not be perceived as the legitimate inheritors of their respective nations.

It is interesting, and perhaps somewhat disconcerting, to observe that the two countries in this study with the most racially and religiously homogenous populations, Scotland and the Republic of Ireland, also have the most political support for a welfare-oriented approach to young offenders. While there is concern about youth crime in those two countries, the politicians do not try to exploit fears about youth in general, and policies are aimed at protecting the public by rehabilitating young offenders.

Conclusion: The Importance of Comparative Study and the Reform of Juvenile Justice

Antisocial behaviour in youth, including criminal behaviour, while not socially acceptable, is not abnormal. Some degree of deviant and offending behaviour is a universal aspect of the adolescent stage of human development. Juvenile justice is thus a concern shared internationally.

Concerns common in the writings of founders of the Illinois Juvenile Court in 1899 are mirrored in the 2001 report of the American Surgeon General on youth violence. Juvenile offending and the social problems to which it is tied are not new problems. The pervasiveness of juvenile offending as a problem makes historical and cross-cultural study of juvenile justice relevant. What is done elsewhere and what has been done in the past can be helpful in formulating strategies to deal with these shared problems.

Currently, there is great controversy over juvenile justice legislation and policy in many countries. Policy makers are looking for ways that are more effective, both in terms of financial and human cost, to reduce and respond to youth crime. Many commentators in the countries studied in this book feel that their juvenile justice systems are in need of substantial reform.

It is vitally important that rigorous research is undertaken to determine what kinds of programs and interventions are most effective in responding to the needs of different youth and, ultimately, in reducing offending behaviour. International comparisons, such as those presented in this book, can play a central role in increasing understanding of different alternatives for reform and in the development of more effective ways to conceive of and administer juvenile justice.

References

Abella, R. (1999). A generation of human rights. *Osgoode Hall Law Journal* 36: 597.

Corrado, R., et al. (1992). *Juvenile justice in Canada: A theoretical and analytical assessment.* Toronto, ON: Butterworths.

Health Canada. (1999). *Toward a healthy future: Second report on the health of Canadians.* Ottawa, ON. Website: http://www.hc sc.gc.ca/hppb/phdd/report/subin.html.

Ignatieff, M. (2000). *The rights revolution.* Toronto, ON: Anansi.

UNICEF International Child Development Centre. (1998). *Juvenile justice. Innocenti Digest 3.* United Nations International Children's Emergency Fund.

U.S. Surgeon General. (2001). *Youth violence: A report of the Surgeon General.* Website: www.surgeongeneral.gov/library/youthviolence/sgssummary.

Zimring, F. (2001). *The common thread: Diversion in the jurisprudence of a century of juvenile justice.* Working Paper No. 41. University of California, Berkeley School of Law Public Law and Legal Theory.

Notes

1   In Canada, there have recently been public inquiries as well as civil suits and criminal prosecutions against staff at many of the juvenile institutions for abuse that occurred in the period from 1940 to 1980.

2   Reservations are unilateral statements countries can make when signing or ratifying a multilateral international treaty. By making such a reservation, a state can exclude or modify the effect of stated provisions of the treaty in their application to that state, without modifying the effect of those provisions on other parties to the treaty. Reservations are permitted so long as they do not defeat the general purpose of the treaty.

3   Australia, Canada, the Cook Islands, Iceland, New Zealand, Switzerland, and the United Kingdom have filed such a reservation on the grounds that they claim such separation is either not feasible in all circumstances or is not appropriate (UNICEF International Child Development Centre, 1998).

4   See, for example *R. v. D.O.L.* [1993] 4 S.C.R. 419 and *Lennox and Addington Family and Children's Services v. T.S.* [2000] O.J. No. 1420 (Ont Fam. Ct.).

5   *Baker v. Canada (Minister of Citizenship and Immigration)*, [1999] 2 S.C.R. 817; *Minister of State for Immigration and Ethnic Affairs v. Ah Hin Teoh* No. WAG118 of 1993 FED No. 182/94 (AUS).

CHAPTER 2

Juvenile Crime and Justice in Canada

Lorne D. Bertrand, Joanne J. Paetsch, and Nicholas Bala

Under Canada's *Constitution Act 1867* the federal government has jurisdiction for enacting criminal laws and procedure, while the provincial and territorial governments have jurisdiction over the administration of justice and the operation of the juvenile court and corrections systems. Accordingly the federal government has responsibility for enacting juvenile justice laws, while the provinces and territories implement those laws with some financial support from the federal government. This makes juvenile justice policy an area where there is a need for intergovernmental cooperation as well as an area of inevitable tension.

The *Juvenile Delinquents Act (JDA)* was enacted in 1908, and it adopted an approach to juvenile justice that, at least in theory, emphasized the welfare of the child offender. In practice, however, the juvenile judges and correctional officials often took a punitive approach in dealing with youths under that Act, and there were problems with the abuse of rights of juveniles, including abuse in juvenile correctional institutions. The *JDA* tended not to distinguish between neglected and delinquent youth, and it had indeterminate sentencing, little protection for legal rights, and gave judges and correctional officials very significant discretion. The *JDA* was replaced by the *Young Offenders Act (YOA)*, which came into effect in 1984. The *YOA* represented a major philosophical shift away from the *JDA* in that it focuses on the protection of society, the rights and responsibilities of young persons, and due process.

Lorne D. Bertrand is the Senior Research Associate with the Canadian Research Institute for Law and the Family, Alberta, Canada.

Joanne J. Paetsch is the Administrator/Research Associate with the Canadian Research Institute for Law and the Family, Alberta, Canada.

Nicholas Bala is a Professor of Law at Queen's University in Kingston, Ontario, Canada, who concentrates his research in the area of family and children's law.

Youth justice issues remain contentious in Canada. A proposal for a new *Youth Criminal Justice Act (YCJA)* to replace the *YOA* has been slowly moving through the Canadian Parliament, but the new Act will come into force early in 2003.

PART I:
PROFILE OF CANADA

Demographic Characteristics

Canada's population in 1997 was just over 30 million people, with 26% aged from 0 to 19. The proportion of youth aged from 0 to 14 decreased from 1980 to 1986, and showed a small increase from 1987 to 1994. Over half of the population resides in two of Canada's ten provinces and three territories: Ontario and Quebec.

According to Statistics Canada, in 1996, 77.9% of the population was urban, up from 76.6% in 1991 (Law, 1997). The provinces with the highest urban populations in 1996 were Ontario (83.3%) and British Columbia (82.1%). The highest rural populations were found in the Northwest Territories (57.5%) and Prince Edward Island (55.8%).

According to 1996 census data, approximately 72% of the population described their ethnic origin as Canadian, British, or French. Visible minorities (defined as persons, other than Aboriginal peoples, who are non-Caucasian in race or nonwhite in colour) accounted for 11% of the population, with 3% identifying themselves as Chinese, 2.4% as South Asians, and 2% as Blacks. Another 1.1 million people (or almost 4% of the total population), reported Aboriginal ancestry in 1996. Sources of immigration to Canada have changed greatly since the 1970s, with many more immigrants coming from non-European countries. Over three-quarters of the immigrant population who came in the 1990s are members of a visible minority group. Almost all visible minorities (94%) lived in a metropolitan area in 1996, compared with 62% of the total population. Seven out of every 10 visible minority persons lived in the three largest cities of Toronto (42%), Vancouver (18%), and Montreal (13%).

Family Types

A total of 69,088 couples divorced in 1998, signaling a rise in the divorce rate for the first time in four years. The crude divorce rate in 1998 was 228 divorces per 100,000 Canadians. Based on these rates, 36% of marriages are expected to end in divorce within 30 years of marriage. In 1998, the average age at divorce was 42 years for men, and 39.4 years of age for women.

Almost three quarters (74%) of families in 1996 were married-couple families, although this proportion declined from 80% of all families in 1986 due to substantial increases in both "common-law" (unmarried opposite-sex partners) and lone-parent families. Between 1991 and 1996, the number of common-law families in Canada increased by 28%, and the number of lone-parent families increased by 19%. Lone-parent families headed by women outnumbered those headed by men by more than four to one, and almost one in every five children in Canada lived with a lone parent in 1996. The average family size in Canada is 3.1 persons.

Socioeconomic Characteristics

Education Levels

Since the early 1950s, Canadians have continued to attain higher levels of education. In 1996, 40% of the population aged 15 and over had graduated from a university or postsecondary institution, up from 29% in 1981, while the proportion of the population that had not completed high school decreased from 48% in 1981 to 35% in 1996.

More recent trends can be seen with the 20-to-29-age group. In 1981, 37% of both men and women had attained either a degree or diploma. By 1996, these proportions had increased to 42% of men and 51% of women in the 20-to-29-age group. The 1996 Census also showed that school attendance rates for young adults aged from 15 to 19 increased. In 1996, 79% of young people were in full-time attendance at school, up from 66% in 1981.

Statistics Canada conducted a School Leavers Survey in 1991, in which nearly 10,000 young people aged from 18 to 20 were interviewed to document the circumstances of their school leaving (Frank, 1996). Two-thirds of the sample were re-interviewed in a follow-up survey in 1995. The 1991 survey found that the school leaver rate of 20-year-olds was 18%. In the follow-up survey in 1995, when the young people had reached age 24, the school leaver rate was down to 15%. One-quarter of the youth who had left school in 1991 had returned to high school and had graduated by 1995. In 1995, males were more likely to have left school (18%) than females (10%). The school leaver rate was highest in Newfoundland (19.7%) and Prince Edward Island (19.2%), and lowest in Ontario (11.7%).

Employment Levels

According to Statistics Canada, just over 11.8 million people were working full-time in Canada in December 1998. The unemployment rate for adults was 6.8%, and the youth unemployment rate was 14.4%, down 1.4% from the year before. Since 1989, the number of self-employed people increased by 42.5%, accounting for 18% of total employment in 1998.

Poverty Levels

Based on Statistics Canada's Low Income Cut-offs, 16.4% of Canadians in 1998 had low incomes, and 18.8% of children under 18 years of age lived in families with low incomes. While a poverty rate of 16.4% is the lowest in Canada since 1992, it was still 41% more than in 1989, the last full year before the last recession (National Council on Welfare, 2000). According to the 1996 Census, poverty rates are highest among Aboriginal peoples (43%), members of visible minority groups (36%), and persons with disabilities (31%). The rate of household poverty has increased in Canada over the past quarter century, and average household incomes have not recovered from the economic recession of the early 1990s. In fact, average household incomes in 1997 were lower than in 1981 (Canadian Council on Social Development, 2000).

Poverty has increased dramatically among young families (i.e., families in which the oldest adult is under 25). In 1998, a young family faced a 47% chance of being poor, compared to a 22% chance in 1981. Lone-parent mothers were at greatest risk of poverty, with a poverty rate of 56% for mothers aged from 25 to 44, and 85% for mothers under 25 years of age. In 1998, there were 1.3 million poor children in Canada. From a juvenile justice perspective, this is a major concern since children in poor families are twice as likely to score in the top 10% in terms of frequency of delinquent behaviours as compared to children in modest-income families, and nearly three times as likely to have high delinquency scores than children in high-income families (Ross & Roberts, 1999).

Social Policy Issues Related to Children and Youth

Childcare Policy

Canada does not have a national childcare policy. In 1994/95, 1.5 million children aged from 0 to 11 were in some form of nonparental childcare while their parents worked (Ross, Scott, & Kelly, 1996). Just over one-third of these children were cared for outside the child's home by a nonrelative, and one-fifth were cared for by a relative. Children spent an average of 21 hours per week in their primary care arrangement. Only 27% of the children in nonparental care were in a regulated childcare program.

Health

In 1994, Canada spent over $73 billion on health expenditures, or $2,496 per capita. (In this chapter all dollar figures are Canadian dollars, which equal roughly $0.65 US.) Health expenditures for children aged from 0 to 14 in 1994 were $7 billion, or $1,170 per capita. Canada has universal, government-funded health insurance that covers most types of medical care. In a few provinces there is government-funded dental care for children, and all jurisdictions have some government funding for prescription drugs for low-income persons.

Canadian children and youth are healthy by international standards, and their level of health has improved considerably over the last decades. According to McIntyre, Connor, and Warren (1998), however, there is room for improvement. In 1994, an estimated 57,000 Canadian families with children under 12 went hungry at least once because their families could not afford to buy food. Children are more likely to experience hunger if they live in large cities, live in a lone-parent household, or are Aboriginal.

As well, despite government funded anti-smoking campaigns, teen smoking rates increased dramatically from 21% in 1990 to nearly 30% in 1996 (Canadian Council on Social Development, 1996). The rate of teen pregnancy also increased from 41 per 1,000 women aged from 15 to 19 in 1987, to 47 per 1,000 in 1995. In 1996, alcohol continued to be the most widely abused drug among Canadian youth. Of youth aged from 15 to 19, 72% drank alcohol regularly or occasionally, and almost 60% of these were regular drinkers.

The suicide rate for Canadian male teens was 23 per 100,000 in 1991, an increase of 400% over the rate of 5 per 100,000 in 1960. Rates for female teens are much lower, but they are hospitalized more frequently for attempted suicide. Aboriginal youth have a suicide rate five times that of other Canadians. According to the World Health Organization, Canada ranks 11th in the world for frequency of suicide among youth aged from 15 to 24.

The National Child Benefit initiative was developed jointly by federal, provincial, and territorial governments, and began in July 1998. The objective of the initiative is to reduce the depth of child poverty, promote attachment to the workforce, and streamline the distribution of benefits (Canadian Council on Social Development, 1998). The federal government's contribution, at $1.7 billion annually, is the Canada Child Tax Benefit for low-income families. Since this money replaces some of the provincial expenditures on social assistance (welfare) benefits to families, provinces and territories have designed programs to reinvest the savings in initiatives to support working-poor families. However, in a number of provinces, pressures to eliminate deficits and reduce taxes as well as more conservative political attitudes have resulted in significant reductions in amounts of support paid to individuals and families on social assistance, as well as less spending on public housing.

In 1999, the federal, provincial, and territorial ministers released a vision paper for a National Children's Agenda (Canadian Council on Social Development, 1999). According to the paper, the goals for Canadian children are good physical and emotional health, safety and security, success at learning, and social engagement and responsibility. These goals are to be achieved by supporting the role of parents and strengthening families, enhancing early child development, improving economic security for families, providing early and continuous learning experiences, fostering strong adolescent development, and creating supportive, safe, and violence-free communities. The National Children's Agenda has received support in Parliament, and possible components include extended parental leave, tax cuts for families with children, divorce law reforms, and new monies for the National Child Benefit.

In September 2000, the Prime Minister announced $23.4 billion of new federal investments over five years to support agreements by First Ministers on Health Renewal and Early Childhood Development. In October 2000, Health Minister Allan Rock announced the establishment of five Centres of Excellence for Children's Well-Being. The Centres are intended to enhance understanding of, and responsiveness to, the physical and mental health needs of children, as well as the critical factors for healthy child development. The Centres are: (1) The Centre of Excellence for Early Child Development, (2) The Centre of Excellence for Youth Engagement, (3) The Centre of Excellence for Child Welfare, (4) The Centre of Excellence for Children and Adolescents with Special Needs, and (5) The Centre of Excellence for Child and Youth-Centred Communities.

Education

Expenditures for all levels of education in Canada (i.e., elementary, secondary, postsecondary and trade/vocational) in 1994 were $58.6 billion, up 83% from the previous decade (Statistics Canada, 1998). This equates to a per capita cost of $2,004 in 1994, up 60% from the 1984 level. Expenditures for elementary and secondary level education account for 61% of the budget, and the majority of financing is provided by the provincial governments. An international study of adult literacy found that nearly one-third of Canadian youth were found to have the highest level of literacy skills, second only to Swedish youth. However, 10% of Canadian youth had poor literacy skills, the third-worst rate out of seven developed countries (Canadian Council on Social Development, 1998).

Crime Prevention Initiatives

In 1996/97, the Canadian government spent $10 billion on justice services, or $337 per capita. The largest proportion (59%) of justice spending was for policing; youth corrections accounted for only 5% of total justice spending ($17 per capita).[1] Adult corrections accounted for 20% of justice spending in 1996/97 ($66 per capita). According to Besserer and Tufts (1999), government spending on police, the courts, and correctional services accounted for 3 cents of every dollar spent by governments in Canada. This is low, compared to that spent on education (14 cents), health (14 cents), and social services (31 cents). Given the large share of government spending on social services, attempts to control costs by reforming Canada's social safety net are highly relevant to the justice sector's focus on crime prevention through social development. In addition, initiatives aimed at diverting cases from the formal court process, such as alternative measures, mediation, family group conferencing, and sentencing circles, are expected to reduce caseloads and costs.

In 1998, the federal government launched the second phase of its National Strategy on Community Safety and Crime Prevention (Canadian Council on Social Development, 1998). The National Crime Prevention Centre oversees the strategy, with an annual budget of $32 million to develop community-based responses to crime. The strategy emphasizes community partnerships and gives priority to funding pilot programs that will benefit children, youth, women, and Aboriginal people.

The Ontario government began an initiative in 1997 that was aimed at improving children's chances in early life (Canadian Council on Social Development, 1998). The "Healthy Babies, Healthy Children" program identifies children aged from 0 to 6 who are at risk of poor social, emotional, cognitive, and physical health. Parents are referred to the program, and have the option of receiving the services of a trained parent who provides advice and emotional support through home visits to help improve parenting skills. The Ontario government estimates that 9,000 children born each year in Ontario will require a home visitor, and has promised to increase funding from an initial $10 million annually to $50 million by 2000. The province has also amended its child welfare laws and changed policies in response to a number of child abuse deaths, and there have been very significant increases in the number of children being brought into state care.

The National Crime Prevention Centre has since contributed funding to similar "Healthy Families" programs in Alberta, Prince Edward Island, and the Yukon, as well as an in-depth evaluation of the initiatives, which will be completed in 2002.

The Ontario government is also funding a long-term, early-intervention program aimed at high-risk children aged 0-4 years and 4-8 years. Community-based projects have been established in eight places in Ontario. The children will be followed for up to twenty years to determine whether these early-intervention programs have an effect on reducing adolescent offending, juvenile pregnancy and school drop-out rates (Peters et al., 2000).

PART II:
TRENDS IN OFFENDING BEHAVIOUR BY JUVENILES

Victimization Rates

Few data on criminal victimization in Canada are available. Canada does not conduct an annual national victimization survey. However, the General Social Survey, conducted annually by Statistics Canada, included victimization cycles in 1988, 1993, and 1999. This self-report survey asks individuals 15 years of age and older about their criminal victimization experiences with respect to eight types of crimes (personal crimes: sexual assault, robbery, assault, theft of personal property; and household crimes: break and enter, motor vehicle/parts theft, theft of household property, vandalism) and their perceptions of the criminal justice system. The following discussion is summarized from Besserer and Trainor (2000).

In 1999, 25% of respondents reported that they had been the victim of at least one of the eight crimes at least once in the past year. This proportion was very close to the 23% reported in the 1993 survey, and very similar to those found for Canada in the International Crime Victims Survey (Mayhew & van Dijk, 1997). The only significant increases in reported victimization rates from 1993 to 1999 were for theft of personal property and theft of household property. Of all incidents reported in the 1999 General Social Survey, approximately one-half involved a personal crime and one-third involved a household crime.

Overall, victimization rates for the four personal crimes were quite similar for males and females; however, females were more likely to have been the victims of sexual assault, while males were more likely to have been the victims of assault and robbery. Higher rates of victimization were reported by city dwellers, young people aged from 15 to 24, and individuals with household incomes of less than $15,000. With respect to household crimes, victimization rates were also higher for city dwellers; however, individuals living in higher income households (greater than $60,000) were more likely to report being the victim of at least one household crime. Rates were also higher for individuals who reported renting as opposed to owning their home.

The survey also found that reporting of victimization incidents to police had declined from 1993 to 1999. In 1999, only 37% of incidents were reported to police while 42% of incidents had been reported in 1993.

A school-based, self-report study conducted in 1999 in the western Canadian province of Alberta examined victimization and delinquency rates of youth aged from 12 through 18 (Gomes et al., 2000). Findings indicated that victimization was more likely to occur at school than elsewhere: over one-half (54%) of the students reported that they had been victimized at least once within the past year at school, while 47% reported that they had been victimized while not at school. The most prevalent types of victimization reported were being slapped, punched, or kicked; having something stolen; being threatened with bodily harm; and having something damaged. The least frequently reported types of victimization were being attacked by a group or gang and being threatened with a weapon.

Overall, male students were more likely to report that they had been victimized in the past year, and females were more likely to report that they had been sexually victimized. Younger students were also more likely to report that they had been victimized than older students. Victimization rates peaked for students in Grade 9 and declined thereafter.

Rates of Reported Crime

The Canadian Centre for Justice Statistics, a division of Statistics Canada, is responsible for collecting data concerning criminal activity in Canada. The aggregate Uniform Crime Reporting Survey (UCR) has collected data annually from 1962 on crime and traffic violations from all police agencies in Canada. Data included in the UCR represent reported incidents that have been substantiated by a police investigation. UCR data are classified into the general categories of violent crime, property crime, other crimes (including such offences as prostitution, offensive weapons, and arson), drugs, other federal statutes (including offences under the customs and immigration acts), and provincial and/or territorial statutes (including highway code). The unit of analysis in the UCR is the incident, and each incident is classified by the most serious offence that occurred. Violent offences are always classified as more serious than nonviolent incidents, which results in underreporting of less serious incidents to the UCR since they are subsumed by the more serious violent incidents.

Table 2.1 presents the annual rates per 100,000 total population of selected violent, property, and other crimes from 1988/99. For violent crimes, there was a general tendency for rates to rise from 1988 through the early 1990s, and then to decline somewhat thereafter. For example, there were 709 per 100,000 population nonsexual assaults reported in 1988; this rate peaked at 891 in 1993 and declined to 765 in 1999. Similarly, the rate for robbery, which was 93 in 1988, rose to 121 in 1991 and then declined to 94 in 1999. Sexual assaults peaked in 1992 at a rate of 140, and have since declined to 78 in 1999, a rate that is lower than that reported in 1988 (109 per 100,000). Homicide rates in Canada have remained relatively stable across this 12-year period at 2 or 3 reported incidents per 100,000 population.

Similar patterns over time have also been observed with the property crimes of break and enter and other theft, with the rates peaking in 1991 and declining thereafter. For break and enter, the rate reached a high of 1,613 in 1991 and declined 35% by 1999 to a rate of 1,044. Other thefts dropped from 3,596 per 100,000 in 1991 to 2,300 in 1999, a decline of 36%. Motor vehicle theft, however, increased quite steadily from 1988 (372 per 100,000) to 1996 (602 per 100,000) and then dropped slightly from 1996 through 1999 (529 per 100,000).

Rates of reported crime for other offences have not displayed as much of a pattern. Drug offences declined from 1989 through 1995, but increased each year from 1996 through 1999. Offensive weapons incidents peaked in 1991 at 77 per 100,000 and declined in subsequent years to a rate of 53 in 1999. The rate of bail violations reached a high in 1998 at 239 per 100,000. Prostitution offences exhibited a steady decline from a high of 40 per 100,000 in 1988 to 17 per 100,000 in 1999.

Table 2.1
Rates of Reported Crime, Canada, 1988/99[1]

Crime	1988	1989	1990	1991	1992	1993	1994	1995	1996	1997	1998	1999
Violent Crimes												
Homicide	2	3	3	3	3	2	2	2	2	2	2	2
Sexual Assault	109	116	119	127	140	139	126	96	90	90	84	78
Nonsexual Assault	709	747	805	870	882	891	873	784	767	780	777	765
Robbery	93	97	104	121	120	107	102	103	105	99	96	94
Property Crimes												
Break and Enter	1,401	1,336	1,430	1,613	1,560	1,468	1,383	1,331	1,335	1,244	1,156	1,044
Motor Vehicle Theft	372	407	453	536	556	584	586	556	602	591	547	529
Other Theft	3,291	3,189	3,349	3,596	3,409	3,166	2,977	2,934	2,863	2,606	2,441	2,300
Other Crimes												
Drugs	230	255	228	211	216	205	216	210	219	222	235	262
Offensive Weapons	70	69	71	77	69	72	71	60	54	54	55	53
Arson	39	37	41	56	59	57	59	45	43	43	43	42
Bail Violations	183	197	204	215	233	233	229	226	224	230	239	237
Disturbing the Peace	218	217	219	231	222	211	195	177	184	192	215	229
Prostitution	40	36	37	38	36	30	19	24	20	19	20	17

1 Rates calculated per 100,000 total population.

Source of data: Canadian Centre for Justice Statistics. Statistics Canada: Policing Services Section and Uniform Crime Reports.

Rates of Youth Charged

In addition to collecting data concerning the number of reported crimes, the UCR also provides information on the number of youth and adults charged with offences. In Canada, young persons aged from 12 through 17 are considered youth and may be charged with criminal offences under the provisions of the *Young Offenders Act*. In 1999, a total of 111,474 youth were charged, representing 18% of all individuals charged. Youth were considerably more likely to be charged with property offences (27% of all property charges laid were against youth) than violent offences (16% of violent charges laid were against youth).

Table 2.2 presents the charge rates of youth for selected violent, property, and other crimes for the period 1988/99. With respect to violent offences, in general, rates of youth charged peaked somewhat later than rates of reported crime for all ages of offenders discussed above. For example, the rate of youth charged with sexual offences exhibited a steady increase from 1988 through 1993, and has declined somewhat since then, although the 1999 rate, at 58 per 100,000, is 5% higher than the 1988 rate. Nonsexual assault charge rates for youth increased steadily and quite substantially from 1988 through 1995, followed by a slight decline in 1996 and slight increases in 1997 and 1998 and a further decrease in 1999. The 1999 rate of 661 per 100,000 is 76% higher than the 1988 rate of 374. Charge rates of youth for robbery increased steadily from 1988 to 1997 and declined in 1998 and 1999, with the 1999 rate of 130 per 100,000 youth being 88% higher than the 1988 rate of 69. Charge rates of youth for homicide remained low and stable across the 12-year period from 1988 through 1999.

The issue of whether the increase in the rate of youth charged with several types of violent offences represents a "real" increase in the actual level of youth crime is very controversial. Some Canadian researchers, such as Corrado and Markwart (1994), argue that there has been a real and substantial increase in the amount of youth violence (other than homicide) in recent years. Other researchers, such as Carrington (1995), argue that such factors as increased reporting to police, increased recording by police, and the adoption of "zero tolerance" policies by school boards may have resulted in what appeared to be an increase in the level of youth crime in the late 1980s and early 1990s, but that there was no real increase in youth crime.

The charge rates of youth for the property crimes of break and enter, motor vehicle theft, and other theft increased steadily from 1988 to 1991 and then declined through 1999. The charge rate for break and enter was 1,183 per 100,000 youth in 1991. This rate had declined by 54% to 550 per 100,000 by 1999. Similarly, the 1991 charge rate for motor vehicle theft was 386 per 100,000 youth. In 1999, this rate had declined by 41% to 227. The charge rate of youth for other theft declined by 54% over the period from 1991 through 1999.

Table 2.2
Rates of Youth Charged with Selected Crimes, Canada, 1988/99[1]

Crime	1988	1989	1990	1991	1992	1993	1994	1995	1996	1997	1998	1999
Violent Crimes												
Homicide	2	2	2	2	2	2	2	3	2	2	2	2
Sexual Assault	55	66	71	84	90	91	80	66	63	61	59	58
Nonsexual Assault	374	450	519	614	634	687	693	709	677	685	687	661
Robbery	69	87	91	121	129	128	127	148	148	155	146	130
Property Crimes												
Break and Enter	1,063	987	1,067	1,183	1,074	942	849	780	758	703	651	550
Motor Vehicle Theft	286	327	352	386	352	352	318	288	285	267	252	227
Other Theft	1,618	1,733	1,884	1,989	1,720	1,471	1,364	1,419	1,322	1,170	1,011	906
Other Crimes												
Drugs	145	139	137	116	115	147	203	213	225	208	227	268
Offensive Weapons	67	76	80	89	83	83	83	71	61	61	60	59
Arson	18	18	20	26	29	26	28	28	23	26	21	24
Bail Violations	156	190	216	290	318	318	298	334	345	346	383	368
Disturbing the Peace	40	47	44	49	43	35	30	31	24	24	25	28
Prostitution	25	20	18	22	15	13	8	11	8	9	8	3

1 Rates calculated per 100,000 youth population aged 12–17.

Source of data: Canadian Centre for Justice Statistics. Statistics Canada: Policing Services Section and Uniform Crime Reports.

The pattern of charge rates of youth for other crimes across the period 1988 through 1999 varied considerably depending on the particular offence. For example, the charge rate for drug crimes increased steadily from 145 per 100,000 youth in 1988 to 225 in 1996, followed by a slight decline to 208 in 1997 and increases to 227 in 1998 and 268 in 1999. Charge rates for offensive weapons peaked in 1991 at 89 per 100,000 youth, and had decreased to 59 by 1999. Charge rates for bail violations increased steadily across the years under consideration to a peak of 383 per 100,000 youth in 1998 followed by a slight decline to 368 in 1999.

There was an increase in the number of female youth charged with both violent and property offences from 1988 to 1999. In 1988, 20% of all charges for violent offences by youth were laid against females; by 1999, this proportion had risen to 25.1%. Similarly, for property offences, in 1988 16.4% of all youth charges were laid against females, compared to 22.5% in 1999.

While public concern in Canada over youth offending remains high, it would appear that in the late 1990s youth crime rates slightly declined. There has not been a good explanation offered for this apparent decline, though it may be associated with a relatively strong economy that is providing greater employment opportunities for youth and their families.

PART III:
THE JUVENILE JUSTICE SYSTEM IN CANADA

Description of Legislation: The *Young Offenders Act*

Canada's *Young Offenders Act*[2] (*YOA*) came into effect in 1984, replacing the *Juvenile Delinquents Act*[3] (*JDA*) which was originally enacted in 1908. The *JDA* had an exclusively welfare-oriented philosophy, status offences such as "sexual immorality," indeterminate sentencing, little protection for legal rights, and gave judges and correctional officials very significant discretion. Despite its theoretical focus on the welfare of children, under the *JDA* there were significant abuses, especially of youths confined to custodial facilities.

The *YOA* established an age jurisdiction for youth court of youth aged from 12 through 17, with offending behaviour by children under 12 dealt with either by voluntary measures or under provincial child welfare laws (Bala, 1997). The *YOA* eliminated status offences, and deals only with the federal criminal law: violations of provincial laws (such as traffic and education statutes) are dealt with in various ways, depending on the province and age of the youth.

Section 3 of the *YOA* sets guiding principles for its implementation, including

- accountability, but ordinarily less accountability than for adults;
- protection of society, including recognition of the importance of rehabilitation and crime prevention;
- recognition of special needs of youth;
- protection of legal rights of youth;
- involvement of parents; and
- use of least possible interference, including diversion from court.

The Act requires that youths who are detained or placed in custody shall be kept separate from adults, and for the designation of "youth courts." In many places there are specifically designated youth police and probation officers, but the *YOA* does not require this. In most provinces youth court judges also deal with adult offenders, albeit usually at a different time, though in some provinces youth courts have more of a family law jurisdiction.

If the police arrest and wish to question a youth about a suspected offence, section 56 of the *YOA* provides that youths must be fully advised of their legal rights. Police officers must advise the youth in "language appropriate to his age and understanding" of the right to silence, and of the right to consult with a parent or lawyer before and during questioning. In more serious cases the police must also warn of the possibility of transfer to adult court.[4] Despite these warnings, in many cases youth waive their rights and make statements confessing guilt.

In less serious cases, the police may decide to deal with a case informally, either by simply discussing the situation with the youth and parents, or by referring the case to an "alternative measures program." These programs may involve community members or victims, and utilize a range of options such as an apology, requiring restitution to the victim or a donation to charity, or community service work. Youths can only be referred to alternative measures if they consent, and if they "accept responsibility" for the alleged offence. If the youth denies responsibility, the case must be referred to youth court for a trial. There are significant variations across Canada in the criteria for eligibility for alternative measures, but in comparison to other countries, only limited use is made of diversion for dealing with youths.

If a youth is charged with an offence, the Crown prosecutor may seek a court order for pre-trial detention. In theory, youth detention should only be ordered on the same basis as for adults, principally to ensure attendance in court, to prevent interference with the administration of justice, or if there is a serious likelihood of a further offence being committed before any trial. Youths may be released pending trial subject to conditions, including parental supervision. In practice, some judges may consider a range of "social factors" in making detention decisions and may, for example, be more inclined to detain homeless youth. Detention, if short term, may involve placement in a jail-like facility (separate from adults), and it can result in a youth being placed in a custody facility with convicted young offenders. Even in a better equipped facility, there is real difficulty in providing good programming for youth in temporary detention.

All youths dealt with in court have a right to counsel. Under the *YOA*, youths who are unable to afford counsel can get a court order for government-paid counsel. While parents may choose to pay for a lawyer for their child, the *YOA* does not require this and most youth have a government-paid lawyer. In some places there are special legal clinics and staff lawyers for youth, though use is also made of lawyers in private practice under a government-paid plan. There are concerns that, in practice, significant numbers of youth waive the right to counsel due to delays in obtaining a lawyer.

The youth court process is "summary," meaning that there is no preliminary inquiry and no jury trial (there is only a right to a jury in youth court in murder cases, as the maximum sentence is 10 years as opposed to 3 years for other offences). In practice most cases in youth court are resolved by a guilty plea, though there are a significant number of trials. Youth court trials are in theory open to the public, but in practice members of the public rarely attend and they may be excluded by court order if their presence might harm a youth. The media may report on youth court proceedings, but cannot reveal the identity of youth except in narrow circumstances, such as if a dangerous youth is at large or a case has been transferred to adult court. There are provisions in the *YOA* to restrict access to youth records, and less serious offences require record sealing or destruction after a crime-free period.

If a youth is found guilty, the case proceeds to "disposition" or sentencing. A judge may order a pre-disposition report before sentencing, and in more serious cases, a psychological or psychiatric assessment may also be prepared for the court. In cases of serious mental disorder, there is a narrow provision for confinement in a mental health facility.

A youth court judge has a range of sentencing options, including fines, community service, restitution to victims, and custody. The most commonly imposed disposition on youth is probation, which typically involves the youth remaining at home and subject to conditions on behaviour (such as school attendance or refraining from contact with other offenders), and some sort of supervision by a youth worker or probation officer. Courts can also require that youth attend counseling or receive treatment as a condition of probation, but there is often a lack of community-based resources for young offenders with significant problems. While sympathetic youth court judges sometimes have tried to order that youth are to receive special treatment paid for by the government, it has been held by appeal courts that judges can only require that young offenders receive treatment or counseling for which the government is willing to pay.

If a youth is placed in custody, the judge must specify the "level" of custody – "open" or "secure" – but provincial and/or territorial correctional officials determine the specific facility within the designated level of custody. Open custody is usually a community-based group home, where a youth will reside, perhaps while attending school in the community. Secure custody is a more secure, usually larger facility. Some use is made of wilderness camps, especially for Aboriginal youth.

There is very significant variation in the nature of custody facilities: some are little more than jails for adolescents with limited programming, while others have quite extensive programming and counseling. A few "boot camps" have been established, with a "strict discipline" approach to programming. All youth custody facilities offer some type of education. A significant number of young offenders have learning disabilities and special educational needs, and some youth make better progress in terms of their schooling in custody than in the community.

The maximum custodial sentence in youth court is 3 years, except for murder, which is 10 years.

Youth court dispositions are subject to review by a judge, which must occur at least once a year if a youth is in custody. Review may, for example, result in transfer from secure to open custody, or release from custody on probation, but there are concerns that too often youths are released into the community without good supervision and support. A more severe disposition can only be imposed at a review hearing if a new offence has occurred, or a youth has violated the terms of the original disposition.

The most serious cases can be "transferred" into adult court for trial and sentencing. Transfer generally only occurs after a youth court hearing under section 16 of the *YOA*. At a transfer hearing the court considers the youth's prospects for rehabilitation and the protection of the public. Transfer is controversial, and the *YOA* was amended in 1992 and 1995 to ensure that protection of the public is paramount. The Act also now provides a presumption that 16- and 17-year-olds charged with the most serious of offences will be dealt with in adult court. Youths who are transferred and convicted may be placed in adult correctional facilities, though even after transfer there is a judicial decision to keep the youth in a youth facility, and there is earlier parole eligibility for youths transferred on murder charges than for adults.

Processing of Youth Cases in 1998/99

As noted above, the *Young Offenders Act* in Canada provided for the establishment of youth courts to deal with criminal offences committed by youth aged from 12 through 17. In addition to conducting the Uniform Crime Reporting Survey, the Canadian Centre for Justice Statistics also completes the

Youth Court Survey (YCS) annually. The YCS has collected data from all youth courts in Canada since 1992-93.[5] Since not all youth charged with criminal offences proceed to youth court, data from the YCS reflect processing of cases through the court system, but are not indicative of the total amount of youth crime in Canada.

Once a police investigation is completed and there are reasonable grounds to believe that an offence was committed by a youth, charges may be laid. A referral may be made, either before or after a charge is laid, to an "alternative measures" or diversion program. Whether an alternative measures program is pre- or post-charge depends largely on the Canadian jurisdiction involved. Except in New Brunswick, Ontario, Manitoba, Alberta, and Yukon, alternative measures are both pre- and post-charge, with the majority of cases being referred at the pre-charge stage. In New Brunswick, Manitoba, and Alberta the alternative measures programs are exclusively pre-charge, while in Ontario, only post-charge alternative measures are available. In the Yukon, the general practice is to refer youth to alternative measures post-charge; in a few cases, however, pre-charge referrals may be made (Carrière, 2000). Alternative measures programs are intended to provide relatively expeditious resolution to less serious cases.

The Canadian Centre for Justice Statistics conducts the Alternative Measures Survey for Youth and Adults annually across Canada. In the fiscal year 1998/99, a total of 33,173 cases involving youth were referred to alternative measures programs (a rate of 1,350 per 100,000 youth). The province of Alberta reported the highest rates of referrals to alternative measures (3,840 per 100,000 youth), while British Columbia and Ontario reported the lowest rates (630 and 660, respectively). Alternative measures referrals were made most often in cases of property-related offences: 57% of all cases referred to alternative measures in 1998/99 were for theft under $5000 (Engler & Crowe, 2000).

Youth cases that are not referred to either a pre-charge or post-charge alternative measures program typically proceed to youth court. Figure 2.1 presents the processing of cases through the youth court system during 1999/2000. During this period, 102,061 (4,174 per 100,000 youth) cases were referred to youth court. Of this total, 72% were aged from 15 through 17. Only 52 cases a year were transferred to adult court. These cases largely involved serious violent offences. Two-thirds (66.8% or 2,783 per 100,000 youth) of referred cases resulted in a conviction, while 32% were acquitted or referred to post-charge alternative measures, and 1.1% received an "other" disposition.

Approximately one-third (34% or 946 per 100,000 youth) of convictions resulted in a disposition to open or secure custody, a very high rate of custody compared to many other countries. Of all cases receiving a custodial disposition, 50% (473 per 100,000 youth) were sentenced to secure custody and 50% were sentenced to open custody. Of all cases resulting in a custodial disposition, 77% were for terms of three months or less, and over 90% were for six months or less (Sudworth & deSouza, 2001). Cases involving violent offences were slightly less

Figure 2.1
Process Model of All Crimes in the Canadian Youth Justice System, 1999/2000

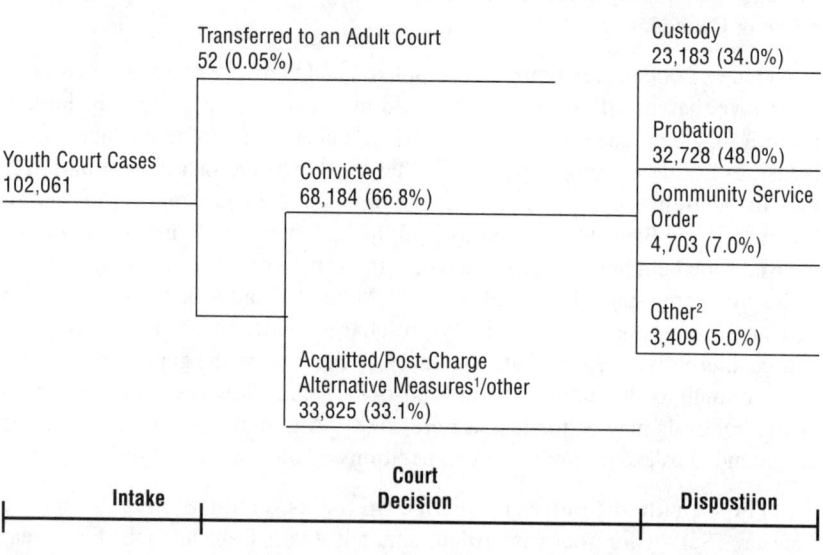

Source of Data: Sudworth, M., & deSouza, P. (2001). Youth court statistics, 1999/2000. *Juristat* 21: 3.

1 Some Canadian provinces and territories allow only pre-charge alternative measures while others allow only post-charge alternative measures. Other jurisdictions use both pre-charge and post-charge alternative measures.

2 Includes a variety of dispositions such as fines, restitution, counseling programs, and discharge.

likely to result in a custodial disposition than cases involving property offences (30% compared to 31%). However, the majority of violent offences were of the least serious type.

The majority of convictions did not result in a custodial disposition. Forty-eight percent (48%) of convicted youth received probation, 5% resulted in other dispositions such as fines, restitution, or discharge, and 7% received a community service order.

System Effectiveness and Efficiency

According to data collected through the Youth Court Survey, in 1999/2000 approximately 35% of all youth court cases resulting in convictions involved repeat young offenders (Sudworth & deSouza, 2001). Repeat young offenders were more likely to be brought to court for property offences than first-time offenders. Conversely, first-time offenders were more likely to be charged with violent offences. In 1999/2000, in cases involving repeat offenders, 53% involved property crimes and 25% involved violent crimes. For cases involving first-time offenders, 48% involved property crimes and 31% involved violent crimes.

In 1999/2000, recidivism rates were higher for males than for females. Of all youth court cases involving males that resulted in a conviction, 37% involved a repeat offender. Of cases involving a female young offender, 29% involved a repeat offender.

Not surprisingly, first-time offenders were more likely to be given a probationary disposition than were repeat offenders. Of cases resulting in a conviction of a first-time offender, 63% received probation as compared to 42% of cases involving a repeat offender. In line with this finding, repeat offenders were considerably more likely to receive a custodial sentence: 42% of repeat offenders were sentenced to custody compared to only 17% of first-time offenders.

Persistent offenders (defined as those with at least three prior convictions) accounted for a disproportionate amount of youth crime: 10% of all youth court convictions in 1999/2000 involved a persistent offender. Consistent with the pattern of youth crime in general, persistent offenders are more likely to be male than female.

System Innovations

There is a widespread recognition among researchers and policy analysts that Canada could do a better job of preventing and responding to youth crime, and there are a number of innovations being undertaken. However, for a variety of political reasons, including disagreements between the federal government and the provinces and territories over policy directions and funding, it has been difficult to affect change.

There is growing awareness of the importance of early intervention strategies with high-risk children to increase the chances that they will be productive adults and reduce the chances that they will be offenders. Some of the discussion is focusing on the importance of the first six years of life (McCain & Mustard, 1999). Some pilot programs have been established to work with pre-school children and children from high-risk families, with long-term research components to assess their impact (Peters & Russell, 1996; Peters et al., 2000).

Although Canada makes more use of youth court and formal charging than other countries, there is an increasing emphasis on diverting young offenders from the formal justice system. Under the *YOA*, section 4 provides a legislative framework for alternative measures, and section 69 encourages community involvement through the use of youth justice committees. Sentencing circles, family group conferences, and other community responses to youth crime are being extended, especially in Aboriginal communities that have high rates of offending. The province of Quebec has a more expansive approach to the role of the state than other Canadian jurisdictions, for example, in regard to support for childcare. It also has a more welfare-oriented approach to youth justice, and makes the most extensive use of various diversionary schemes for young offenders. In comparison to other provinces, Quebec also links its youth justice system most closely to its child welfare system, and has the lowest reported rates of youth crime and use of youth court.

There is also a growing awareness that more effective policing can help reduce the incidence of certain types of youth offending. Communities are increasingly establishing partnerships between police forces, schools, and community agencies. Police are more frequently patrolling in schools and involved in teaching about values, drugs, and law, as well as engaging in counseling and intelligence gathering.

There are also a number of new intervention strategies being introduced, at least on a pilot basis, to deal with youth who have already committed offences. In a number of provinces, Conservative politicians have established boot camps, modelled on those already established in some American states (Anand, 1999). The motivation for this action was clearly political, as some of these politicians ran for office promising to "get tough" on youth crime. Fortunately, the boot camps that have been established have significant counseling and educational components, and community follow-up. While initial findings from an evaluation of a boot camp in Ontario show reduced recidivism, further research evaluations are necessary to determine whether the decrease in offending is statistically significant (T3 Associates Training and Consulting, 2001; Anand, 1999).

Another innovation is a pilot program of community-based multi-systemic therapy, based in several Ontario centres (Cunningham, 2000). This program is aimed at youth with serious anitisocial and criminal behaviour, and is modelled on similar successful American programs. It is a family and present-oriented therapeutic program that develops a tailored program to meet the needs of individual youth and their parents, aimed at reducing criminal behaviour. It takes referrals from probation officers and other sources. This program is being subjected to rigorous control group studies to determine cost-effectiveness.

Issues and Controversies: The *Youth Criminal Justice Act*

There is considerable controversy over youth justice in Canada, with over 70% of respondents to public opinion polls reporting a lack of confidence in the youth justice system. In 2000, the two conservative opposition parties attempted to make youth justice a major issue in the federal election. One of the conservative parties, the Canadian Alliance, included in its election platform promises to reduce the age jurisdiction from the current 12 to 18 years to a proposed 10 to 16, to increase the number of youths dealt with in adult court and to allow more identifying publicity about youths in the justice system. On the other hand, the more progressive opposition Quebec separatist party opposed any efforts that might result in more youths being sent to adult jails, or that would increase federal control over provincial youth corrections policies.

In some provinces, provincial politicians have also made youth crime an issue, charging that inadequate legal responses, and in particular the federal *Young Offenders Act,* are a problem. In three provinces, British Columbia, Manitoba and Ontario, Conservative governments have enacted legislation to allow victims of crimes committed by youths to sue the parents of offenders. In practice these laws are rarely used, and parents may use a defence of reasonable supervision, but these laws are intended to "send a message."

While many politicians and members of the public, stirred by media reports that devote disproportionate attention to violent youth crimes and youth gangs, focus on "getting tough" with youth crime, as this chapter documents Canada makes more use of youth court charging and custody than other countries. These responses are relatively expensive and often not very effective in reducing youth crime. There is also a concern that Aboriginal and visible minority youth are disproportionately represented in youth court and correctional facilities. While this may in part reflect poverty and social problems among these groups, there are also charges of racism made against police and other justice system professionals.

The federal government has embarked on a "Strategy for the Renewal of Youth Justice" (Department of Justice Canada, 1998) that involves plans for both an increase in spending and new legislation. The Strategy is intended to have more youths diverted from youth court and youth custody, though for a relatively small group of serious violent offenders there is a more punitive response. The Strategy aims to make more use of community-based options for rehabilitating most youth offenders, as well as increasing access to rehabilitative services and community follow-up support for youth in custody. For a public that is demanding a "get tough" approach, there is also the prospect of longer sentences for the most serious offenders. The federal government has been negotiating with the provincial and territorial governments about how much to increase its spending and how to shift resources towards community-based programs.

An important part of the Strategy is the proposed new *Youth Criminal Justice Act.*[6] The *YJCA* is a complex piece of legislation. It attempts to place a greater emphasis on community-based responses to youth offending behaviour without interfering with the important areas of responsibility of judges and provincial and territorial governments. Thus, for example, there are a number of provisions that encourage the use of a range of pre-court screening and diversion options, but the new Act clearly gives the final responsibility for making decisions to police, prosecutors, and local agencies and does not give any youth the "right" to seek diversion.

The new Act states that custody is to be a "last resort" sentencing option, reserved for youth who have committed violent offences or who have violated the terms of community-based sentences. For youth who receive a custodial disposition in youth court under the *YCJA*, there is a provision that each sentence is to include one third under "community supervision." This provision is intended to increase community follow-up, though there is the possibility of the supervision being suspended or release occurring before the court-imposed release date. A new sentencing option is being added for serious offenders, that of "intensive rehabilitative custody." This provision might allow a court, with the approval of correctional officials, to place a youth in a facility where treatment will be provided, though even for youths in these facilities there will be restraints on involuntary treatment.

For the most serious violent offenders, the *YCJA* increases the prospect of an adult sentence. For youths 14 and older convicted of a very serious offence, there will be the presumption of an adult length sentence, with the first portion likely to be served in a youth custody facility. The *YCJA* will simplify and expedite the process for deciding whether an adult sentence may be imposed, replacing the pre-trial "transfer" hearing under the *YOA* with a post-conviction process, though giving the right to trial by jury to youths facing this type of sanction. The test for deciding whether to deal with a youth as an adult will focus more on accountability and less on rehabilitation. The *YCJA* will also allow for the publication of identifying information about youths convicted of serious offences even if not subject to an adult sentence.

A controversial provision of the proposed new law will allow provincial and territorial governments to establish programs to seek reimbursement from parents for legal services provided to their children. There is a real concern that this may result in parents pressuring their children to waive the right to counsel, and hence plead guilty even if innocent or not receive appropriate advocacy for sentencing. Another contentious proposal will give judges some discretion to admit confessions of youth to the police, even if the police have not fully complied with the cautioning requirements for adolescents.

The proposed *YCJA* has been criticized by conservative politicians for not being "tough enough" on youth crime, while Quebec has criticized it for undermining its treatment-focused philosophy for young offenders and for intruding on areas of provincial jurisdiction. The *YCJA* has recently been enacted and it will come into force early in 2003.

The ultimate effect of the *YCJA* will depend on the extent to which provincial and territorial governments establish and support appropriate programs and facilities. It will also depend on the approaches of police, prosecutors, judges, probation officers and correctional officials. There are plans for major professional education programs to coincide with the introduction of the new Act, in part intended to help shape attitudes and values.

References

Anand, S.S. (1999). Preventing youth crime: What works, what doesn't, and what it all means for Canadian juvenile justice policy. *Queen's Law Journal* 25: 177-213.

Bala, N. (1997) *Young offenders law*. Concord, ON: Irwin Law Publishing.

Besserer, S., & Trainor, C. (2000). Criminal victimization in Canada, 1999. *Juristat* 20. Ottawa, ON: Canadian Centre for Justice Statistics.

Besserer, S., & Tufts, J. (1999). Justice spending in Canada. *Juristat* 19. Ottawa, ON: Canadian Centre for Justice Statistics.

Canadian Centre for Justice Statistics. (2000). *Youth court data tables, 1998-99*. Ottawa, ON: Statistics Canada.

Canadian Council on Social Development. (2000). *The Canadian fact book on poverty 2000*. Ottawa, ON: Canadian Council on Social Development.

Canadian Council on Social Development. (1999). *The progress of Canada's children into the millennium: 1999-2000*. Ottawa, ON: Canadian Council on Social Development.

Canadian Council on Social Development. (1998). *The progress of Canada's children 1998: Focus on youth*. Ottawa, ON: Canadian Council on Social Development.

Canadian Council on Social Development. (1996). *The progress of Canada's children 1996*. Ottawa, ON: Canadian Council on Social Development.

Carrière, D. (2000). Youth court statistics, 1998/99 highlights. *Juristat* 20. Ottawa, ON: Canadian Centre for Justice Statistics.

Carrington, P.J. (1995). Has violent youth crime increased? Comment on Corrado and Markwart. *Canadian Journal of Criminology* 37.

Corrado, R.R., & Markwart, A. (1994). The need to reform the *YOA* in response to violent young offenders: Confusion, reality or myth? *Canadian Journal of Criminology* 36.

Cunningham, A. (2000). *Implementing multisystemic therapy in Canada*. www.amicusmst.org

Department of Justice Canada. (1998). *A strategy for the renewal of youth justice*. Ottawa, ON: Canada Communications Group-Publishing, Public Works and Government Services Canada.

Engler, C., & Crowe, S. (2000). Alternative measures in Canada, 1998-99. *Juristat* 20. Ottawa, ON: Canadian Centre for Justice Statistics.

Frank, J. (1996). After high school: Initial results of the school leavers follow-up survey. *Education Quarterly Review* 3 (4): 10-22.

Gomes, J.T., Bertrand, L.D., Paetsch, J.J., & Hornick, J.P. (2000). *The extent of youth victimization, crime and delinquency in Alberta, 1999*. Calgary, AB: Canadian Research Institute for Law and the Family.

Law, B. (1997). *1998 Canadian sourcebook*. Don Mills, ON: Southam Information Products.

Mayhew, P., & van Dijk, J.J.M. (1997). *Criminal victimization in eleven industrialized countries*. London: Home Office.

McCain, M., & Mustard F. (1999). *Reversing the real brain drain: Early years study.* Toronto, ON: Ontario Children's Secretariat.

McIntyre, L., Connor, S., & Warren, J. (1998). *A glimpse of child hunger in Canada.* Ottawa, ON: Human Resources Development Canada.

National Council on Welfare. (2000). *Poverty profile 1998.* Ottawa, ON: National Council on Welfare.

Peters, R., & Russell, C. (1996). Promoting development and preventing disorder: The better beginnings, better futures project. In R. Peters & R. McMahon (Eds.), *Preventing childhood disorders, substance abuse and delinquency* (Thousand Oaks, CA: Sage), pp. 19-47.

Peters, R. et al. (2000). *Developing Capacity and Competence in Better Beginnings. Better Futures Communities: Short-term Findings Report.* (Kingston, ON: Better Beginnings, Queen's University). http://bbbf.queensu.ca.

Ross, D.P., & Roberts, P. (1999). *Income and child well-being: A new perspective on the poverty debate.* Ottawa, ON: Canadian Council on Social Development.

Ross, D., Scott, K., & Kelly, M.A. (1996). Overview: Children in Canada in the 1990s. In Human Resources Development Canada/Statistics Canada, *Growing up in Canada: National longitudinal survey of children and youth* (Ottawa, ON: Minister of Industry), pp. 15-45.

Statistics Canada. (1998). *Education in Canada, 1997.* Ottawa: Minister of Industry.

Sudworth, M., & deSouza P. (2001). Youth court statistics, 1999/2000. *Juristat* 21. Ottawa, ON: Canadian Centre for Justice Statistics.

T3 Associates Training and Consulting. (2001). *Project Turnaround outcome evaluation: Final report.* Toronto, ON: Ontario Ministry of Correctional Services.

Notes

1 It should be noted that costs for youth courts are included in the "Courts" category and not in "Youth Corrections." Thus, the amount of spending under "Youth Corrections" is an underestimate of spending on youth justice.

2 R.S.C. 1985, c. Y-1.

3 R.S.C. 1970, C. J-3.

4 *R. v. T.(E.)* (1993), 26 C.R. (4th) 246 (S.C.C.).

5 Unlike the Uniform Crime Reporting Survey, which collects data on a calendar year basis, the Youth Court Survey collects data on a fiscal year basis, i.e., April 1 through March 31.

6 S.C. 2002, chap. 1, Royal Assent Feb. 19, 2002.

CHAPTER 3

Juvenile Crime and Justice in the United States of America

Howard N. Snyder

The United States of America does not have a national juvenile justice system. Juvenile justice systems vary substantially from state to state, though the U.S. Constitution, federal policies and legislation, and political pressures produce significant common features. These separate systems, which are controlled largely by state legislation, differ from each other in mission, scope, and procedure. These inherent variations provide many opportunities to test different approaches and new programs and to learn from others, but they make it difficult to describe succinctly the delivery of juvenile justice in the United States.

Juveniles in eighteenth-century America were subject to the same legal regime as adults by the criminal justice system, though age was often considered a mitigating factor in sentencing. The "child saver" movement in the nineteenth century was a response to the concerns of social reformers who believed increasing industrialization, urbanization, and immigration was causing moral decline and exposing children to crime and vice. "Houses of refuge" and reformatories were established in urban areas. These institutions were seen as substitutes for families that were not capable of protecting and nurturing their own children. Poor, orphaned, and immigrant children were taken to these institutions. Although these institutions were intended to protect and rehabilitate children, by the end of the nineteenth century, critics of these "reformatories" argued that they were little more than prisons for poor, urban, and vagrant youth living on the margins of society.

In response, a separate juvenile justice system was born in the United States. The first juvenile court was established in the State of Illinois in 1899. Nearly all states had a juvenile court by the 1920s. These civil (i.e., noncriminal) courts

---

Howard N. Snyder is the Director of Systems Research for the National Center for Juvenile Justice in Pittsburgh, Pennsylvania, USA.

were guided by the principle that their actions should be in the *best interest of the child*. Juvenile justice in the United States was molded by the concept of *parens patriae*, which saw the state in the role of a parent. As a parent, the state had a responsibility to intervene in the lives of children when the child was in need of care due to the inability of the natural parents to provide appropriate care or supervision. Within this framework, a child violating the criminal law was considered to be a delinquent in need of the court's "benevolent intervention." Court hearings were informal with few of the procedural requirements of a criminal court. While it is likely that most interventions included some element of punishment, the juvenile justice system saw its primary mission as treatment and rehabilitation. During their early histories, juvenile courts in the United States were bolstered by the expectation that the newly developing social sciences offered hope for successful interventions to "reform" delinquent youth.

However, by the 1960s and 1970s, many doubted whether rehabilitation was possible, or at least whether the practices of the juvenile justice systems were effective in rehabilitating the youth under their care. A U.S. Supreme Court Justice in an opinion written in the 1960s characterized juveniles caught up in the juvenile justice system as possibly receiving the worst of both worlds, receiving neither the procedural safeguards of the criminal justice system nor the rehabilitative promise of the juvenile justice system.

Beginning in the late 1960s, rulings by the United States Supreme Court substantively changed the character of the juvenile courts. The informality of the juvenile courts was greatly diminished when they were ordered to give accused delinquents many of the same legal rights adults had when charged with a criminal act (e.g., protection against self-incrimination, the right to receive notice of the charges, the right to present and question witnesses, the right of indigent youth to have an attorney provided by the state, and the right to have the charges against them proven beyond a reasonable doubt). These rulings diminished the procedural differences between the juvenile and criminal justice systems.

Juvenile justice policy in the United States was altered significantly in the 1990s by concerns surrounding a substantial increase in violent crime arrests of youth and growing public concern about juvenile crime. In reaction, many states revised their juvenile justice legislation to modify the mission of the juvenile justice system to include (and in many instances give priority to) *public safety* concerns. Nearly every state in the 1990s changed its legislation to enable more juveniles to be tried as adults in the criminal justice system — exposing them to all the sanctions available to adults. As the differences between the juvenile and criminal justice systems blur and as more juveniles are processed as adults, some in the United States today are questioning if there will be a separate justice system for juveniles in the next 20 years.

PART I:
PROFILE OF THE
UNITED STATES OF AMERICA

Demographic Characteristics

In 1998 the United States had a population of 270 million people. Twenty-six percent (26%) of the population (i.e., 70 million persons) was below the age of 18. Since the 1960s, persons under age 18 have been a decreasing proportion of the U.S. population. The racial and ethnic composition of the U.S. population has changed within the last generation. The percentage of nonHispanic white youth decreased from 74% in 1980 to 65% in 1998. The percentage of Hispanic youth increased from 9% to 15% between 1980 and 1998, while Asian/Pacific Islander youth doubled (from 2% to 4%). The proportions of nonHispanic black youth and of American Indian/Alaskan Native youth remained essentially constant over the period at 15% and 4% respectively. The increases in Hispanic and Asian/Pacific Islander youth were due to both immigration and the higher birth rates of these ethnic groups.

The population of the United States is spread over 50 states and the District of Columbia (the independent capital city). California, the largest state, had a population of 33 million in 1998. Wyoming, the state with the smallest population, had less than 500,000 inhabitants. In the United States about 30% of the children live in central cities, 47% live in the metropolitan areas surrounding the central cities, and 23% live in rural areas. Most black and Hispanic youth live in the central cities, while most white youth live outside the central cities.

Living Arrangements

In the United States the number of two-parent families is on the decline. In 1970, 85% of youth lived with two parents; in 1998 it was 68%. Twenty-three percent (23%) lived with only their mothers, 4% lived only with their fathers, and 4% lived with neither parent. In recent decades the proportion of youth living with two parents has been decreasing among all racial and ethnic groups, though white children were much more likely to live with both parents (76%) than were Hispanic (64%) or black children (36%).

One reason for this change in the composition of American families has been the sharp rise in births to unmarried mothers. In 1997 one of every three births in the United States (32%) was to an unmarried mother, compared to just 5% of births in 1960 (Federal Interagency Forum on Child and Family Statistics, 1997). This is related to the large increase in the proportion of women of childbearing age who are unmarried (from 29% in 1960 to 46% in 1994), the increase in nonmarital cohabitation, and the nearly 50% decline in the birth rate of married women. However, nearly two-thirds of children living with only their mothers in 1995 were living with mothers who had been married but were either divorced, separated, or widowed.

Socioeconomic Characteristics

Employment and Poverty

In 1997, 40% of persons living in poverty in the United States were children under age 18 (Federal Interagency Forum on Child and Family Statistics, 1999). One in five American children (19%) lived below the poverty level, a proportion that has held relatively constant since the early 1980s and is above the levels of the 1970s (15%). While most children who live in poverty were nonHispanic whites, a smaller proportion of nonHispanic white children than black and Hispanic children live in poverty. In 1997, 11% of white children lived in poverty, compared to 37% of black and 36% of Hispanic children.

Family structure is related to poverty levels. Forty-nine percent (49%) of children in female-headed households lived in poverty in 1997, compared to 10% of children living in married-couple families. In 1997 three-fourths (76%) of all children living with parents had at least one parent who worked full time all year. Two-parent families (88%) were more likely to have at least one parent who was a year-round, full-time worker than were families headed by a single father (70%) and families headed by a single mother (41%). A major change in the United States over the last generation has been the increase in the proportion of two-parent families in which both parents work full time out of the home, an increase from 17% in 1980 to 31% in 1997. The children of these families and the children in one-parent families where the parent works full time outside the home have been labeled "latch-key children," children who are likely to come home from school to an empty home. Research in the United States has found that this unsupervised time is a period of high risk for both victimization and offending (Snyder & Sickmund, 2000).

Health Care

In the United States in 1996, parents reported that 81% of children were in very good or excellent health (Federal Interagency Forum on Child and Family Statistics, 1999). Children living in poverty were less likely to be in good health than were children living in families at or above the poverty line (65% compared to 84%). The United States does not have universal health care. Health insurance is a common benefit of employment. Many children in families where the parent is unemployed, underemployed, or who has inadequate private health insurance receive health care through the public welfare system. However, in 1998, 15%

of America's children had no health insurance, compared to just 1% of persons over age 64. Poor children (23%) were more likely to lack the necessary health insurance than were nonpoor children (13%). In 1997, Hispanic children (29%) were more likely to lack health insurance coverage than were black (19%) or white (11%) children. Children living in families without adequate health insurance can receive publicly paid emergency treatment, but they lack access to preventive and supportive health care.

Education

In the United States nearly one of every seven youth drops out of school before graduating from high school (Federal Interagency Forum on Child and Family Statistics, 1999). In 1997, 86% of Americans between the ages of 18 and 24 had completed the equivalent of 12 years of schooling (i.e., a high school education). The percentage was higher for whites (91%) than blacks (83%). The level was far lower for youth of Hispanic origin (67%). In 1998 about one-third (31%) of high school graduates aged 25 to 29 had received a college degree, which was substantially above the 22% figure reported for 1971. White high school graduates aged 25 to 29 were twice as likely as black and Hispanic graduates to have earned a college degree (35% versus 18% and 17% respectively).

Reported Drug Use

Each year researchers in the United States ask a large representative sample of high school seniors (persons averaging ages 17 to 18) about their drug use. Their confidential responses show that illicit drug use decreased substantially between 1978 and 1992 (Johnston, O'Malley, & Bachman, 1995). In 1978 37% of high school seniors reported using an illicit drug in the previous month; this figure had dropped to 14% by 1992. Since 1992 reported illicit drug use has been on the rise, reaching 26% in 1998. Younger students have reported similar increases in recent years.

Alcohol use also declined during much of the last two decades. In 1980 41% of high school seniors reported having five or more drinks in a row in the prior two weeks. This percentage dropped to 27% in 1993, before increasing again thereafter and reaching 31% by 1998.

Social Policy Issues Related to Children and Youth

Crime Prevention Initiatives

As with the juvenile justice system, crime prevention strategies in the United States are predominately locally determined. In general, the role of the federal government is (1) to develop, test, and promote model crime prevention programs; and (2) to encourage the implementation of these programs by providing states and local jurisdictions with funds that may be spent on such programs. As a result, there are many crime prevention programs in the United States, ranging from pre-natal home nurse visitation programs targeted at reducing the criminal behaviour of young mothers and their babies to pre-school education programs for children who are at risk of academic failure. There are also crime prevention initiatives in some states that have produced rigid criminal sentencing policies that result in long terms of confinement for repeat offenders. To summarize all crime prevention initiatives would be impossible, but a brief description of a few may give the reader a sense of them.

In recent years local jurisdictions have begun to adopt a new (or possibly a very old) approach to policing, namely community-oriented policing. As popularly described, such programs move police officers out of their patrol cars and have them walk their beats to acquaint them with the citizens and their problems. It is believed that community policing will help citizens develop a greater level of trust in law enforcement. Where community-oriented policing is most effective, the law enforcement officers are either aware of problems before they happen, or find ways to deal with offenders that satisfy the needs of the community, prevent a reoccurrence of the problem, and reduce the community's dependence on the formal justice system.

A popular, school-based, drug abuse prevention program is DARE (Drug Abuse Resistance Education). This program is found in most school districts across the United States. Targeted at juveniles aged 11 and 12, this program uses law enforcement officers to teach children about the harm associated with drug use and attempts to give the children coping skills that may help them resist the initial social pressure to experiment with drugs. While rigorous evaluations of these programs have shown little (if any) positive long-term effects on juvenile drug use, the program is well promoted and has captured the hearts of many parents and local officials. The DARE logo is seen everywhere — on T-shirts, caps, bumper stickers, and even painted on the sides of police cars.

Juvenile curfews are common in many jurisdictions, introduced to attempt to reduce juvenile offending and victimization. However, until recently these curfews were often poorly enforced, and there is no reliable research to demonstrate that curfews are effective in reducing youth crime. Research in the United States has clearly shown that most of the violent crime committed by juveniles is committed in the few hours between the end of the school day and dinner time (Snyder & Sickmund, 2000). Whether targeting crimes committed by the general population of juveniles or by members of juvenile gangs, this specific time period calls out for crime prevention programs. With empirical evidence that violent crime is more concentrated in the after-school hours than in the late night hours (the traditional curfew period), many communities are establishing after-school programs with the help of crime prevention funds. These programs provide adult supervision for activities ranging from academic programs to sports during the hours when many youth would otherwise be unsupervised. Federal, state, and local governments have devoted substantial funding in recent budgets for after-school programs.

At the other end of the continuum are the crime prevention initiatives based on a philosophy of incapacitation and deterrence. These initiatives are premised on the belief that the longer offenders are incarcerated, the fewer crimes will be committed. In addition, realizing the high likelihood of lengthy sentences, other potential offenders will hopefully be discouraged from committing crime. After a strong negative public response to high-profile failures in early prison-release programs, some states passed *Truth in Sentencing* legislation. These laws prohibit early release from prison and require convicted adult offenders to serve a high percentage (e.g., 85%) of the prison sentence imposed by the judge before being eligible for parole. Some states have also passed *Three Strikes* legislation. Using a reference to the sport of baseball, such legislation requires a judge to sentence an adult offender convicted of a third felony to life in prison (i.e., three strikes and you're out). These policies have had anticipated and unanticipated consequences. Prison construction has soared, placing significant strains on state budgets. In jurisdictions where plea bargains were the norm in felony prosecutions, court dockets are now overwhelmed as offenders fight even their first strike. And while the crimes committed by the incarcerated offenders are certainly diminished, there is evidence (especially with drug offences) that other offenders have stepped in to fill the criminal void resulting from the incarceration, diminishing the crime prevention effect of incarceration.

The impact of *Truth in Sentencing* and *Three Strikes* legislation is felt only gradually after introduction. Under these systems, the flow of adult offenders into the prison system generally does not increase, but with time the prison population swells as length of stay increases. The real cost of these policies is seen 5 or 10 years after the legislation is enacted, when the prison budget is commanding more and more of the state's revenues. Recent research has found that funds spent on prevention programs that target persons before they enter the juvenile and adult criminal justice systems (i.e., primary prevention programs) are more cost-effective than are funds spent on programs that incarcerate offenders for longer periods of time (Greenwood et al., 1996). Support for more primary prevention programs is growing in the United States as the sheer cost of incarceration is being recognized.

PART II:
TRENDS IN OFFENDING BEHAVIOUR BY JUVENILES

Rates of Reported Crime

The Federal Bureau of Investigation (FBI) monitors the levels of crime reported to law enforcement agencies in the United States using two indices, one for violent crime and one for property crime. The committee designing the FBI's Uniform Crime Reporting Program in the 1930s wanted to develop indices that would be sensitive to changes in the volume and nature of reported crime. They decided to incorporate specific offences into these indices based in part on the seriousness of the offence, but also on the likelihood of the offence being reported to law enforcement agencies, its frequency of occurrence, and its pervasiveness in all geographical areas of the country. The Violent Crime Index and the Property Crime Index are each combinations of offences that the developers of the reporting series believed to be effective barometers of the crime types they were designed to monitor. The components of the indices are:

- **Violent Crime Index** — murder and nonnegligent manslaughter, forcible rape, robbery, and aggravated assault.
- **Property Crime Index** — burglary, larceny-theft, and motor vehicle theft.

All information on reported crime trends in the United States is limited to a tabulation of these seven crime types.

The Property Crime Index (i.e., reported Property Crime Index offences per 100,000 persons in the United States population) was at its lowest level in over two decades in 1998 and 24% below the peak year of 1980 (Federal Bureau of Investigation, 1981-1999). Trends in the individual offences within the index did not follow this general pattern. Motor vehicle theft and larceny-theft rates declined moderately over this period (by 9% and 14% respectively). In sharp contrast to these relatively small changes, the burglary rate in the United States dropped by 49% between 1980 and 1998. Some have attributed this large decline to the substantial improvement in the U.S. economy and to the proliferation of home and business security systems.

The relative stability followed by a decline in the property crime rate in the United States in the 1980s and 1990s was not replicated by the violent crime rate trends. Between 1980 and 1991 the rate of reported violent crimes in the United States increased by 27%. However, violent crime rates fell each year between 1991 and 1998. By 1998 the rate had fallen 25% to near the lowest level in the last two decades.

The United States has one of the highest rates of homicide in the world. In 1980, the homicide rate in the United States peaked at a level of 10.2 homicides for every 100,000 persons in the resident population. Between 1980 and 1996 the homicide rate fluctuated, returning almost to the peak level in 1991 (9.8). But the most recent figures are encouraging. By 1998 the homicide rate in the United States had fallen substantially to 6.3, down 38% from the peak year of 1980 and to its lowest level since 1967.

The rates for other components of the Violent Crime Index also peaked in the early 1990s and have fallen since then. The rate of reported forcible rapes in 1998 (34.4) was near the average level of the last 20 years. Robbery rates have fluctuated over the last two decades, but the low rate of reported robberies in 1998 (165.2) was at a level that had not been seen since the 1970s. In contrast to the other components of the Violent Crime Index, reported incidents of aggravated assault increased substantially (48%) between 1980 and 1992. By 1998 the rate had fallen back to the level of 1988, but it was still significantly above the levels of the mid-1980s.

The increase in reported aggravated assaults may have more to do with policy change than a change in the behaviour of the American population. During this period of growth in reported assaults, many states changed their laws and many law enforcement agencies revised their procedures to cope with the problems of domestic violence. It was not uncommon in decades past for law enforcement officers to handle domestic violence calls (e.g., a disturbance call in which a husband and wife are fighting or in which a juvenile is fighting with a parent) informally—for example, asking the individual to calm down, or having the husband or wife stay with a relative for the evening while tempers cooled or the effects of the alcohol wore off. With the increased understanding of the harm domestic violence causes to the family, the children, and the community, many law enforcement officers are now required to arrest and remove from the home for a period of time one of the primary actors in the dispute. These policy changes have resulted in more arrests and, therefore, more law enforcement reporting of domestic assault crime statistics. In addition, these policy changes may also have caused more domestic violence incidents to be reported to police by the participants, neighbours, or friends, knowing that some action would be taken. Therefore, the large increases in reported aggravated and simple assaults probably do not reflect actual increases in these types of behaviours, just more reporting to and by law enforcement.

Juvenile Arrests

In 1998 law enforcement agencies made more than 2.6 million arrests of persons under age 18. Not all of these youth are classified as juveniles by the U.S. justice system. This is because in some states all persons come under the authority of the criminal (i.e., adult) justice system when they turn age 17, while in a few other states the age of adult criminal jurisdiction begins at age 16. To complicate the matter even further, even for some persons whose age alone would classify them as a juvenile in their state, state legislation places their alleged behavior (generally a prescribed set of serious crimes) under the authority of the adult criminal justice system. Whether state statutes place all 16- or 17-year-old alleged offenders under the jurisdiction of the criminal justice system or their acts alone make them adults in the eyes of their state's justice system, these youth are exposed to the same set of sanctions as any adult, including in some cases the death penalty. Therefore, not all of the 2.6 million arrests in 1998 were the arrest of a juvenile according to state statutes, but for simplicity they will be labeled *juvenile arrests* in the remainder of this section.

Eighteen percent (18%) of all persons arrested in the United States in 1998 were under age 18. Juveniles were involved in a much smaller proportion of violent crime arrests (17%) than property arrests (33%). About one-quarter (27%) of the persons arrested for robbery were under age 18, substantially above the juvenile arrest proportions for the other violent crimes of forcible rape (17%), aggravated assault (14%), and murder (12%). In contrast, juveniles were involved in 52% of arson arrests, 42% of vandalism arrests, 36% of motor vehicle theft arrests, 35% of burglary arrests, and 32% of larceny-theft arrests in 1998. In 1998 13% of all persons arrested on a drug offence were under the age of 18, and 24% of persons arrested for a weapons law violation were juveniles.

In the United States in 1998 there were 86 juvenile arrests for every 1,000 persons aged 10 through 17 in the population. Twenty-six percent (26%) of juvenile arrestees were age 17, 23% were age 16, and 19% were age 15. Nine percent (9%) of juvenile arrestees in 1998 were below the age of 13. In 30% of all juvenile arrests, the most serious charge was a property offence. In another 15% of arrests the juvenile was charged with a violent offence (i.e., murder, forcible rape, robbery, aggravated assault, simple assault, and weapons possession). Sixteen percent (16%) of arrested youth were charged with an alcohol or other drug offence, 7% with disorderly conduct, 7% with running away from home, and 6% with a curfew violation.

Twenty-seven percent (27%) of juveniles arrested in 1998 were female. Females were overrepresented in only one offence category; while females were 49% of the United States population aged 10 through 17 in 1998, they were involved in 58% of arrests in which the youth was charged with the status offence of running away from home. Other crime types in which females had relatively high proportions of the juvenile arrests were larceny-theft (35%), liquor law violations (30%), and curfew and loitering law violations (30%). Males were most overrepresented in juvenile arrests for forcible rape (98%), murder (92%), weapons offences (91%), robbery (91%), and burglary (89%).

In 1998, 79% of the United States population between the ages of 10 and 17 were racially classified as white (including Hispanic), with 15% black, and smaller proportions of Native Americans (1%) and Asian/Pacific Islanders (4%).[1] Racial minorities were overrepresented in juvenile arrest statistics. The youth was white in 71% of all juvenile arrests in 1998, while 26% were black, 1% were Native American, and 2% were Asian/Pacific Islanders. Nonwhite youth were involved in 30% of property offence arrests, 34% of weapons law violation arrests, 34% of drug arrests, and 45% of violent crime arrests. Minority youth were most overrepresented in murder arrests (53%). Minority youth in 1998 were involved in relatively small percentages of juvenile arrests for liquor law violations (8%) and driving under the influence of alcohol or drugs (9%). These low percentages probably reflect the fact that these arrests are most common in nonurban areas, where minority populations are relatively small.

Juvenile Arrest Trends

In general between 1980 and 1996 the juvenile arrest rate for property crimes remained essentially constant (see Table 3.1). The rate, however, dropped substantially between 1996 and 1998, so that in 1998 the juvenile arrest rate for property crimes was 24% below its 1980 level. Arrest rates for specific property crimes also declined over this period but to different degrees. For example, during this period the juvenile arrest rate for burglary declined 53%, while the arrest rate for larceny-theft dropped by 9%, and for motor vehicle theft, by 19%.

While juvenile arrests for drug abuse remained essentially constant between 1980 and 1992, the rate increased markedly in the next six years. By 1998 the juvenile arrest rate for drug abuse violations was double the 1992 rate. This increase occurred during a period when self-report drug abuse surveys showed little change in the use of illicit drugs by juveniles in the United States. However, the increase did correspond with a new federal government initiative labeled "The War on Drugs." This policy initiative reflected the public's concern over drug abuse by America's youth and provided funds to pay for up to 100,000 new law enforcement officers to serve in local jurisdictions across the country. Therefore, the increase in juvenile drug abuse arrests can, to a great extent, be attributed to changes in public attitude and law enforcement policy, rather than changes in juvenile behavior. It is also interesting to note that curfew arrest rates also abruptly increased in the early 1990s after an empirically unsubstantiated idea gained public credibility that enforcement of juvenile curfew laws would reduce juvenile violence.

The large increases in juvenile arrests for violent crime offences between 1988 and 1994 were used as justification for significant changes in the juvenile justice system in the United States. In the period between the mid-1970s and the late 1980s the juvenile violent crime arrest rate remained relatively constant. The rate then broke out of its traditional levels in 1989 and continued to increase to the peak year of 1994. Between 1988 through 1994 the juvenile violent crime arrest rate in the United States increased over 60%, causing the media, the public and legislators to call for changes in the juvenile justice system to handle the apparent *"new breed"* of juvenile offender. With the increased media attention on juvenile crime, the American public grew to believe the new type of offender, the juvenile "superpredator," was the reason for the increase in juvenile violence. This reasoning placed the blame for the increasing juvenile violence on a small core of youth who were beyond the rehabilitative powers of the juvenile justice system. Through this argument, it was logical not to utilize or develop treatment options; what was appropriate was to send these youth to the criminal justice system and lock them away for long time periods. State legislation was enacted to respond to this perceived problem of the "superpredator." However, while the resulting changes were being made, juvenile violent crime arrest rates declined each year from 1995 through the 1998, falling to a level below that of 1989, essentially erasing all of the increase that stimulated the changes.

Table 3.1
Juvenile Arrest Rates in the United States, 1980/98

	1980	1982	1984	1986	1988	1990	1992	1994	1996	1998
All Offences	7,414	7,345	6,766	7,505	7,600	8,033	8,239	9,275	9,522	8,570
Violent Crime Index	334	314	297	317	326	428	482	527	464	370
Murder	6	7	5	6	8	12	12	13	10	7
Forcible Rape	16	17	20	21	19	22	22	20	19	17
Robbery	167	151	132	128	117	155	175	199	178	109
Aggravated Assault	144	140	140	161	181	239	273	294	257	237
Property Crime Index	2,562	2,373	2,221	2,427	2,419	2,564	2,523	2,546	2,387	1,960
Burglary	794	701	568	575	506	513	507	481	438	375
Larceny-theft	1,521	1,488	1,474	1,603	1,593	1678	1,656	1,720	1,668	1,380
Motor vehicle theft	222	163	156	227	297	347	331	311	251	179
Arson	25	22	23	23	24	26	29	34	29	26
Selected Other Offences										
Simple assault	300	301	319	388	448	538	623	716	770	771
Fraud	29	77	73	75	56	43	62	78	86	36
Stolen property offences	134	117	102	125	146	157	153	153	138	113
Vandalism	398	344	362	390	391	450	482	496	454	404
Weapons violations	92	94	97	113	126	147	204	220	178	149
Prostitution and comm. vice	11	13	12	10	7	6	5	4	5	5
Sex offences	41	44	58	58	57	60	68	59	55	50
Drug abuse violations	384	317	306	306	367	304	343	558	727	685
Driving under the influence	109	106	88	97	82	72	49	47	58	68
Liquor law violations	511	497	447	570	588	577	416	404	517	524
Drunkenness	150	140	101	111	83	88	63	62	78	82
Disorderly conduct	448	476	350	378	414	444	502	578	727	615
Curfew	245	327	281	307	318	320	309	454	650	635
Runaway	503	472	483	582	577	620	601	850	646	542

Rates are arrests of persons aged 10 to 17 per 100,000 persons aged 10 through 17 in the resident population.
Source: Snyder, H. (1999). *Juvenile arrests 1998*. Washington, DC: Office of Juvenile Justice and Delinquency Prevention.

Magnifying the public's concern over violent juvenile offenders in this period, the juvenile murder arrest rate in the United States more than doubled (up 111%) between 1987 and 1993. The rate declined substantially after 1993, erasing all of the increase by 1998. Trends for violations of weapons laws closely paralleled the pattern for juvenile murder arrests. Juvenile arrest rate for weapons law violations doubled between 1987 and 1993, and then by 1998 returned to the levels of the late 1980s. A study of murders by juveniles reinforces the connection between firearms and juvenile murders. Between 1980 and 1998 the number of murders committed annually by persons under age 18 in which no firearm was used (i.e., murders resulting from physical assault or the use of other types of weapons such as knives and clubs) remained essentially constant. What increased between the late 1980s and 1993 were murders in which the juvenile used a firearm; similarly, the subsequent decline in murders by juveniles was a decline in firearm-related murders.

A further understanding of the connection between juvenile crime and firearms comes from an interview study of male juvenile arrestees in 1995 (Decker, Pennell, & Caldwell, 1997). Those interviewed were mostly youth who were being held in secure detention; therefore, their responses reflect the behaviours of a group of offenders who were more serious than those in the general population of juvenile arrestees. About one in five of those interviewed said they carried a gun all or most of the time. Only about one of every four juveniles who had guns said they had stolen their guns. Of those youth who had a gun, about one in four said they had used the gun in a crime. About half of the juveniles said someone had shot at them at least once and about one in six said they had actually been wounded by a gunshot. When asked why they carried a gun, two-thirds said it was for self-protection or defence. Others said it was to gain the respect of their crowd.

After a dramatic increase in the level of juvenile violence in the late 1980s and early 1990s, juvenile crime rates have declined. Many reasons have been offered for this decline: the improving economy, the changing drug markets, increased intervention by law enforcement, the growth in the prison population, the decline of juvenile gangs, increased sanctions for firearm crimes. However, the actual influence of any of these factors has been difficult to validate. Regardless of the reasons for the increase (and then decrease) in juvenile violence, the growth in the juvenile violent crime rates resulted in significant changes in the juvenile justice system in the United States. Some have attempted to argue that these changes actually caused the decline in juvenile violence, but it seems clear from the trends that the declines began before the changes were in place.

PART III:
THE JUVENILE JUSTICE SYSTEM IN THE UNITED STATES

Description of Legislation

The federal government in the United States has little direct control over the structure and daily activities of the state-based juvenile justice systems. The U.S. federal government provides state juvenile justice systems with a very broad legal framework, through the United States Constitution and a small number of relevant rulings by the United States Supreme Court. Along with this broad legal framework, the federal government also recommends some practice standards. States are encouraged by the federal government to adopt these standards (e.g., the sight and sound separation of juveniles and adult in jails) by giving the states a relatively small amount of funds if the states comply with the federal standards. In addition, the federal government also influences state policies by giving more funds designated for use in specific areas (e.g., the improvement of state criminal history record repositories). The federal government also affects the day-to-day operations of the U.S. juvenile justice system by providing a substantial amount of funds to support the costs of services delivered at the local level.

Nearly every aspect of the juvenile justice system is controlled by state legislation. Large increases in violent crime arrests of juveniles in the early 1990s (especially for murder) produced political pressure for state governments to "toughen" their juvenile justice legislation. Previously, the purpose clauses of most state juvenile justice legislation said that the guiding principle for the juvenile system was to act in the *best interest of the child*. Changes in the 1990s have modified these purpose clauses to increase the emphasis on public safety. As a result, new legislation removed some or all of the confidentiality surrounding the juvenile justice system. Many courtrooms were opened to the public. In many jurisdictions the names of juvenile offenders handled in the justice system are made public, are reported to their schools, and can even be found on the Internet.

In addition, nearly every state made it easier to transfer juveniles who are charged with serious crimes to the criminal (i.e., adult) justice system to be processed as an adult. In the late 1990s in the United States persons as young as 14 could be processed in the adult justice system in nearly every state. In many states children below the age of 14 (even as young as 7) charged with certain crimes may be handled as an adult, and are open to all adult sanctions including placement in adult prisons. A number of states allow for capital punishment of those convicted of murder, even though under the age of 18 at the time of the commission of the offence. Capital punishment is not permitted for those under

16 at the time of the offence, and there is a tendency to commute death sentences for those 16 and 17 years of age at the time they commit a murder.

Previously, the decision to transfer a juvenile to the adult criminal justice system was generally made by a juvenile court judge. In these cases the prosecutor would request a transfer hearing and attempt to prove that the youth was not amenable to rehabilitation within the juvenile justice system. If the judge believed the youth could not be rehabilitated, the judge transferred the matter to the adult criminal court. Increasingly, in recent years, other system actors have been given the decision-making authority to transfer a juvenile to criminal court. Prosecutors in many states now may file a juvenile case directly in the adult criminal court, a process labeled prosecutorial discretion. Legally this is accomplished by the legislature classifying a set of crimes or offenders as being under the concurrent jurisdiction of both the juvenile and criminal justice systems and empowering the prosecutor to select the appropriate venue for the case.

In many states the legislators themselves have assumed the responsibility for making the transfer decision. In these states, legislation has been passed that requires that certain types of charges must be handled in criminal court if the child is at least a certain age and/or charged with one of a defined list of crimes. (Technically, these legislative exclusions are not transfers because the case was never in juvenile court.) In all, the additional pathways into the criminal justice system has likely increased the flow of juveniles into the adult justice system, although no hard data exist to document this conclusion. It has been roughly estimated that 200,000 persons under the age of 18 are annually processed as adults in the criminal justice system in the United States, mostly because many states classify all their 17-year-olds (and a few, their 16-year-olds) as adults.

Description of Practice

After arrest, the role of law enforcement officers is to either send the matter deeper into the juvenile (or possibly criminal) justice system or divert the case out of the system, sometimes into alternative programs. Usually this decision is made after talking to the victim, the juvenile, and the parents, and after reviewing the juvenile's prior contacts with the juvenile justice system. Federal regulations discourage confinement of juveniles in adult jails and lockups. Law enforcement officers may decide to detain a juvenile in secure custody for a brief period in order to contact a parent or guardian, or to arrange transportation to a juvenile detention facility. Federal regulations require that a juvenile can be securely detained in a police station for no longer than 6 hours, and then only in an area that is not within sight or sound of adult inmates. In 1998 22% of arrested juveniles, generally those involved in less serious incidents, were processed within the law enforcement agency and then released — usually with a warning against further misconduct. About 1% of arrested juveniles were referred to a child welfare agency. The others were referred to a juvenile or criminal court for further justice system processing.

Most juvenile court cases are referred to the court by law enforcement officers. If law enforcement decides to send the case deeper into the justice system, law enforcement documents the incident, suggests which laws have been violated, and sends the information on to court intake for further processing. Other referrals to court intake are made by parents, victims, schools, and probation officers. The court intake function is generally the responsibility of the juvenile probation department and/or the prosecutor's office. At this point a decision is made either to dismiss the case, handle the matter informally, or request formal intervention by the juvenile court. To make this and the charging decision, an intake officer or a prosecutor first reviews the facts of the case to determine if there is sufficient evidence to prove the allegation. If there is not, the case is dismissed. When there is sufficient evidence, intake decides if the case should be handled formally.

In 1997, as is indicated in Figure 3.1, almost half (43%) of all delinquency cases referred to juvenile court intake were handled informally (i.e., non-petitioned) at the intake level.[2] As noted above, even before the juvenile court process begins, 22% of arrested juveniles are diverted by the police, resulting in a total diversion rate in the USA that is over 50%.

About half (44%) of the cases informally processed by the juvenile courts were dismissed due to legal insufficiency, or because intake workers believed no further action was necessary. In the other informally processed cases, the juvenile voluntarily agreed to specific conditions for a specific time period. These conditions are often outlined in a written agreement. Conditions may include such items as victim restitution, school attendance, drug counseling, or a curfew. In most jurisdictions a juvenile may be offered an informal disposition only if he or she admits to committing the act. The juvenile's compliance with the informal agreement is often monitored by a probation officer. Consequently, this process is sometimes called "informal probation." If the juvenile successfully complies with the informal disposition, the case is eventually dismissed and no formal record is maintained. If, however, the juvenile fails to meet the conditions, the case will proceed just as it would have if the intake decision had been to handle the matter formally.

In contrast to informally handled cases where the youth "volunteers" to abide by sanctions recommended by intake, formally handled (i.e., petitioned) cases involve the prosecutor asking the court to assume control over the youth and force the youth to abide by the sanctions ordered by the court. If the decision is made to formally handle the case in juvenile court, the prosecutor may file two types of petitions. A delinquency petition states the allegations and requests the juvenile court to *adjudicate* (or judge) the youth a delinquent, making the juvenile a ward of the court. In response to the delinquency petition, an adjudicatory hearing is scheduled. At the adjudicatory hearing, witnesses are

Figure 3.1

Juvenile Court Processing of Delinquency Cases in the United States, 1997

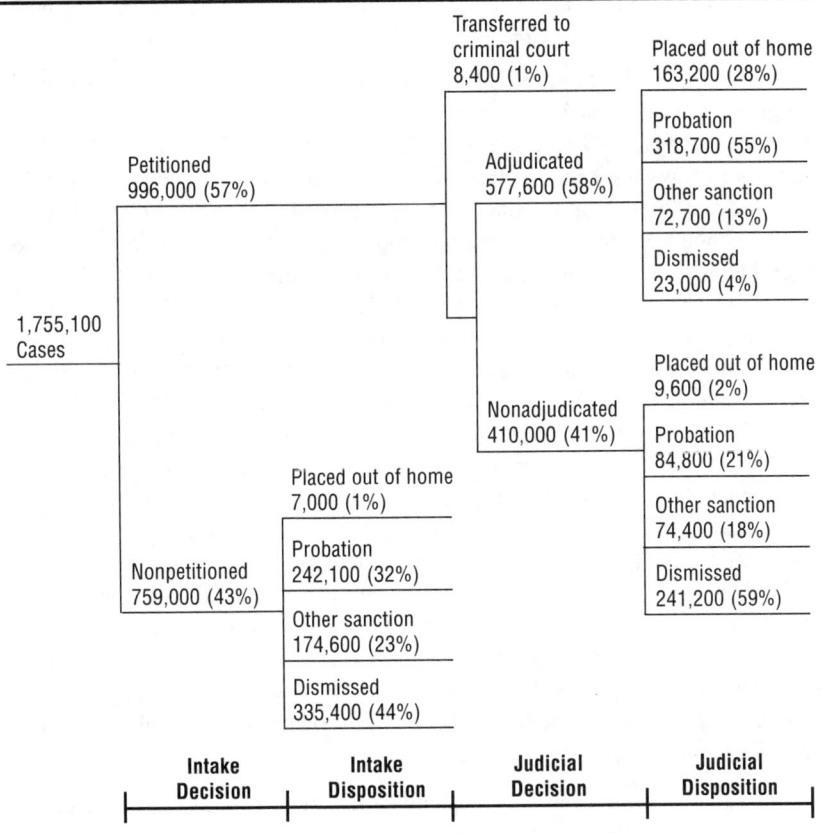

Note: Detail may not add to totals because of rounding.

Source of data: Puzzanchera, C., Stahl, A., Finnegan, T., Snyder, H., Poole, R., & Tierney, N. (1999). *Juvenile court statistics 1997*. Washington, DC: U.S. Department of Justice, Office of Juvenile Justice and Delinquency Prevention.

called and the facts of the case are presented. In nearly all adjudicatory hearings the determination of whether the juvenile was responsible for the offence(s) is made by a juvenile court judge, although in some states, for more serious offences, the juvenile is given the right to a jury trial. In 1997, juveniles were adjudicated delinquent in 58% of cases petitioned to juvenile court.

In 41% of petitioned cases in 1997 the youth was not formally adjudicated a delinquent. In most (59%) of these cases, the case was dismissed. In the rest, the youth voluntarily agreed to some sanction in lieu of being adjudicated delinquent. In many of these cases, the judge warned the juveniles that if they do not successfully complete their promises, they would be brought back into court, adjudicated delinquent, and ordered to comply with a set of sanctions. By voluntarily agreeing to comply with sanctions at an adjudicatory hearing, juveniles have one last chance to keep an adjudication of delinquency from being placed on an official court record.

The second type of petition (i.e., a waiver or transfer petition) is filed when the prosecutor believes that a case under jurisdiction of the juvenile court would be more appropriately handled in criminal court. The court decision in these matters follows a review of the facts of the case during which the youth's attorney may present a defence. If there is probable cause to believe that the juvenile committed the act, the juvenile court then considers whether jurisdiction over the matter should be transferred to criminal court. This decision generally centres on the issue of whether the juvenile is amenable to treatment in the juvenile justice system. The prosecution may argue that the juvenile has been adjudicated several times previously and that interventions ordered by the juvenile court have not kept the juvenile from committing subsequent delinquent acts. The prosecutor may argue that the crime is so serious the disposition that the juvenile court may impose will not be sufficient to rehabilitate the youth. The youth's attorney would generally present the counter arguments. If the judge agrees that the case should be transferred to criminal court, juvenile court jurisdiction over the matter is waived and the case is filed in criminal court. If the judge does not approve the waiver request, an adjudicatory hearing is scheduled in juvenile court. In 1997 juvenile court judges transferred about 1% of formally processed delinquency cases to criminal court. This number has declined in recent years as alternative and expanded routes to criminal court (i.e., prosecutorial discretion and legislative exclusion) have been established by new juvenile justice legislation.

During the processing of a case, a juvenile may be held in a secure detention facility if the court believes it is in the best interest of the community or the child. After arrest a youth is often brought to the local juvenile detention facility by law enforcement. Juvenile probation officers or detention workers review the case and decide if the juvenile should be held pending a hearing by a judge. In all states a detention hearing must be held within a time period defined by statute, generally within 24 hours. At the detention hearing a judge reviews the case and determines if continued detention is warranted. As a result of the detention hearing the youth may be released or detention continued. In 1997 juveniles were detained in 19% of delinquency cases processed by juvenile courts. Detention may be for one day or may extend for months, until the adjudicatory and dispositional hearings are completed. In some cases crowded juvenile facilities require that detention continue beyond the date of court disposition until a bed becomes available in a juvenile correctional institution or treatment facility.

Between the adjudication decision and the disposition hearing, probation staff prepares a pre-sentencing report on the adjudicated youth. To prepare this plan, probation staff develop an understanding of the youth and assesses available support systems and programs. To assist in preparation of the dispositional recommendations, the court may order psychological evaluations, diagnostic tests, or a period of confinement in a diagnostic facility. The sentencing recommendations are presented by the probation officer to the judge at the disposition hearing. These recommendations are based on a range of factors, generally including the nature of the offence, the youth's prior court history, the needs of the victim, public safety, the needs of the youth, and the availability of services. Also the prosecutor and the defence counsel may make dispositional recommendations. After considering the options presented, the judge orders a disposition in the case.

In the United States in recent years many jurisdictions have adopted the policy of ordering dispositions in juvenile court cases that address the needs of the offender, the victim, and the community. Using this "balanced" approach to disposition decision making, the court asks what the offender requires to decrease his or her likelihood of re-offending, what the victim needs to feel the harm done by the offender has been mended, and what the community needs to be protected from the offender. Consequently, most juvenile court dispositions are multi-faceted. For example, a probation order may include an indeterminate period of supervision by a court probation officer, plus the additional requirements of drug counseling, weekend confinement in the local detention centre, and community or victim restitution.

Review hearings may be held to monitor the juvenile's progress on probation and to hear reports from probation staff. After conditions of the probation have been successfully met, the judge terminates the case. In 1997, 55% of adjudicated delinquents were placed on formal probation.

At the dispositional hearing the judge may order the juvenile committed to a residential placement. Residential commitment may be ordered for a specific or indeterminate time period. In 1997, 28% of adjudicated delinquents were placed in a residential facility. The facility may be publicly or privately operated and may have a secure, prison-like environment or a more open, community-based setting. The United States has a wide variety of residential options. Boot camps have become popular in recent years, although research has questioned their effectiveness without strong aftercare (i.e., re-entry) programs. Boot camps are modelled on the training experiences of military recruits upon induction into the armed services. Marching, physical fitness, and strict discipline to rules are hallmarks of these programs that last generally from three to nine months. There are wilderness programs that teach youth through outdoor experiences (on the sea, on mountains, and in forests) to be both self-sufficient and to contribute to the well-being of the group. There are other facilities that are essentially juvenile prisons.

In many states, when the judge commits a juvenile to the state juvenile corrections agency, the agency determines where the juvenile will be placed and when the juvenile will be released. In other instances the judge controls the type and length of stay. In both situations, review hearings are held to assess the progress of the juvenile. Following release from an institution, the juvenile is often ordered to a period of aftercare or parole. During this period the juvenile is under supervision of the court or the juvenile corrections department. If the juvenile does not follow the conditions of aftercare, he or she may be recommitted to the same facility or to another facility. In most states the juvenile justice system may maintain supervision and control over juveniles once they are adjudicated a delinquent to the age of 21. This means that most states have the ability to hold a juvenile for at least three years in a secure facility.

In recent years some state legislation has given juvenile court judges the option of imposing both a juvenile and a criminal court sanction for serious offences. In these situations the judge orders and then immediately suspends the criminal court sentence as long as the youth complies with the juvenile court sanction. For example, the judge may order and then suspend sentence to adult prison and then place youth in a juvenile treatment facility. If the youth does well in the juvenile facility, at the point of review, the judge will dismiss the adult sentence and release the youth from the juvenile facility. If, however, the youth does not respond to the juvenile sanction, the suspension on the adult sanction will be withdrawn and the youth will be placed in the adult prison for the term dictated by the judge.

A one-day census in 1997 found that there were nearly 77,000 offenders committed to juvenile correctional facilities (Snyder & Sickmund, 2000). Viewed another way, on a typical day in that year, 256 of every 100,000 juveniles aged 10 and above in the U.S. resident population were living in a residential correctional facility because the courts had determined they had committed a law-violating act and needed this type of treatment intervention. Sixty-seven percent (67%) of these youth were held in publicly operated facilities, while the others were held in privately operated facilities.

Another 28,000 juveniles were being held in detention awaiting their adjudicatory or disposition hearing on an average day in 1997, a daily juvenile detention rate of 95 juveniles for every 100,000 juveniles aged 10 and above in the U.S. resident population. In this study, at the time of the count, the youth had already been in detention for an average of 18 days, while the typical committed youth had been in the residential placement facility for 113 days. The average length of time youth spend in these facilities before release was probably double these figures. On this typical day in 1997, 63% of youth in detention and residential placement were racial minorities and 86% were male.

Most states give youth the option of expunging (i.e., destroying) their juvenile court records if they reach a certain age and have had no contact with the justice system for a prescribed period of years. In reality, few youth avail themselves of this option. If the record is not expunged and a young adult is brought into criminal court, his or her juvenile records may be used to determine the amount of bail set and/or the sentence given if convicted. States are also beginning to store electronically the fingerprints of adjudicated juveniles. Modern fingerprint scanning and recognition technology will enable law enforcement agencies across the country to search these records during investigations of crimes now and in the future.

Recidivism

There are no national measures of the effectiveness of the juvenile justice system in the United States. Individual research studies have documented the recidivism of juveniles referred to court. One study investigated the court careers of 69,000 youth who had been referred to two large juvenile courts (Snyder, 1988). Overall, 56% of youth referred to juvenile court were referred again for a new offence before their 18th birthday. The recidivism rate was higher for younger juveniles (who had more time to commit a new offence before their 18th birthday) and for juveniles with more prior referrals. More specifically, only 41% of youth (46% of males and 29% of females) referred to juvenile court for the first time returned for a new offence. Recidivism rates increased to 74% by the fifth referral (76% for males and 65% for females). The recidivism rates for first-time offenders below age 15 averaged about 57%, while 33% of 16-year-olds with on average 1.5 years to recidivate returned to juvenile court.

A more recent study tracked the court career lengths of 151,000 youth referred to a juvenile court in a major metropolitan area in the southwestern United States (Snyder, 1998). These youth turned age 18 between 1980 and 1995. The study tested the assumption that the length and offence seriousness of court careers were increasing in the more recent birth cohorts. The study found that the youth who *graduated from the juvenile justice system* (i.e., turned age 18) in 1995 had on average been referred to court more times (i.e., had longer "careers") than the youth who graduated in the early 1980s (2.4 compared to 2.1 referrals per career). This was true for both males and females. Also over these graduating "classes" the proportion of youth with a violent crime referral in the court career increased from 8% to 10%. However, the probability that a youth would be referred for a second violent crime offence remained constant, with just one of every six youth referred for a violent offence returning charged with a new violent crime.

This study of the court careers of violent offenders shows that the recidivism of juveniles who turned 18 in the early 1980s were similar to those who graduated in the mid-1990s. This implies that the large increase in officially recognized youth violence in the United States during the period from 1980 through 1994 was not due to an increase in the frequency of violence committed by a small group of chronic offenders, but by an expansion of the proportion of the juvenile population involved in committing violent crime. It also implies that, for the court to reduce youth violence, it must stop youth from committing their first officially recognized violent crime, since few return for a new violent offence. Institutionalizing a growing proportion of the juvenile population in the United States will not be effective, either morally or economically, in reducing violent youth crime. Prevention programs hold the most promise.

Justice System Expenditures

In 1990 the justice system in the United States cost federal, state, and local governments a total of $74 billion, or approximately $300 for every man, woman, and child in the country (Lindgren, 1992). Reflecting their primary responsibility for the justice system in the United States, $7 of every $8 spent on justice were spent by state and local governments. State and local governments spent more than $260 per citizen on the justice system. Nationally, police protection cost $32 billion, or 43% of justice expenditures. Judicial and legal services (i.e., courts, prosecution, and public defence) cost $17 billion, or 22% of justice expenditures. Corrections cost the United States $25 billion, 34% of justice expenditures.

Justice system expenditures were 3.3% of every governmental dollar spent in the United States in 1990. The federal government devoted less than 1% of its budget to justice, while state and local justice system expenditures were between 6% and 7% of their total budgets. Compared to justice expenditures, federal, state and local governments spent in 1990 six times as much on social insurance programs, almost five times as much on national defence and international relations, four times as much on education and libraries, more than three times as much on interest on debt, twice as much on housing and the environment, and almost twice as much on public welfare.

Since 1971 (the first year for which comparable data were available) justice system expenditures have increased substantially in the United States. Between 1971 and 1990 the cost of justice activities increased 61% in constant dollars per capita. Over this time period, spending increases were 16% for police protection, 58% for courts, 152% for legal services and prosecution, 154% for corrections, and 259% for public defence. Between 1971 and 1990 the proportion of the correctional dollars spent on institutions increased substantially, while the proportion spent on probation and parole diminished. Between 1979 and 1990 state expenditures for building prisons increased by more than 600%, so that by 1990 state governments were spending nearly 4% of their total budgets for corrections.

Between 1985 and 1995 the number of persons in secure custodial facilities in the United States more than doubled (Bureau of Justice Statistics, 1997). In 1995, on a typical day, there were approximately 1.7 million persons (i.e., juveniles and adults) in a secure facility such as a prison, jail, or juvenile detention centre in the United States. Another approximately 4 million persons were on probation or parole. Therefore, in 1995, more than 2% of the U.S. population were living under the supervision of the justice system.

System Innovations

Juvenile justice in the United States is a local responsibility. As a result, system-wide innovations are rare, but innovations are often being tried at the local level. A primary role of the federal government in the juvenile justice system is to develop and/or discover and test models of good practice and to make programs and accompanying training materials available to local jurisdictions. The increasing juvenile violent crime rates of the early 1990s and the transfer of more juveniles into the adult justice system have stimulated the search for more effective, earlier interventions to divert troubled youth from the path that leads deeper into the criminal system. Research findings have been used to support the development of successful interventions. For example, research studies showing that recognizable behaviors at ages of 7 and 8 can be indicators of future serious delinquency behavior have led to, among others, the establishment of school-based crime prevention programs for children in grade school and justice system programs for high-risk youth who come into the system before age 10 (see Loeber & Farrington, 1998). Other studies showing that the majority of violent crime by juveniles occurs in the hours immediately following the end of the school day (a time period associated also with high rates of drug use and behaviours that lead to unwanted pregnancies) have led the federal government to encourage communities to establish after-school programs.

For the juvenile justice system, the federal government has developed and has been encouraging local juvenile justice systems to establish a comprehensive set of intervention programs designed to meet the range of needs of troubled juveniles in their communities (Wilson & Howell, 1993). This comprehensive strategy is based on a system of graduated sanctions, a continuum of reasonable, fair, and humane interventions that hold the youth accountable for their actions while providing treatment and rehabilitation. This strategy is sometimes compared to a tourniquet—with the juvenile justice system first assessing the risks and needs of the youth, then applying the appropriate sanctions (i.e., pressure). If the sanctions fail to deter the delinquent's unacceptable behavior, sanctions are increased. Recognizing that juvenile needs and risk factors vary from jurisdiction to jurisdiction, the strategy encourages each local juvenile justice system to assess the needs and risks of their youth, and to have available the range of sanctioning options needed to address their specific problems. In the more than 3,000 counties across the United States, correctional workers, probation officers, judges, prosecutors, and law enforcement officers are trying to determine what will help a troubled youth and what can be done to prevent juvenile crime in their communities.

References

Bureau of Justice Statistics. (1997). *Correctional populations in the United States, 1995.* Washington, DC: Bureau of Justice Statistics.

Decker, S., Pennell, S., & Caldwell, A. (1997). *Illegal firearms: Access and use by arrestees.* Washington, DC: National Institute of Justice.

Federal Bureau of Investigation. (1981-1999). *Crime in the United States series.* Washington, DC: U.S. Government Printing Office.

Federal Interagency Forum on Child and Family Statistics. (1999). *America's children: Key national indicators of well-being, 1999.* Washington, DC: U.S. Government Printing Office.

Federal Interagency Forum on Child and Family Statistics. (1997). *America's children: Key national indicators of well-being, 1997.* Washington, DC: U.S. Government Printing Office.

Greenwood, P., Model, K., Rydell, C., & Chiesa, J. (1996). *Diverting children from a life of crime: Measuring costs and benefits.* Santa Monica, CA: RAND.

Johnston, L., O'Malley, P., & Bachman, J. (1995). *Monitoring the future study.* Washington, DC: U.S. Department of Education.

Lindgren, S. (1992). *Justice expenditure and employment, 1990.* Washington, DC: Bureau of Justice Statistics.

Loeber, R., & Farrington, D. (1998). *Serious and violent juvenile offenders: Risk factors and successful interventions.* Thousand Oaks, CA: Sage.

Puzzanchera, C., Stahl, A., Finnegan, T., Snyder, H., Poole, R., & Tierney, N. (1999). *Juvenile court statistics 1997.* Washington, DC: U.S. Department of Justice, Office of Juvenile Justice and Delinquency Prevention.

Snyder, H. (1988). *Court careers of juvenile offenders.* Washington, DC: Office of Juvenile Justice and Delinquency Prevention.

Snyder, H. (1998). Serious, violent, and chronic juvenile offenders: An assessment of the extent of and trends in officially-recognized serious criminal behavior in a delinquent population. In R. Loeber & D. Farrington (Eds.), *Serious and violent juvenile offenders: Risk factors and successful interventions.* Thousand Oaks, CA: Sage.

Snyder, H. (1999). *Juvenile arrests 1998.* Washington, DC: Office of Juvenile Justice and Delinquency Prevention.

Snyder, H., & Sickmund, M. (2000). *Juvenile offenders and victims: 1999 national report.* Washington, DC: Office of Juvenile Justice and Delinquency Prevention.

Wilson, J., & Howell, J. (1993). *A comprehensive strategy for serious, violent and chronic juvenile offenders: Program summary.* Washington, DC: U.S. Department of Justice, Office of Juvenile Justice and Delinquency Prevention.

Notes

1. Another large minority group in the United States is persons of Hispanic origin, an ethnic not a racial classification. Hispanics are found in all racial groups. Arrest statistics in the U.S. do not distinguish the arrests of Hispanics.
2. Delinquency is a law-violating act that would be a crime if committed by an adult.

CHAPTER 4

Juvenile Crime and Justice in England and Wales

John Graham

The juvenile justice system in England and Wales has recently undergone a radical overhaul. A number of events led up to this, including the change of government in May 1997 and the publication of two highly significant reports from the Home Office (Graham & Bowling, 1995) and the Audit Commission (1996). The first report, a national survey of self-reported offending by 14- to 25-year-olds in England and Wales found that, contrary to popular belief, many young men do not appear to grow out of crime during the transition from childhood to adulthood (i.e., from ages 14 to 25). This led the new government to question earlier policies based on the assumption that, given the relative ineffectiveness (and even counter-productiveness) of criminal justice interventions, juvenile offenders should be diverted from formal proceedings. It also provided evidence of the importance of intervening as early and as quickly as possible in order to "nip offending in the bud," which is one of the main philosophical planks underpinning the new approach to juvenile justice.

The same report also identified the main influences on starting to offend and this, along with other research evidence (see, for example, Farrington, 1996), has fundamentally affected the current shift in thinking away from reacting to a crime after the event and towards a more proactive approach that emphasizes the need to prevent children from committing offences in the first place. This was subsequently endorsed by the Audit Commission's study of youth crime, which recommended shifting some resources from the juvenile justice system to more proactive, preventive work with children at risk of offending (Audit Commission, 1996).

John Graham is Deputy Director of the Strategic Policy Unit, Home Office, London, England.

The Audit Commission's report criticized the lack of effectiveness and inefficiency of the youth justice system and the services that support it. It concluded that

- the time taken from arrest to sentence was unnecessarily long (four months on average);
- most of the £1 billion per annum spent on young offenders is taken up by processing and administration costs, with virtually no money being specifically used to address their offending behaviour (£1 equals about $1.50 US);
- the management of the youth justice system was largely uncoordinated, inconsistent, unsystematic, and inefficient; and
- too little was undertaken to prevent children and young people from becoming offenders in the first place (Renshaw, 1998).

The Audit Commission made a number of recommendations, some of which are reflected in the *Crime and Disorder Act 1998*, others in more recent legislation. This new legislation reflects a number of important shifts in thinking. The new legislation introduced a wide range of new measures that reflect in law much of the new discourse on the nature of juvenile crime and ways to combat it. These include a move away from the "welfare versus punishment" debate, a widening of the notion of criminal responsibility beyond the offender him/herself, the introduction of the principle of restoration, and a departure from an emphasis on the more time-honoured notions of retribution, deterrence, and rehabilitation.

This chapter provides an account of recent developments in juvenile justice in England and Wales, including a discussion of the new discourse. It describes recent patterns and trends in juvenile crime, drawing on self-reported as well as recorded crime data, describes the operation of the current juvenile justice system in England and Wales (including the new measures), presents a limited analysis of the cost-effectiveness of this system, and concludes with a discussion of some of the most significant issues that are emerging in the wake of these new developments. First, however, in order to provide the necessary context for international comparison, the chapter begins with a brief description of some of the main demographic and socioeconomic characteristics of England and Wales, and the characteristics of contemporary life as it affects children and young people.

PART I: PROFILE OF ENGLAND AND WALES

This first section describes some of the main demographic and socioeconomic features that characterize England and Wales, with particular reference to the lives of children and young people, which are very different today from what they were only 20 years ago. In some respects their outlook has improved – they are physically healthier, their life expectancy is longer, they are better educated, and they have considerably more spending power. But compared with 20 years ago, today's children and young people are also more likely to

- live in poor households or in households with no adult in work;
- live in a home where parents cohabit rather than marry;
- experience the separation or divorce of their parents;
- be brought up in single or stepparent families;
- experiment with psychoactive drugs;
- suffer from psychosocial disorders (especially depression, suicide among young men, and eating disorders among young women); and, last but not least,
- engage in criminal behaviour.

At the same time, many of the support mechanisms on which young people have traditionally relied have eroded or been weakened, as communities have become more fragmented and families less stable (Social Exclusion Unit, 2000). It is within this context that the role of the juvenile justice system needs to be understood.

Demographic Characteristics

The population of England and Wales is just under 50 million people. As in other developed countries, children and young people have become a decreasing proportion of the total population during this century as fertility rates have declined and improvements in mortality rates have led to an overall aging of the population. There are currently about 5 million juveniles (those aged 10 to 17 inclusive) in England and Wales, which constitutes about 10% of the total population. In the last 10 years, the proportion of the population made up by juveniles has declined by 1.2%.

Ethnic Distribution

Just under 6% of the population of England and Wales are members of visible minority groups, of which nearly one-third are of African-Caribbean origin and over half are of Asian origin (mostly from India, Pakistan, and Bangladesh).

Nearly half of all visible minority members in the country were born in England and Wales. In contrast to the majority of the population, visible minority groups have markedly different age structures. Whereas about one in five of the white population is aged under 16, one in three people from visible minorities is under 16, with nearly one in two Pakistanis and Bangladeshis being under the age of 16. Furthermore, whereas two out of five whites are aged under 30, the majority of people from visible minorities – three out of five – are under 30. In 1991, the number of under 16s from visible minorities was more than 10 times that of those aged 65 and over, whereas for the white population the numbers were roughly equal (Office for National Statistics, 1996). Since visible minority groups have a relatively large youth population, juvenile crime issues are especially significant for these groups.

England and Wales cover approximately 150,000 square kilometers and have a density of 335 inhabitants per square kilometer. Much of the population live in urban areas, with London, the largest city, having some 7 million people. The 10 largest cities account for over one-fifth of the total population of England and Wales. Visible minority groups tend to cluster in specific areas in England, and in some urban areas the proportion of the population from visible minorities is high. In Leicester, for example, a fifth of the total population is of Indian origin (Office for National Statistics, 1996).

Family Structure, Formation, and Breakdown

Of the total population aged 16 and over, 48% of males and 45% of females are married. Over the last 25 years, the age at first marriage has risen steadily and today the average age of first marriage is 25 for women (21 in 1971) and 27 for men (23 in 1971). The decline in marriage rates has been accompanied by a steep rise in cohabitation rates, although this has only partly replaced marriage. Young people are therefore less likely to marry, more likely to cohabit, and where they do marry, will do so at an older age (Bone, 1996). This, in turn, has led to an extension of the transition from childhood to adulthood.

As with marriage, childbearing is being deferred and the proportion of young adults who are childless is increasing. The proportion of births outside marriage is also increasing, and today about one in three births is outside marriage (although of these four out of five are registered jointly by both parents). Among mothers under the age of 20, the proportion of births outside marriage has increased steeply from under one in four in the mid-1960s to more than four in five today.

An important contemporary influence on the lives of young people is the prevalence of marital dissolution. Approximately one in three marriages end in divorce, and about one in five children now live in single-parent households, which represents a 130% increase in the last 20 years. Approximately 8% of dependent children and youth (over 1 million) live in stepfamilies, and today twice as many children experience their parent's divorce compared with 20 years ago. About half of all African-Caribbean children live in lone-mother households, compared with less than one in ten Asian children.

Socioeconomic Characteristics

Education

In England and Wales, where the minimum statutory school leaving age is 16, there are approximately 3 million children in secondary education. Overall, educational standards are rising and young people are remaining in school longer. Ten years ago, 45% of 19- to 21-year-olds had completed secondary school, whereas today approximately 65% achieve this level. The proportion of school leavers who have not completed secondary school has declined in the last decade, although it is now leveling out and the gap between those who achieve in school and those who do not is widening (Payne, 1999). Furthermore, with the exception of Portugal, the United Kingdom (UK) has the highest proportion of school leavers in the European Union (EU) with poor qualifications, at nearly 50% above the EU average (Social Exclusion Unit, 2000). Levels of literacy and numeracy are also low compared with other industrialized countries (Moser, 1999), and the UK has lower rates of participation in post-16 education than many other European countries (Social Exclusion Unit, 1999).

A small proportion (somewhere between 5% and 10%) of young people in their last year of compulsory education are persistently truant (i.e., stay away from school for at least one day per week; Social Exclusion Unit, 1998). While there are no reliable data to indicate whether trends in truancy, persistent or otherwise, are worsening or not, there has been a considerable increase in the number of children permanently excluded from school. During the 1990s, the number of those excluded has more than trebled to over 12,000 per year, with youth of African-Caribbean origin being approximately five times more likely to be excluded from school than white students. Two-thirds of school-age children sentenced in court have either been excluded from school or are known as persistent truants (Renshaw, 1998).

Employment and Training

The total economically active population in England and Wales is just under 24 million, of which just over half (57%) are men. Of those employed, approximately three-quarters work in service industries. Compared with a decade ago, a slightly higher proportion (about 4%) of the UK population of working age are employed.

Since the beginning of the 1980s, the proportion of married mothers in full-time employment has increased, whereas for lone mothers it has declined. In three-fifths of married-couple families with dependent children, both adults were in employment in the late 1990s, whereas in the early 1980s it was about half.

The proportion of families where only the male is employed has, in contrast, declined from about two-fifths to a quarter (Office for National Statistics, 1998).

In 2000, there were approximately 2 million unemployed people in the UK (approximately 8.3% of the economically active population), although precise measures of unemployment are notoriously problematic. In Britain, more than 8% of 18- to 24-year-olds were unemployed, of whom 20% were unemployed for six months or more (Social Exclusion Unit, 2000). However, the unemployment rate for this age group nearly halved since the early 1990s and the long-term unemployment rate also declined steeply (Social Exclusion Unit, 2000).

Over the last 20 years, there has been a noticeable shift for young people leaving school from seeking employment to continuing training. In the 1970s, over half of all school leavers went into jobs, whereas in 1996 only 7% of school leavers entered the employment market. Currently, about 70% of 16-year-olds stay on in some form of further education (compared with 50% only 10 years ago) and a further 10% take up places on government training schemes. However, the take-up of youth training by school leavers has been steadily declining (from 24% of school leavers in 1989 to 11% in 1994), leaving a disadvantaged group of school leavers (nearly 10%) who are not in employment, education, or training. In 1988 Social Security legislation removed entitlement to Income Support for 16- to 17-year-olds, which leaves those who are not in employment, education, or training dependent on their families for income, or forced to resort to begging, prostitution or crime to support themselves. Some three-quarters of 16- to 17-year-old males who appear before the Youth Court are not in education, training, or employment (Social Exclusion Unit, 1999).

Unemployment rates for visible minorities are higher than for whites, with approximately a quarter of blacks and those of Pakistani/Bangladeshi origin unemployed, compared with one in eight of Indian origin and one in twelve whites. Young black and Pakistani/Bangladeshi people are the most likely to be unemployed. Approximately 36% of 16- to 24-year-old youth of African-Caribbean origin were unemployed in 1996/97 in Great Britain, compared with 31% of youth of Pakistani/Bangladeshi origin, 26% of youth of Indian origin, and 14% of young white people (Office for National Statistics, 1998).

Poverty

Over the last 15 years, the proportion of children living in households with below half the national average disposable income rose from one in ten to one in three (i.e., from about 1.25 million to about 4.3 million children; Department for Social Security, 1999). Most of this change occurred in the latter half of the 1980s. Since the proportion of the whole population living in households with below average income increased by less than this (from about one in eleven to one in four), children are increasingly being concentrated in less prosperous households. Households with below half the national average income are also approximately 10% worse off in absolute terms than they were 20 years ago.

Therefore children living in the poorest households are both absolutely and relatively more deprived than they were 20 years ago.

Social Policy Issues Related to Children and Young People

Expenditure

It is not possible to provide reliable estimates of the proportion or amount of total public expenditure that is spent on children and young people in England and Wales. However, there is evidence to suggest that government expenditure on children aged 0 to 15 seems to be greater in regions of high deprivation, but that expenditure on young people aged 16 to 24 living in similarly deprived areas is less than in more affluent areas (Social Exclusion Unit, 2000).

The amount spent on education increased over the decade from 1986 to 1996 from £31 billion to £39 billion; in 1996 education spending was nearly 13% of the total public expenditure budget, whereas in 1986 it was just 12%. During the same period, expenditure on public order and safety rose from £11 billion to £15 billion. This represents an increase from 4.2% of the total public expenditure budget in 1986 to 4.9% in 1996 (Office for National Statistics, 1998). Although it is also very difficult to determine how much is spent on crime prevention, figures for 1994-95 show that expenditure on crime prevention amounted to only a tiny fraction of this public order budget (about £260 million) (Home Office, 1996).

Child Welfare

Approximately 55,000 children are currently in the care of local welfare authorities in England, Wales, and Northern Ireland, which represents about 4.5 children per 1,000 population below the age of 18. This is a considerable decline on the numbers in care in 1981 at 99,000 or 7.5 children per 1,000 population below 18 (although the numbers have increased in the last five years). During this same period, the use of residential group homes has declined considerably. Today, only one in six children in care (6,300 in total) is in a residential group home, compared with over one in four in 1981.

The proportion living in foster care has increased by more than 50% since the early 1980s, but the number of children on child protection registers has declined in the last eight years from 45,000 to 36,000. Much of this decline occurred following the implementation of the *Children Act* in 1991, a central aim of which is to keep families together wherever possible. Somewhat paradoxically, the number of reports to the National Society for the Prevention of Cruelty to Children (NSPCC) for help in relation to children suspected of suffering abuse, neglect, or cruelty rose from 41,000 in 1990/91 to 66,000 in 1996/97 (Office for National Statistics, 1998).

PART II:
TRENDS IN OFFENDING BEHAVIOUR BY JUVENILES

This section provides a picture of recent trends in crime. In theory, there are three ways of measuring crime trends: through crimes recorded by the police, through victimization surveys, and through self-report surveys. All three measures have their limitations. Crimes recorded by the police are by no means an accurate measure of criminal behaviour or even "crime" rates. They do not include all crimes (e.g., computer crime, tax and benefit fraud, and environmental pollution) and of course they do not include crimes that are not reported. Furthermore, many crimes that are reported to the police are, for various reasons (see Maguire, 1997), not recorded.[1] Official police data on offending also tends to be skewed in terms of age, gender, race, and class (see Walker, 1995), with the young, males, those from specific visible minorities (primarily African-Caribbean) and the lower socioeconomic classes overrepresented.

Victim surveys include more of the offences that go unreported or that are unrecorded, but cannot capture victimless crimes, such as drug use, or crimes against organizations, such as shoplifting and fraud (unless specifically designed to do so). And of course they are unable to provide useful information on the characteristics of offenders, including the offender's age, class, ethnicity, and gender. Self-report surveys are probably the best method of establishing trends in offending behaviour, especially by young people, but they have limitations also (see, for example, Hindelang, Hirschi, & Weis, 1981; Coleman & Moynihan, 1996), and in England and Wales there is only limited-time series self-report data.[2] Given the limitation of using recorded crime rates in determining trends in *juvenile* crime (because they are unable to distinguish the age of offenders), the only data available for estimating such trends is that which is collected on known offenders (i.e., those who are cautioned by the police or convicted by the court of an offence). But, as shown below, these data are also inadequate for determining trends in juvenile crime.

The discussion that follows provides an overview of trends in crime based on crimes recorded by the police, victimization data, and self-report data. In practice, the trends captured by each of these measures are broadly similar. It also includes trend data on *known offenders*, which is broken down by age where possible.

Recorded Crime

There were 5.1 million "notifiable" (or serious) offences[3] recorded by the police in 1998/99, of which 84% were against property. The recorded crime rate increased from 7,400 offences per 100,000 in 1988 to 10,900 per 100,000 in 1992/93, and then declined to 8,600 in 1998/99. Over the decade, there was a 16% increase, but crime rates are declining from a peak in the early 1990s.

Although there are significant difficulties in making international comparisons,[4] Joutsen (1997) has found similar patterns in other Western European countries, and the data in this book suggests a similar trend for North America.

Given that property crime comprises such a large proportion of all recorded crime, overall trends are largely a reflection of those in property crime. It is therefore important to look at trends in specific offence categories.

Crimes against Persons[5]

In 1998/99, 5% of all recorded crime was for violence against persons, which compares with 4.5% in 1989. However, the number of recorded violent offences has increased by about 30% in the last 10 years (from 350 per 100,000 in 1989 to 440 per 100,000 in 1998/99). Between 1989 and 1998/99, *serious* violent crime (i.e., those offences that endanger life) increased even more steeply at a rate of, on average, 10% per year. In contrast to recorded crime overall, the violent crime rate rose between 1995 and 1997/98, but fell back in the next year by over 10%. Again, similar trends are found in other Western European countries (Joutsen, 1997).

Since 1989, offences such as crimes against persons other than rape, burglary and theft, and handling stolen goods have increased at a similar rate to the overall recorded crime rate. The main important exceptions, in addition to violent crime discussed above, are robbery (average increase of 10% per annum since 1989) and rape (average annual increase of 13%). Other European countries have experienced similar increases in robbery and rape, although the possibility that a large number of rapes are unreported means that even trend data needs to be considered with caution (Joutsen, 1997).

Maguire (1997) reports that in addition to rape, the other offences that have increased the most in England and Wales over the last 10 years are drug trafficking and serious woundings. Drug trafficking has increased by, on average, over 10% per annum, whereas serious woundings have increased by 9% per annum. Given that the latter are less susceptible to changes in reporting and recording behaviour, Maguire (1997) concludes that there has been a real and significant increase in serious woundings in the last decade.

Police Clearance Rates

Approximately one in four offences (1.3 million) was cleared by the police in 1997/98.[6] Since 1989, the overall police clear-up rate fell from 34% to 28%. For some offences, such as fraud and forgery, the decline in clearance rates during the last 10 years has been quite considerable (from 66% to 47%), but for other offences, such as violence against the person, it has remained fairly stable at around 77%. The overall clearance rate remains relatively low due to the fact that a large proportion of property crimes are not cleared by identification of the offender and laying of a charge.

Victimization

The British Crime Survey (BCS), which was first undertaken in 1981, provides an index of crime based on experiences of victimization. The latest BCS, undertaken in 1997 and published in 1998, estimated that 16.5 million crimes were committed against adults living in households in 1997.[7] This is more than three times the number of crimes recorded by the police, and over 50% more victimization than in 1981, when the BCS was first undertaken. However, as with recorded crime rates, victimization rates fell in the late 1990s. Since the previous survey conducted in 1995, the overall level of household victimization has declined by 14%.

According to the BCS, only one in four offences is actually recorded by the police. At the peak of victimization in 1995, there were at least three times as many domestic burglaries committed as recorded by police, four times as many thefts from vehicles, seven times as many incidents of vandalism, and eight times as many robberies and thefts from the person (Mirrlees-Black, Mayhew, & Percy, 1996).

The BCS also shows that, between 1981 and 1995, the incidence of self-reported domestic violence increased by 242%, acquaintance violence (those who are acquainted with each other but not in a domestic relationship) by 123%,[8] muggings (robberies, attempted robberies, and snatch thefts) by 54%, and stranger violence by 12%. During the same period, burglaries increased by just over 100%, attempted burglaries by nearly 160%, thefts of cars by about 50%, thefts from cars by about 75%, and attempted vehicle thefts (both from and of vehicles) by a staggering 600%.

Over the 1980s, the BCS showed a less steep increase in crime than offences recorded by the police, which probably reflected an increase in reporting to the police by victims, for example, of domestic violence. In the 1990s, the BCS showed a steeper increase than police figures between 1991 and 1993, and a leveling off between 1993 and 1995. Police figures stabilized earlier (between 1991 and 1993) and since 1995 have been gradually falling.

The most important exception would seem to be for violent crime, which has increased on both measures since 1991. Between 1993 and 1995, for example, violence increased by 17% on BCS figures and by 6% on police figures. But between 1995 and 1997, while incidents of wounding as measured by the BCS increased by 18%, recorded woundings declined by 17%. Further details, including the precise definitions of offence categories and detailed explanations for the differences between recorded and survey rates, can be found in Mirrlees-Black, Mayhew, & Percy (1996) and Mirrlees-Black et al. (1998).

Child Victimization

No trend data exist on the victimization of children and young people, but there are some prevalence and incidence data. The fourth sweep of the BCS, which was undertaken in 1992, included a sample of 1,350 12-to-15-year olds. They were asked about victimization in six areas: thefts of unattended property, thefts and attempted thefts from the person, assault, harassment by adults, harassment by young people, and sexual harassment. One-third reported being assaulted on at least one occasion in the previous six to eight months, two-fifths had something stolen, one-fifth had been harassed by someone their own age, and one-fifth by someone older than 16. About 70% of victims had experienced more than one incident, and 20% of victims had experienced too many victimizations to say precisely how many. Incidents were commonly perpetrated by boys who were known to the victim, at or near school. Only a quarter of all incidents were considered by victims to be crimes, with four-fifths of assaults and nonsexual harassments considered "noncriminal" by the victims. The risk of assault was found to be as high among 12- to 15-year-olds as among 16- to 19-year-olds, and higher than for those aged 20 or over.

The only other reliable source of data on victimization among the young comes from the Youth Lifestyles Survey (YLS), undertaken in 1993. This national household survey, which covered 14- to 25-year-olds, found that half of all respondents had been victimized in the previous 12 months. Approximately a quarter (23%) were victims of vandalism, nearly a third (29%) were victims of theft and one in six (16%) reported being a victim of violence.

Known Offenders

Both the recorded police crime data and data acquired from victimization surveys provide information on *offences*, but not *offenders*. Information on the age of offenders can be obtained in two ways – either through the police statistics on known offenders or through surveys of self-reported offending. Both data sources provide some indication of who is responsible for committing offences, but there are important differences between them. The official police statistics on known offenders are restricted to those who are cautioned by police or convicted for an offence, whereas self-report surveys cover a much wider population, including those offenders who have not been detected, and those who may have been detected or recorded by the police.

As mentioned above, there have only been two national self-report surveys of offending behaviour, one in 1993 and the other in 1999. Over this six-year period, the proportion of 14- to 17-year-old boys who admitted offending doubled from 18% to 36%. For girls the same age, the rise was much smaller – from 7% to 23% (Flood-Page et al., 2000). The increase in offending by boys was mainly due to the proportion admitting to fighting and criminal damage to property (vandalism), which increased by 12% and 7% respectively between 1993 and 1999. However, it is not reliable to estimate trends on the basis of two surveys six years apart, so this section describes trends in known offending based on the number of individuals formally processed by the criminal justice system.

In 1998, the total number of known offenders cautioned or found guilty of indictable offences (i.e., excluding summary and motoring offences – unless stated otherwise, all references to official crime data refer to indictable offences) was 533,000. This is somewhat lower than the number of offences recorded by the police, and considerably lower than the total number of offences committed. The attrition rate – the proportion of all indictable offences that end up in a caution or a conviction – has been estimated to be in the region of 3% (i.e., 1 in every 33 offences ends up in a caution or a conviction; Home Office, 1995). Since some offenders will be charged with more than one offence, the proportion of offenders who end up with a caution or a conviction will be higher, but there are still considerable deficiencies in the capacity of the criminal justice system to deal with the overall problem of crime.

Of the total number of just over half a million known offenders in 1998, 127,000 were aged 10 to 17 (i.e., 24%). Approximately four out of five were male and nearly half of all offenders were cautioned or convicted for burglary, theft, or handling stolen goods. The overall rate of offending by males was nearly 2,000 per 100,000 of the male population and just over 400 per 100,000 of the female population. For those aged 10 to 17, the rates were 3,700 for boys and 1,100 for girls. The peak age of known offending for males in 1998 was 18 for males and 15 for females.

The trend in the numbers of all known offenders over the last 10 years has been relatively stable. In 1988, there were slightly fewer known offenders than in 1998, but only marginally so. More significantly, there has been a clear shift in the composition of the known offender population over the last decade. Those who are formally dealt with are much more likely to be cautioned or convicted of drug offences (nearly a fourfold increase since 1988) and less likely to be cautioned or convicted of burglary (a drop of over a third in the same period). Other changes include a 25% rise in the number of females cautioned or convicted of violence against the person and a reduction of about a quarter in the number of males cautioned or convicted for theft and handling stolen goods. For those under the age of 18 there is only limited information available.

Known Juvenile Offenders

The total number of known juvenile offenders[9] in 1997 was 127,000, which is 17% less than in 1988. Taking into account changes in demographics, this represents a fall from approximately 3,000 young offenders per 100,000 persons aged 10 to 17 in 1988 to 2,400 in 1998 (a reduction of 20%). Given the considerable overall rise in crime as measured by the British Crime Survey during this period and the fact that approximately one-quarter of all known offenders are juveniles, it seems unlikely that this represents an accurate picture of the trend in juvenile crime.

A number of reasons have been suggested for the reported decline in the known juvenile offending rate in the last decade. These include

- the re-classification of three offences as nonindictable offences in 1988 (common assault, taking a motor vehicle without consent, and criminal damage over £400 but under £2,000);
- an increase in the use of informal (unrecorded) warnings;
- an increasing tendency for charges to be heard together;
- an increase in the number of persistent young offenders who commit many offences, but are only counted as one offender in the official police statistics;
- a fall in the detection rate; and
- a fall in the proportion of young offenders found guilty in court.

The Audit Commission (1996) concludes that once these factors have been taken into account, the known offending rate by young people does not appear to have declined. Farrington (1992) suggests that juvenile crime has probably increased. In reality it is simply not known (and not knowable) whether offending by young people is increasing or not, although some indication of recent trends can be ascertained from the two national self-report surveys conducted during the 1990s. However, before turning to what is known about juvenile crime from self-report data, it is worth briefly summarizing some of the main characteristics of the current known juvenile offender population and how it differs from those dealt with by the police and the courts 10 years ago.

Compared with a decade ago, there are six times as many juvenile offenders cautioned or convicted for drug offences and about twice as many for robbery. There has also been an increase in the number of juvenile offenders cautioned or convicted for violence against the person, but this is due entirely to a 50% increase among females. In contrast, cautions and convictions for burglary and theft and handling stolen goods have fallen by nearly 60% during the same period. Other offences have remained relatively stable.

Self-Reported Offending

The best source of national self-report data on offending comes from two surveys conducted in 1993 and 1999. The first survey, which was based on a sample of 1,721 young people aged 14 to 25, asked respondents to report on their involvement in 23 offences, ranging from arson, drug use, and shoplifting to credit card fraud and serious assaults. The findings show that offending is widespread among this group, with one in two young men and one in three young women committing an offence at some time, and one in four young men and one in eight young women admitting to committing an offence in the previous year. The majority committed no more than one or two offences, and a disproportionate amount of offending was committed by a small minority of offenders, with 3% of offenders responsible for a quarter of all offences (Graham and Bowling, 1995).

Similar findings were found in the second survey, which albeit had a larger sample (4,850) and covered a wider age range (12 to 30). Nearly half (47%) admitted to ever committing an offence,[10] with more young men admitting offending than young women (57% versus 37%). Again, one in four men admitted offending in the previous year, but slightly fewer young women did so (one in nine as opposed to one in eight).[11] Just over half admitted to committing one or two offences in the last year, and about 10% of offenders were found to be responsible for nearly half of all offences (Flood-Page et al., 2000).

The peak age of self-reported offending in the first survey was found to be 21 for males and 16 for females (compared with 18 and 15 for known offenders). In the second survey, the peak ages of self-reported offending were much closer to the known offender peaks at 18 for boys and 14 for girls. In both surveys, young women grew out of crime earlier than young men. A controversial finding from the first survey was that young men, at least up to the age of 25, did not grow out of property crime, with prevalence rates remaining the same from the age of 18 up to 25. As they got older, they switched from relatively risky property offences, such as shoplifting and burglary, to less visible and less detectable offences, such as fraud and theft from the workplace (Graham and Bowling, 1995). A similar pattern was discernible from the second survey (with fraud and theft from the workplace continuing to increase up to the age of 30), although property offending prevalence rates among young men began to decline overall in the early to mid 20s (Flood-Page et al., 2000). The fact that young men tend to switch to offences with lower detection rates as they get older influenced policy on juvenile crime away from diversion from court and towards a policy of responding quickly and effectively at the first signs of trouble. This new approach to "nipping offending in the bud" is outlined later in this chapter.

PART III:
THE JUVENILE JUSTICE SYSTEM IN ENGLAND AND WALES

Legislation

The first juvenile courts were established in England and Wales by the 1908 *Children Act*. With the exception of murder, the juvenile courts dealt with all offences committed by young people aged 7 to 15, unless the offences were committed with an adult. Following the introduction of this Act, only children aged 14 and over could be sentenced to imprisonment.

In 1933, the first *Children and Young Persons Act* introduced the concept of welfare provision into the juvenile justice system, placing a duty on magistrates to have regard for the welfare of the child in making an appropriate disposition. The 1933 Act also extended the jurisdiction of the juvenile court to 16-year-olds, introduced approved schools, which provided juvenile offenders with education and training in a secure setting, and remand homes, which kept juveniles who were remanded in custody pending conclusion of their proceedings separate from adult prisoners.

After the Second World War, corporal punishment in juvenile institutions was abolished by the 1948 *Criminal Justice Act*, which also marked the beginning of a trend towards increasing restrictions on the use of imprisonment for juvenile offenders. The age below which an offender could not be sentenced to imprisonment (with the exception of certain grave crimes) was raised to 15 years of age, and detention centres were introduced for short periods of custody (usually three months, but exceptionally six months). The 1948 Act also introduced attendance centres, the main purpose of which was to punish offenders by depriving them of their leisure time while allowing them to continue to reside in their communities. In the same year, the *Children Act* set up local authority (local government) children's departments, which, among other things, ended the placement of neglected children together with young offenders in approved schools.

In 1961, a new *Criminal Justice Act* removed from juvenile courts the power to sentence young offenders to prison for more than six months (with a few exceptions). The Act also reduced the maximum period of Borstal training schools from three years to two years and lowered the minimum age for admission from 16 to 15. Section 53 of the *Children and Young Persons Act 1933*, which provided for the detention of young people for certain grave crimes, was expanded for those aged 14 and above to all offences for which an adult sentence of 14 years or more might be imposed. Two years later, the *Children and Young Persons Act 1963* raised the minimum age of criminal responsibility from 8 to 10.

The trend towards a welfare-oriented system culminated with the passing of the *Children and Young Persons Act* in 1969, which shifted the emphasis away from matters of justice and legal rights, and towards the welfare of the child and his or her immediate needs. The 1969 Act also shifted the balance of power away from magistrates and towards the local authority, which became responsible for implementing some of the sentences of the juvenile court. Approved schools and remand homes were amalgamated into community homes, which were run by local authorities, and committing an offence became one of the grounds on which child welfare proceedings could be brought.

In practice, the 1969 Act was never fully implemented, and by the end of the 1970s, the welfare approach was increasingly being questioned. Arguments prevailed for a return to a "just deserts" model, for proportionality in sentencing, for determinate penalties, and for greater protection of the legal rights of juveniles (and their parents). Legislation passed during the 1980s went some way towards achieving these objectives.

The *1982 Criminal Justice Act* abolished indeterminate sentences (Borstal training school was replaced by youth custody with a maximum period of 12 months). It also shortened sentences of imprisonment in a detention centre from a minimum of three and a maximum of six months to 21 days and four months respectively, introduced criteria for restricting the use of custody, and allowed new requirements to be attached to community supervision orders. In the following year, the Department of Health issued a Circular announcing the allocation of funds for diverting young offenders from custody through intensive intermediate community treatment programs and encouraging local authorities to set up interagency committees to deal with young offenders. This, it has been suggested, constituted a first step towards a more integrated system of juvenile justice (Allen, 1991).

The *1988 Criminal Justice Act* raised the criteria for imposing a custodial sentence and replaced detention centres and youth custody with a single custodial sentence known as "detention in a young offender institution" for those aged 15 and above. A year later, the *Children Act 1989* finally removed all child welfare proceedings from the juvenile court, leaving it to deal exclusively with criminal matters.

Up to the end of the 1980s, the history of juvenile justice was characterized by contrasting views on the causes of (and hence remedies for) offending. Legislation and criminal justice policy and practice swung towards and then away from a welfare approach to juvenile offenders, at times emphasizing the needs of the child, at others, the importance of punishment. During the latter part of this period, the recognition that certain categories of offenders are best dealt with outside the formal court system was underlined by the increasing use of the formal police caution. A series of Home Office Circulars encouraged the use of police cautioning, which culminated in 1990 with the introduction of National Standards (revised in 1994). The 1980s also witnessed a decline in the use of custodial measures for juvenile offenders.

At the beginning of the 1990s, the enactment of the *1991 Criminal Justice Act* reflected a clear move away from a welfare approach and towards a "just deserts" approach. Responsibility for dealing with young offenders shifted again, this time away from the criminal justice system and towards the community. It confirmed in legislation the move towards diverting young offenders from court and custody, and brought 17-year-olds within the jurisdiction of a new youth (as opposed to juvenile) court. On the basis that their offending rates were found to be almost identical, 16- and 17-year-olds were identified by the 1991 Act as "near adults" and sentenced on the basis of their maturity rather than their age (although 17-year-olds continued to be dealt with as adults for remand and other pre-trial purposes). This change brought the sentencing of 17-year-olds into line with the age of majority and with sentencing practices in other Western European countries (Gibson et al., 1994) and with the U.N. *Convention on the Rights of the Child.*

As part of a trend towards gradually removing those aged under 14 from the formal jurisdiction of the courts (Gibson et al., 1994), the 1991 Act explicitly distinguished between "children," who are aged 10 to 13, and "young persons," who are aged 14 to 17 inclusive. This trend was temporarily halted following a Court of Appeal judgement in 1994 (Court of Appeal in *C [a minor] v Director of Public Prosecutions* [1994]), which ruled that children aged 10 to 13 were *doli incapax,* which meant that they were not considered legally capable of having criminal intent. The House of Lords, however, subsequently overturned this decision on the grounds that such matters were properly a matter for Parliament to decide. With the implementation of the *Crime and Disorder Act 1998,* the doctrine of *doli incapax* for 10- to 13-year-olds was finally abolished (this is discussed further below).

The 1991 Act had a twin track approach to young offenders, with distinctions being drawn between a minority of violent, dangerous, and persistent offenders for whom custody was considered to be the right option, and a majority of mostly petty property offenders for whom community-based sentences were considered more appropriate. The Act specified that remands in *adult* custody for 15- and 16-year-old boys were to be phased out and the maximum term of detention in a Young Offenders Institution would be reduced to 12 months. It also required parents, for the first time, to be more accountable for the offences of their children through the introduction of parental bind-overs. A parental bind-over is a fine up to £1,000 where the court feels that a parent or guardian has failed to exercise proper care or control over a juvenile who re-offends.

Following the implementation of the 1991 Act in October 1992, the climate surrounding the issue of juvenile offending changed dramatically. Urban disturbances, the advent of theft of automobiles for "joyriding," the rise of the persistent young offender, and the horrific murder of the toddler Jamie Bulger by two 10-year-old boys in February 1993 all served to fan the flames of a "moral panic" about young offenders (see Newburn, 1997). A Parliamentary Committee was set up to report on the problem of juvenile crime (Home Affairs Select Committee, 1993), and in March 1993 the first of a number of changes in legislation was announced. These changes included the introduction of secure training centres for 12- to 15-year-olds, which reflected the public's increasingly punitive attitude towards the young who offend.

In 1993, the Conservative Government enacted the *Criminal Justice Act*, revising a number of key provisions in the 1991 Act. In 1994, the *Criminal Justice and Public Order Act* introduced a number of measures revising the diversionary trend of the 1980s. The planned secure training order for persistent young offenders became law, and the provisions allowing for detention in prison custody for grave offences were extended to 10- to 13-year-olds. The 1994 Act also doubled the maximum length of detention in a Young Offenders Institution from 12 to 24 months for 15- to 17-year-olds, and allowed courts to remand 12- to 14-year-olds as well as 15- and 16-year-olds to "secure accommodation." The 1994 Act also provided courts with new powers to bind over parents to ensure their child's compliance with a community sentence.

In the same year, a government Circular placing limits on the use of multiple cautions by the police was issued, and in the final months of the Conservative Government, a number of ideas from America were imported, such as boot camps and military-style custodial regimes. Three year later, the *Crime (Sentences) Act 1997* extended the discretion of magistrates in Youth Courts to allow the names of juveniles to be publicly released following conviction, where this is considered to be in the public's interest.

In November 1997, the new Labour Government (a more progressive Social Democratic government replacing the Conservative government) published a White Paper entitled "No More Excuses," which outlined its strategy for tackling youth crime (Home Office, 1997a). It represented a comprehensive overhaul of the youth justice system by shifting the focus away from crisis intervention and making the primary statutory aim of the youth justice service the prevention of offending.[12] The preventive focus of the new strategy is reflected in a number of measures, some of which directly affect the workings of the youth justice system and some of which are directed at external agencies. The new strategy included new sentencing options for juvenile court, while the involvement of external agencies is primarily intended to identify children and young people at risk of becoming involved in criminal activity and changing their behaviour before bad habits take root.

In addition to these two aims – preventing offending, and intervening early with children at risk of offending – the new legislation

- increased the responsibility of parents for the offending of their children;
- introduced a number of measures for reducing delays and improving the efficiency of procedures from arrest to sentence; and

- introduced multi-agency partnerships at the local level – Youth Offending Teams – to coordinate and deliver a more efficient and effective system.

The main legal changes introduced to achieve these aims were

- the abolition of *doli incapax* (presumption of legal incapacity for children under 14), making younger children liable for crimes without the Crown having to prove mental capacity;
- the introduction of a number of new sentences or orders, including the child safety order, parenting orders, action plan orders, reparation orders, and detention and training orders;
- the introduction of local child curfews for children under the age of 10[13];
- the replacement of the current, nonstatutory cautioning system with a new Final Warning scheme; and
- the introduction of a range of measures for speeding up the time taken from arrest to sentence, particularly for persistent young offenders.

Two other important changes were

- the setting up of a Youth Justice Board for England and Wales to provide leadership, set standards, and monitor performance; and, in the longer term,
- measures to help the courts move towards a more open, less adversarial system, which will pay greater attention to the needs of victims, offenders, and their parents.

Most recently, the *Youth Justice and Criminal Evidence Act 1999* (now consolidated in the *Powers of Criminal Courts [Sentencing] Act, 2000)* introduced new Youth Offender Panels for young offenders pleading guilty and convicted for the first time. Based on restorative principles, the Youth Offender Panel consists of at least two volunteers from the local community and one member of the Youth Offending Team. The Panel draws up a contract with the offender, which will include a program of activity aimed at preventing re-offending and making reparation to the victim or the wider community. Victims can attend Panel hearings, as can any responsible adult capable of having a good influence on the offender. Parents (or guardians) must attend where the offender is under the age of 16. Contracts may contain a variety of measures, including reparation, mediation, community service, home curfews, attendance orders (school or work), and a requirement to attend special courses on, for example, addressing offending behaviour or drug misuse. Contracts can also require the offender to stay away from specific persons or places.[14] Non-compliance can lead to referral back to court for sentencing.

Most of the changes are ultimately concerned with improving the efficiency and effectiveness of the youth justice system. Some are more controversial than others, and some are quite innovative. Those that raise fundamental questions relating to notions of justice are, arguably, of most interest and three elements of the new legislation – the abolition of *doli incapax*, the introduction of the parenting order, and the child safety order – are considered further below.

Current Practice

Most proceedings in respect of people under 18 are brought in specially constituted magistrates' courts known as Youth Courts. The procedure in Youth Courts, which is adversarial in nature, is simpler and less formal than in adult magistrates' courts. Members of the public are generally not admitted to sittings of Youth Courts, but the press may attend and report on the proceedings. However, such reports must not identify any young people involved unless the court itself has allowed identification (e.g., to prevent injustice to a juvenile or facilitate a serious offender's apprehension). The magistrates who sit in Youth Courts are chosen from a special panel. The court must be made up of not more than three magistrates, among whom there must normally be at least one man and at least one woman. Most magistrates are unpaid, or "lay" members of the public who rely on justices' clerks for advice on matters of law. In some large cities, district judges (formerly known as stipendiary magistrates) are appointed; they are full-time, salaried professionals with legal qualifications who adjudicate alone.

Under certain circumstances, a child or young person will be tried in the adult Crown Court rather than the Youth Court (although they can still be remitted to the Youth Court for sentence). These circumstances include those charged with homicide, those charged with an offence for which a person aged 21 or over could be sentenced to at least 14 years imprisonment, those charged with the offence of indecent assault, and those charged jointly with a person aged 18 or older (who may also be committed to an adult magistrates' court).

Currently, the youngest age at which a child can be brought to court in criminal proceedings is 10 years. This is known as "the age of criminal responsibility." A child below the age of 10 cannot be found guilty of a criminal offence. The judicial arrangements for dealing with young offenders (those aged 10 to 17) can be divided into four main sections: reprimands and final warnings, prosecution, remand arrangements, and sentencing.

Police Cautions

Reprimands and Final Warnings[15]

When dealing with a young offender, the police have considerable discretion in deciding how to respond. They may decide, in the less serious cases, that an informal warning is sufficient, either given on the spot or at the police station. In either case no further action will be taken. Informal warnings are not formally or systematically recorded, and cannot be used in court in later proceedings. If an informal warning is not considered appropriate, the police may decide to issue a Reprimand or a Final Warning. A record is kept by the police of Reprimands and Final Warnings. A community intervention program, involving the offender and his or her family to address the causes of the offending, will usually follow the Final Warning. No offender will be able to receive more than one Reprimand, and a second Final Warning is only possible if at least two crime-free years have lapsed since the first was issued.

Prosecution

If a decision is taken not to caution but to pursue a prosecution, the case is then referred to the Crown Prosecution Service (CPS), who decides whether there is sufficient evidence to secure a conviction and whether it is in the public interest to proceed with the prosecution. If not, the CPS will discontinue proceedings, sometimes referring the case back to the police with a recommendation for some form of caution. Since the introduction of the Crown Prosecution Service in 1986, the proportion of cases discontinued has increased considerably.

Remand Arrangements

Once a decision has been taken to prosecute an offender, he or she will appear in court. *The Bail Act 1976* applies to juveniles in the same way that it applies to adults, and while there is a general presumption in favour of release (bail) for all defendants, this is particularly emphasized in the case of juveniles. Under the 1976 Act, the presumption is that defendants will be granted bail unless the court is satisfied that there are substantial grounds for believing that the defendant, if released on bail, would

- fail to surrender to custody; or
- commit an offence while on bail; or
- interfere with witnesses or otherwise obstruct the course of justice.

Additionally, defendants may be refused bail if the court is satisfied that they should be kept in custody (or local authority accommodation) for their own protection or, if they are under 17, for their own welfare. The 1994 *Criminal Justice and Public Order Act* tightened some of the conditions under which bail may be granted. A Government Circular issued in 1994 offers those involved in making bail decisions guidance on risk assessment and how to improve bail information.

In many areas bail information schemes are available, although these currently only apply to juveniles aged 17. These provide detailed and verified information about the defendant and his or her domestic circumstances, which helps courts decide whether or not the general presumption in favour of bail release should be overruled. In 1993, the Home Affairs Select Committee on Juvenile Offenders recommended that the use of bail information schemes by the courts when dealing with offenders under the age of 17 should become standard practice. New national standards on bail information schemes were subsequently produced, and these came into effect in March 1995. In some parts of the country community programs, provided either by the voluntary sector or by local authorities, are available for work with defendants who might be at risk of being refused bail in the absence of some kind of support and/or supervision.

If bail is refused, a juvenile offender may be either remanded to local authority accommodation or to prison. Defendants under 17 who are refused bail are normally remanded to local authority accommodation, usually in the area in which the young person resides or where the offence was committed. In exceptional cases, local authorities may apply to the court for a "secure accommodation order." For a local authority to obtain a secure placement, it must satisfy the courts that the juvenile offender has committed a serious violent or sexual offence, or is likely to abscond from nonsecure accommodation, or is likely to injure him or herself or other people if not in secure accommodation.

A wide range of alternative forms of residential provision are available for juveniles remanded to local authority accommodation, depending on the circumstances of the young person concerned. The placement possibilities include a community home (sometimes in secure conditions), remand fostering, supported lodgings, placement with relatives, or placement in his or her own home under supervision.

Accommodation in a Community Home. A high proportion of young people remanded to local authority accommodation are accommodated in community homes. These provide an alternative to the family home for those who have difficulties with their families. Under certain circumstances, juveniles held on remand in community homes may be held in secure accommodation. Only those with a high risk of absconding, or those charged or convicted of a serious offence (violent, sexual, or punishable in the case of an adult with 14 years imprisonment or more) are likely to be held in secure accommodation. The 1991 Act provided for 15- and 16-year-olds (but not 17-year-olds) to be remanded in secure accommodation rather than prison custody. The 1994 *Criminal Justice and Public Order Act* extended the age range of children on whom courts are empowered to impose a "security" requirement from 15 and upwards to 12 and upwards.

Remand Fostering. As an alternative to accommodation in a community home, a young person may be placed with remand foster parents, who will usually have been specially recruited and trained for the purpose. Fostering can be more effective than a community home placement, allowing for more individual attention, supervision, and support. The number of remand foster schemes is small, but growing.

Supported Lodgings. Where a local authority decides that a young person is not in great need of supervision or support, it may place him or her in private lodgings. The host family is not usually expected to fulfil a parental role, but to offer a degree of support.

Placement with Relatives. Placement with relatives may be used when factors associated with the juvenile's own home suggest that a removal from this environment would be desirable, and where relatives are willing and able to offer support and supervision but risk to the community is low.

When a defendant is remanded to local authority accommodation, the court may impose other special conditions, such as requiring the defendant to remain indoors between certain hours, to refrain from attending a particular place or meeting particular individuals, or to report to a police station. The court can also impose requirements on the local authority, such as stipulating that the defendant shall not be placed (i.e., accommodated) with a named person. For example, the court may take the view that the home circumstances of the defendant provide insufficient support or supervision and may decide, therefore, to require the local authority not to allow him or her to return to live at home.

Since the mid-1970s it has been the aim of successive governments to phase out the remanding of juveniles to penal establishments, and between 1977 and 1981, the powers of the court to remand juveniles in custody were progressively restricted. Fourteen-year-old girls were excluded from the procedure in 1977, 15- and 16-year-old girls in 1979, and 14-year-old boys in 1981. Since then custodial remands for juveniles have been available only for 15- and 16-year-old boys and the numbers remanded in prison fell substantially during the 1980s, only to begin rising again in the 1990s.

Remands in prison are subject to similar criteria as for placement in secure accommodation, with the added criterion of protecting the public from *serious harm* from the young person. Before remanding a young person to prison the court is required to consult a local authority social worker or a probation officer. No young person may be remanded to prison without having been given the opportunity of applying for legal aid. The *Criminal Justice Act 1991* contains the power to replace prison remands with remands to local authority secure accommodation for 15- and 16-year-olds, and it is possible that prison remands for all 15- and 16-year-olds will be phased out in the future.

The Labour Government initiated a review of secure accommodation and young people held on remand with a view to rationalizing remand arrangements. *The Crime and Disorder Act 1998* now provides the courts with powers to remand children aged 12 or over to secure accommodation.

Sentencing

If a youth is convicted in a Youth Court, the powers of the courts to sentence offenders under 18 are governed by a number of key principles. The first of these is the statutory principle aim of the youth justice system of preventing re-offending. For magistrates the main impact has been an expectation to think more in terms of what will change behaviour. New court sentencing powers introduced in June 2000 are designed to provide effective early intervention with young offenders which tackles the factors associated with the young person's offending behaviour and is most likely to prevent further offending. Sentences should also provide a proportionate response to the seriousness and persistance of offending. Where the offence is so serious or, in the case of a violent or sexual offence where the court considers it necessary to protect the public from serious harm from the offender, the Youth Court has the power to pass a custodial sentence.

From April 2000, a detention and training order may be imposed on 15- to 17-year-olds and for 12-to-14-year olds deemed by the court to be persistent offenders. The maximum sentence is two years, one half of which is spent in secure accommodation and the second half under supervision in the community. A new program, the Intensive Supervision and Surveillance Programme (ISSP), was introduced in 2001 to provide an alternative to custody for the most active repeat young offenders. Courts also remain subject to the general principle set out in the *Children and Young Persons Act 1933* that, in dealing with a child or young person, whether as an offender or otherwise, they shall have regard to the welfare of the child or young person.

Another important principle is that of parental responsibility. In the case of defendants under the age of 16, parents are expected to attend court, and may be required to pay fines or compensation to the victims. Courts are required to bind parents over to take proper care of and exercise proper control of their child where this is desirable in the interests of preventing the youth from committing further offences. The 1994 *Criminal Justice* and *Public Order Act* extended these powers by allowing courts to include in any bind-over a requirement that the parent or guardian must ensure that a child complies with the requirements of a community sentence. Since June 2000, the courts can impose a parenting order requiring parents to attend a parenting program or to comply with other conditions to help prevent further offending by their children. More is said about parenting orders below.

Finally, 16- and 17-year-olds are regarded as being in a transitional stage between childhood and adulthood, and for them it is believed that a flexible approach to sentencing is desirable. The full range of community sentences, both those available to younger juveniles and those currently available for adults, can be imposed and courts have *powers* to order the parents to be involved (as opposed to the duty for parents to be involved that applies in respect to younger offenders). In determining how to use these powers, courts are required to take account of a range of factors relating to the offender's stage of development and maturity.

Before imposing custody (except for the most serious offences [indictable only] or where the sentence is prescribed in law), or certain more demanding community sentences (e.g., community service orders and combination orders), the court should consider a pre-sentence report (PSR). The report, usually submitted by a probation officer or a social worker, provides information about the youth, family, and circumstances of the offence, and any mitigating circumstances. National Standards for Pre-Sentence Reports (PSR) were published in 1992 and new standards were published in March 1995. The 1994 *Criminal Justice and Public Order Act* provided the courts with the discretion to dispense with the requirement to obtain a PSR before sentence where it is satisfied that it can properly sentence without one *and* if it has considered an existing PSR on the offender. (If more than one such report exists, the most recent one must be considered.) It has been suggested that, in practice, courts would be unlikely (Wilkinson, 1995) or unwise (Faulkner, 1995) to dispense altogether with PSRs for juvenile offenders. In the case of very grave offences, Section 53 of the *Children and Young Persons Act* allows for an adult-length sentence that may include prison custody.

The Processing of Cases in 1998

Cautioning[16]

In 1998, as indicated in Figure 4.1, the majority (about two-thirds) of all juvenile offenders known to the police were cautioned. For those aged 10 to 11, 91% of males and 97% of females were cautioned. For those aged 12 to 14, the equivalent figures were 72% and 88%, and for 15- to 17-year-olds, 48% and 67% respectively. About three-quarters of all cautions were for theft and handling stolen goods, 10% were for burglary, and about 12% were for violence against the person (Home Office, 2000).

From 1986 to 1993, the proportion of known juvenile offenders cautioned (as opposed to convicted) for indictable offences increased, particularly amongst 14- to 17-year-olds. In 1986, nearly half of 14- to 17-year-old male offenders were cautioned, whereas in 1993 nearly two-thirds were cautioned. For females, the equivalent rise was from 70% to 84%. With the restrictions placed on multiple cautioning in 1994, the use of cautioning fell to 54% for males and 76% for females by 1998. For those aged 10 to 13, the proportion that received cautions remained relatively high.

Prosecution

In 1998, about 80,000 juveniles were prosecuted for an indictable criminal offence. This represents an increase of approximately 10,000 over 1995 and 20,000 over 1993, but is about the same number as in 1988. The decline in prosecutions from 1988 to 1993 reflects the increase in the number of juveniles diverted from court, while the increase since 1993 reflects the reversal of this trend following the government's policy to end multiple cautions. Approximately one in four prosecutions against young people (for summary as well as indictable offences) are discontinued by the Crown Prosecution Service or dismissed by the court (Audit Commission, 1996).

Figure 4.1
Process Model of Youth Crimes in England and Wales, 1998

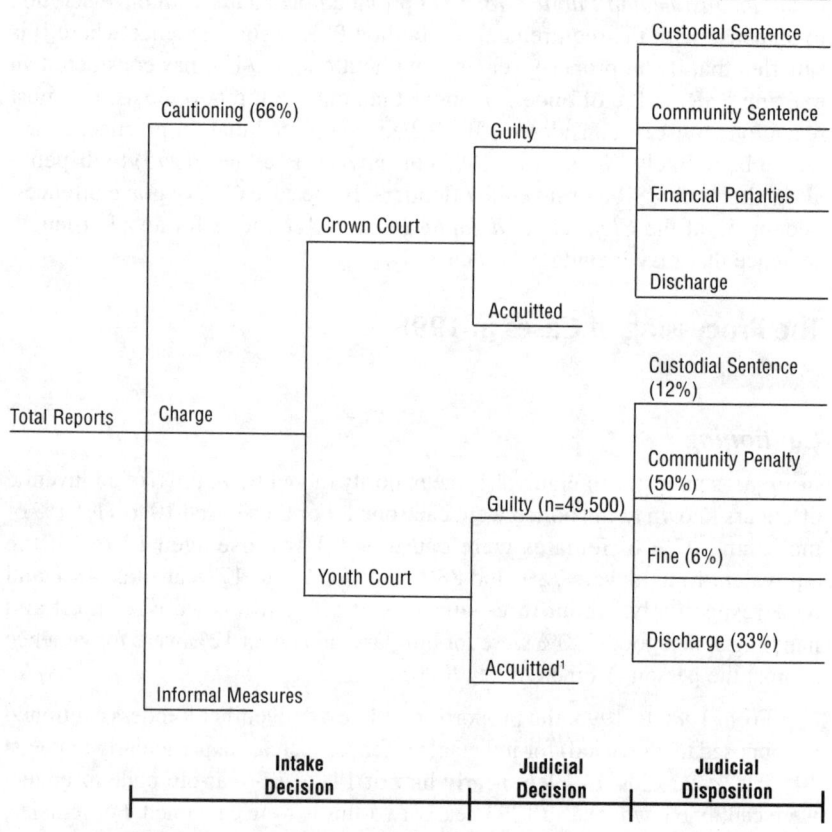

1   While exact numbers are not available, approximately 25% of youth cases heard in magistrates court were discontinued or withdrawn.

Sentencing

In 1998, as indicated in Figure 4.1, there were 49,500 juveniles sentenced by Youth Courts for indictable offences. Of these, approximately 9,400 were aged 10 to 14 (8,100 males and 1,300 females), and the rest (40,100) were aged 15 to 17 (35,000 males and 5,100 females). Of all juveniles sentenced in 1998, a third received an absolute or conditional discharge, half received a community penalty, 6% received a fine, and 12% were sentenced to immediate custody. In 1988, there were 63,000 juveniles sentenced for indictable offences, which is 25% more than in 1998. During the same period, the proportionate and absolute use of fines declined markedly, whereas an increasing proportion of youth who have been convicted by the court are discharged. Compared with 1988, fewer young people are found guilty by the courts (partly because fewer plead guilty). These changes in sentencing led the Audit Commission (1996) to conclude that less is done now to address offending behaviour than a decade ago. This led to the introduction in April 2000 of reparation orders,[17] which have substantially displaced conditional discharges for less serious offences.

The Use of Custody

The use of custody (i.e., placement in juvenile prison accommodation) for juvenile offenders, whether on remand or under sentence, is currently restricted to 15- to 17-year-olds (although secure training centres for 12- to 15-year-olds also take small numbers of offenders). The total number of juvenile offenders in custody on 30 June 1997 was 2,500 (i.e., the juvenile prison population). Of these, approximately 800 were on remand (untried or convicted but awaiting sentence). The vast majority was male.

In 1998, 8,300 juvenile offenders were sentenced to custody, of whom 600 were females. This is similar to the numbers sentenced to immediate custody in 1988 (although the number of females was lower). However, after the 1988 *Criminal Justice Act* came into force with its provisions to encourage community-based sentences, custody declined to a low of 3,900 in 1993. After the 1993 *Criminal Justice Act* came into effect, use of custody rose again. In 1988, approximately 13% of juveniles who were convicted in court were sentenced to immediate custody, which fell to less than 10% by 1990 before rising again to about 13% by 1998.

In addition to custodial sentences, young offenders can be held in adult prison custody if sentenced under section 53 of the *Children and Young Persons Act 1933* for committing grave offences (now consolidated in section 91, *Powers of Criminal Courts (Sentencing) Act, 2000*). In October 1992, section 53 was extended to 17-year-olds and in 1994 the *Criminal Justice and Public Order Act* further extended section 53 to cover younger offenders (10- to 13-year-olds). Trends in the use of section 53 therefore need to be interpreted carefully. However, since 1994, the number of juveniles sentenced under section 53 has risen considerably. In 1997, about 700 juveniles were sentenced under section 53, and in 1998 about 600, a considerable increase over the early 1990s (even allowing for the addition of 17-year-olds), when only about 100 juveniles were sentenced under section 53. This is possibly one of the most worrying trends in the sentencing of juvenile offenders.

Cost-Effectiveness

Costs

Since 1993, the government has developed a "Flows and Costs" model of the criminal justice system although, as yet, it does not contain separate calculations for the Youth Court. Nevertheless, best estimates of the cost of processing a typical Youth Court case suggest that it costs between 10% and 100% more than the cost of a comparable adult case. Assuming a factor of 50%, it is estimated that the processing of an indictable offence through the Youth Court costs approximately £3,600 per case. This includes police, prosecution, court, legal aid, probation, remand, and custody costs. The cost can be broken down into police case preparation £400; trial at Youth Court £2,000; and sentence £1,200. Where a juvenile case is heard in the Crown Court, the costs are much higher, at approximately £18,800 per case.

The Audit Commission (1996) produced a very similar estimate of the cost of processing a juvenile offender at, on average £3,700. However, the Audit Commission estimates includes £1,200 for the police, which is based on the full investigation and processing costs, whereas the "Flows and Costs" model only includes police costs incurred in case preparation for court.

The Audit Commission (1996) has also published estimates of the costs of processing cases with different sentences. Those which end up with a caution cost, on average £1,200; with caution plus referral to a community program £1,900; with a court imposing a discharge £3,600; with an attendance centre order £3,800; with supervision/probation £5,600; and with custody, just over £9,000. They conclude by estimating that the cost of juvenile crime to society is in the region of £1 billion per annum.

The estimated cost of a probation order is £200 per month; community service £150 per month; and a supervision order £190 per month. Estimates of the cost of a placement in youth custody range from £1,500 to £2,500 per youth per month.

A study of the total costs of offending by 15- to 17-year-olds sentenced to custody concluded that each offender costs, on average, about £75,000. The costs included in the overall estimate were the costs of the offence, the costs of the official response to the offence, and the costs of care and community interventions. Offence costs averaged about £23,000; response costs £27,000; and care and community intervention costs about £25,000. Extrapolating to the total population of 15- to 17-year-olds in custody, this amounts to about £188 million (NACRO, 1998).

Effectiveness

Cautioning[18]

The effectiveness of cautioning can be assessed by considering the proportion of juvenile offenders who receive cautions who are convicted within a two-year-period following the caution. In 1985, the proportion of cautioned juveniles who were convicted after two years was 17%. In 1988, it was 20%, and in 1991, it was 21%. For males the conviction rates were 20% in 1985, 22% in 1988, and 25% in 1991. For females, the equivalent figures were 8%, 9% and 11% respectively. In 1994, 19% of known juvenile offenders who were cautioned were convicted of a standard list offence within two years (22% of males and 11% of females).[19]

The effectiveness of cautioning (as measured in terms of subsequent convictions) appears to have remained relatively stable since the mid-1980s. The drop in the proportion of cautioned offenders who were subsequently convicted in 1994 is probably the result of the introduction in March of a Government Circular that discouraged repeat cautioning and the use of cautions for the most serious offences. The 1994 sample, which was taken in November, therefore comprises a less serious group of offenders, both in terms of the offences for which they were cautioned and the number of previous cautions. Following the introduction of the 1993 Circular, the proportion of cautioned offenders who had previously been cautioned was lower than in earlier years. The proportion of cautioned male juveniles who had a previous caution fell from 32% in 1991 to 20% in 1994, and for females, the drop was from 18% to 12%.

The effectiveness of cautioning, as measured by subsequent conviction rates, appears to decline after the first caution. In 1994, 14% of juveniles with no previous cautions were convicted within two years, whereas 37% of those with one previous caution and 48% of those with two or more cautions were subsequently convicted (Home Office Statistical Bulletin, 1994). There is evidence to suggest that, after three occasions prosecution is more effective in reducing re-offending than cautioning (Audit Commission, 1996). In a few parts of the country, there are caution "plus" schemes, which attempt to supplement the caution with community-based interventions to address the offender's behaviour, but no data currently exist on the effectiveness of such schemes.

It should be stressed that convictions after two years are not an accurate measure of re-offending. In a smaller sampling exercise undertaken in 10 police force areas, it was found that 45% of juveniles cautioned in 1991 were either convicted or re-cautioned within two years (31% were re-cautioned, 24% were convicted, and some were both re-cautioned and convicted). There will also be others who will have offended but who were not caught and were therefore neither re-cautioned nor convicted within the two year follow-up period. The extent of the true rate of re-offending is unknown.

Sentencing

Re-conviction rates following a sentence for a criminal offence tend to be particularly high for juvenile offenders, with the highest rates among the most serious offenders, and hence following the most serious sentences. In 1994, the latest year for which re-conviction data is available, the re-conviction rates of those convicted of a standard list offence are shown for different disposals in Table 4.1 below.

Table 4.1
Proportion of Juveniles Convicted of a Standard List Offence in 1994 and in the First Half of 1997 Who Were Re-convicted within Two Years by Disposal

Sentence	1994 %	1997 %
Conditional discharge	58	61
Fine	66	67
Attendance centre order	72	75
Supervision order	79	80
Probation	87	82
Community service order	74	74
Custodial sentence*	81	90

* Excludes detentions under section 53 of the *Children and Young Persons Act 1933*.

As Table 4.1 shows, the re-conviction rate of those sentenced to probation is the highest, at 87%, but caution should be exercised in interpreting re-conviction rates and in drawing comparisons between disposals. The re-conviction rate for juvenile offenders (16- and 17-year-olds) commencing probation in 1994 was substantially higher than in 1993, when it was 78%. This is likely the result of the small sample available in 1994, which was just 85 cases. A more extensive sample of those commencing probation in 1994 reveals a lower re-conviction rate of 76%. However, with re-conviction rates being so high, they may not in themselves provide an adequate indication of effectiveness. The nature and number of re-convictions may also be important. Furthermore, the characteristics and previous offending records of offenders sentenced to different sentences varies, and for those sentenced to custody, part of the follow-up period will have been spent in custody, where the risk of re-conviction is considerably lower. If the first day of release from prison is taken as the first day of the two-year follow-up period, then the re-conviction rate rises to 87% (i.e., based on a sample of discharged prisoners rather than a sample of sentenced offenders).

As part of the study, a "predictive" model of re-offending was developed, based on a logistic regression model taking into account the gender, age, current offence and previous criminal history. Comparisons of predicted and actual re-conviction rates are more reliable indicators of the effectiveness of different sentences (although even here changes in the sentencing framework, or changes in social factors such as financial means or home circumstances, which could not be taken into account in determining predicted rates, may account for some observed differences). These cautionary concerns notwithstanding, comparisons of predicted and actual re-conviction rates suggest that fines and conditional charges tend to produce slightly better outcomes compared with predictions, whereas other sentences tend to produce slightly worse outcomes.

Not surprisingly, the re-conviction rates of juvenile offenders increase with the number of previous court appearances. So whereas just over half of all juveniles with no previous court appearances sentenced to custody are re-convicted within two years of release, the proportions with one, two, or three previous appearances are 82%, 91%, and 95% respectively within the same time span (based on 1994 figures). A similar pattern exists for other sentences.

Re-conviction rates also vary according to the type of offence for which a juvenile offender is originally sentenced. The highest re-conviction rates of those discharged from youth prison are for those who were originally convicted of theft and handling stolen goods (93%) and burglary (90%), although in both cases such offenders are likely to have had a number of previous court appearances and the high re-conviction rate may simply be a reflection of this.

Issues and Concerns

The new legislation, and in particular the *Crime and Disorder Act 1998*, is likely to have a considerable impact on the way that society responds to juvenile crime. Its philosophy represents an attempt to move away from the tired dichotomy between welfare and punishment, and towards the more utilitarian aim of preventing crime. Reducing costs and improving performance are the driving forces behind a new "managerialism," with an emphasis on devising plans, setting targets, measuring performance, and reviewing progress. Many of the new measures have been piloted (they were implemented nationally in June 2000), which reflects a desire to develop pragmatic rather than ideological solutions. These are welcome developments, but some features of the new proposals have not been universally welcomed. In particular, the abolition of *doli incapax* and the introduction of new orders for aberrant families and children have attracted some criticism.

The Abolition of doli incapax

Prior to the enactment of the *Crime and Disorder Act 1998*, before a juvenile aged from 10 to 13 could be convicted of a criminal offence, the prosecution had to prove that he or she not only intended to commit the offence, but also that in so doing appreciated that what he or she did was seriously wrong. Known as the principle of *doli incapax* (Latin for "incapacity to do wrong"), the idea was to recognize that a child's understanding, knowledge, and ability to reason is not the same as that of an adult. The *doli incapax* defence developed at common law, to recognize that some children lack the intellectual and moral development to be held accountable through the criminal justice system.

Doli incapax was abolished for a number of reasons. First, it was argued that it is extremely difficult (if not impossible in some cases) for the prosecution to provide the necessary evidence to show that a child had knowledge *and* appreciation that his or her act was seriously wrong. In practice, to rebut the presumption that a child knew and appreciated that an act was wrong, the prosecution needed to adduce evidence that showed that the defendant was of normal mental and moral development for his or her age. Second, it was argued that the doctrine is inherently contradictory. How can evidence that shows that a child is "normal" be used to rebut the presumption of *doli incapax*, when the doctrine itself presumes that it is *normal* for children of that age *not* to know right from wrong? And third, the government believed that abolishing *doli incapax* would ensure that children would receive appropriate interventions to prevent further offending. There are, however, those who consider the abolition of *doli incapax* to be wrong.

Bandalli (1998) argues that it was actually quite easy for the prosecution to rebut the presumption of *doli incapax*, and that even if there were practical difficulties, these could be overcome if the doctrine were retained but the presumption were reversed. It would then be presumed that a child aged from 10 to 13 could distinguish right from wrong, unless the defence could show otherwise. However, this proposal would not help to reduce the delay associated with the existence of the *doli incapax* defence, and might even increase delays if the defence decided to raise the issue in every case.

The argument that abolishing *doli incapax* ensures that appropriate interventions occur is based on the assumption that children who offend require some form of intervention, irrespective of whether they appreciate that their offending behaviour was wrong or not. However, if a child is held not to be responsible for his actions on the basis that he did not appreciate that the acts were wrong, then technically speaking, no crime has been committed and there are therefore no grounds, at least within the parameters of criminal law, for imposing criminal sanctions (i.e., interventions). Furthermore, even if such interventions were totally benign, the child is still found guilty of committing a criminal offence and receives a criminal record.

Perhaps more importantly, Bandalli (1998) points out that since the vast majority of children who appear before the Youth Court plead guilty, the issue of *doli incapax* rarely arises. This then begs the question as to whether its abolition has much practical significance, and leads to the wider question of whether, *in principle,* children as young as 10 should be held as accountable in the criminal justice system for their actions as older youths or adults. According to accepted wisdom in the field of child development, individual children develop and mature at different rates and at different times, and one of the key ways in which they learn to distinguish right from wrong is by testing boundaries. The key issue therefore should not simply be one of age, but should be one of maturity.

In 1993, in the English Court of Appeal, Justice Laws supported the abolition of the *doli incapax* defence, arguing

> ...the fact that in an earlier age [when the defence of *doli incapax* developed] there was no system of universal compulsory education and perhaps children did not grow up as quickly as they do nowadays (Penal Affairs Consortium, 1995).

Morrison (1997), in his detailed account of the murder and trial of the toddler Jamie Bulger by two 10-year-old boys in 1993, suggests that it is a myth that children "grow up" more quickly than their ancestors. He states:

> A hundred years ago, children had much shorter childhoods, were more quickly introduced to work, marriage, parenthood and death. In 1860, a ten year old could legally have sex. In 1993, ten year olds are thought too immature for sex, though mature enough to [be legally accountable for] murder.

In most European countries, children under the age of 14 are not held criminally responsible for any of their acts, and in some countries (e.g., France, Spain, and Germany), the principle of limited responsibility applies to children up to the age of 18.

Given the small number of cases where the prosecution had to rebut the presumption of *doli incapax*, and the doubts as to whether such a rebuttal was in practice so difficult to achieve, one might ask whether the abolition of *doli incapax*, at this moment in the history of English criminal law was not, at least in part, a reaction to the shocking murder of the toddler Jamie Bulger in 1993 by two 10-year-old boys. While the Crown in the Bulger case was able to rebut the *doli incapax* defence, there was concern that it *might* have succeeded. Had it not been for this tragic killing, the government might not have so easily accepted the notion that children are capable of extreme evil and the government might not have been so easily convinced of the need to abolish an age-old doctrine.

The Parenting Order

The parenting order is one of the most recent developments in the continuing shift towards placing more emphasis on holding parents responsible for the offending behaviour of their children. It can also be seen as one of a number of new measures for supporting parents in bringing up children to avoid a wide range of social problems, of which criminality is just one. In the first instance, a Youth Court may require a young offender's parents to attend regular counseling or guidance sessions for a period not exceeding three months, or to comply with other conditions to help them control their children. The order is available where a child or young person has been convicted of an offence or made the subject of a child safety order, an antisocial behaviour order, or a sex offender order. It is also available for parents who have been convicted of failing to send their child to school.

In some cases, courts may impose additional requirements, such as requiring parents to ensure their children attend court or school, or that the children are at home during certain hours of the day or night. Such additional requirements may apply for up to one year, and where a parent fails to comply with the terms of an order, they may be liable to a fine of up to £1,000. Before imposing a parenting order, the court is expected to assess the effects of such an order on the offender's family circumstances.

Research has consistently shown that family relationships and lack of appropriate parental supervision are important influences on offending (see, for example, Graham & Bowling, 1995; Farrington, 1996).

Prior to their introduction, a number of concerns were expressed about the value of a court-imposed parenting order, including the potentially counter-productive effect of exerting coercion on dysfunctional, uncooperative, or lone-parent families, and the possibility of increasing the chances of child abuse, family breakdown, and children ending up in state care (Family Policy Studies Centre, 1998). For poor parents, the imposition of a fine in cases of breach may also be counter-productive and alternative, non-financial penalties may be preferred by the courts in these cases. In practice, it is up to the courts to ensure that the potential for misusing this new power is not realized.

Early indications suggest that whilst a handful of parents were resentful of the compulsory nature of the order and for being held responsible for the offending of their children, the majority have really welcomed the opportunity to improve their parenting skills. Professionals (i.e., members of Youth Offending Teams) as well as offenders themselves have also expressed positive views about the new parenting programs. In the first year alone, (April 2000 to March 2001), over 900 parenting orders were made.

The Child Safety Order: An Early Intervention Response

In addition to the authority to seek a child protection order in cases of parental abuse or neglect, the child safety order permits intervention for children under the age of 10 who are at risk of becoming involved in crime or who have started to display antisocial or criminal tendencies. It can be used where the local authority can show that

- a child under the age of 10 has done something that would constitute an offence if he or she were over 10;
- a child's behaviour indicates that he or she was at risk of offending;
- a child's behaviour is disruptive or harassing to local residents; or
- a child has breached a local curfew order.

The order can specify that certain conditions be undertaken to support the child, protect him or her from the risk of being drawn into crime, and to attempt to ensure proper care and control. To secure this, the Family Proceedings Court (cases are not heard in the Youth Court) may require a child, for example, to attend school, be at home at certain times, or stay away from certain people or places. The order normally lasts up to three months, but in exceptional circumstances, may last up to one year.

By providing support and protection to children under the age of criminal responsibility, the child safety order represents a move towards the Scottish Children's Hearing System, where such decisions are embedded within the criminal justice system. This is also consistent with some of the longer-term aims of the Labour Government to move towards a less adversarial juvenile justice system. However, the Family Policy Studies Centre (1998) has suggested that it could lead a child who has committed no offence to see him or herself as an offender, and to a *defacto* lowering of the age of criminal responsibility.

Along with the parenting order, the child safety order reflects the state's increasing involvement in the private sphere of the family, which in turn reflects widespread concern about changing family structures and the "breakdown of the family." It allows state intervention for children who have not committed an offence *but are considered to be at risk of so doing*. It reflects the growing concern about increasingly younger out-of-control children, but it remains to be seen whether this response provides a solution. So far, the signs are that it will not – only a few child safety orders[20] have been imposed since the piloting of the new orders began.

The Shift Towards Prevention

The current government is committed not just to being "tough on crime," but also to being "tough on the causes of crime." The 1997 White Paper devoted a chapter to tackling the causes of crime and outlines a range of government-wide initiatives for achieving this. These include

- measures to support families, which are to be coordinated by a new Ministerial Group on the Family, chaired by the Home Secretary;
- the development of policies to reduce social exclusion, which are being developed by a new Cabinet Office Unit, accountable directly to the Prime Minister;
- new programs to reduce youth unemployment, early school leaving and expulsions, school failure, truancy, and welfare dependency;
- the appointment of a new UK Anti-Drugs Coordinator (the so-called "Drugs Tzar") to develop a new ten-year drugs strategy;
- the introduction, through the *Crime and Disorder Act 1998*, of a new statutory duty on local authorities and the police to prevent crime and disorder.

Subsequently, the government funded a number of preventive initiatives, such as the Crime Reduction Programme and Sure Start (an early intervention program for 0- to 4-year-olds). Most recently, work undertaken by the Social Exclusion Unit with young people living in poor neighbourhoods has led to a recommendation to set up a national Children's Fund (Social Exclusion Unit, 2000).

Within this preventive context, the *Crime and Disorder Act 1998* consistently refers to the importance of changing the behaviour of offenders. The introduction of the new reparation order, for example, reflects an attempt to make offenders face the consequences of their actions by seeing the harm they have perpetrated on their victims and to make amends for so doing. The new youth offending teams will provide local areas with a multi-agency network for tackling youth crime as well as improving the delivery of youth justice services. The introduction of the child safety order, local child curfews, and the Final Warning ("to nip offending in the bud") are all justified by reference to research findings that show that the younger the age at which children begin to offend, the more likely they will become career criminals (see Home Office Statistical Bulletin, 1987). It is encouraging that much of the government's current efforts to tackle youth crime are firmly grounded in research-based evidence on the causes of crime. The key issue, however, is whether any of the considerable resources that are currently tied up in identifying and processing young offenders can be shifted to the potentially more effective strategy of preventing children from becoming offenders in the first place.

Following the publication of the Audit Commission's report in 1996, which recommended shifting to a more proactive approach to tackling youth crime, the Commission undertook further follow-up work on tackling youth crime. The report (Renshaw, 1998) based on data collected by district auditors in 1997, identified a number of ways in which savings could be made. Financial savings could be achieved by speeding up the court process, increasing opportunities to address offending behaviour, improving communication and coordination of agencies, and improved monitoring of re-offending. The following are among the most significant savings identified:

- £12 million by reducing the average number of court appearances before sentence from 3.63 to 3.00;
- £23 million by diverting those first- and second-time offenders who received a discharge, a fine, or an attendance centre order to a caution plus community intervention scheme that addressed their offending behaviour;
- £24 million by diverting half of all first- and second-time offenders given community penalties to caution-plus schemes and ensuring all those with two or more previous offences who were cautioned were also given caution plus;

- £34 million by replacing pre-trial custodial remands with bail support schemes.

By improving the effectiveness of the juvenile justice system, considerable additional resources (in the region of at least £90 million) could be released for prevention. Since a relatively small number of offenders commit most of the offences that result in a caution or conviction (about 3%), resources that effectively target those at risk of offending may, at least potentially, be much more cost-effective. There is now a limited body of literature that documents what works in preventing crime and criminality (see, in particular, Sherman, 1997), although much more high-quality evaluations of preventive programs are needed, particularly in countries outside the U.S.

In 1996, RAND, a non-profit institution that advises on various aspects of public policy in the U.S., published the findings of a study that measured the cost-effectiveness of a number of crime prevention strategies, including early interventions with children and families at risk and the Californian "three strikes and you're out" incarceration program (Greenwood et al., 1996). The results are highly encouraging; parent training, graduation incentives, and delinquent supervision were all found to be more cost-effective than incarceration. While the authors caution that these findings must be carefully assessed before being applied, they suggest that shifting resources from the criminal justice and penal system to a more proactive approach may be financially and socially sensible. Governments seriously interested in preventing offending should pay greater attention to evidence of this kind, rather than continue to seek the solution to juvenile crime solely within the narrow horizons of the criminal justice system.

References

Allen, R. (1991). Out of jail: The reduction in the use of penal custody for male juveniles 1981-88. *Howard Journal* 30 (1): 30-52.

Audit Commission. (1996). *Misspent youth*. Abingdon: Audit Commission Publications.

Bandalli, S. (1998). Abolition of the presumption of *doli incapax* and the criminalisation of children. *The Howard Journal of Criminal Justice* 37 (2): 114-123.

Bone, M. (1996). *A statistical map in: The Carnegie young people initiative*. Carnegie United Kingdom Trust. Leicester: Youth Work Press.

Coleman, C., & Moynihan, J. (1996). *Understanding crime data: Haunted by the dark figure*. Buckingham: Open University Press.

Department for Social Security. (1999). *Opportunity for all: Tackling poverty and social exclusion*. First Annual Report (CM 4445). London: The Stationery Office.

Family Policy Studies Centre (1998). *The crime and disorder bill and the family*. London: Family Policy Study Centre.

Farrington, D. (1992). Trends in English juvenile delinquency and their explanation. *International Journal of Comparative and Applied Criminal Justice* 16 (2): 153-163.

Farrington, D. (1996). *Understanding and preventing youth crime*. York: Joseph Rowntree Foundation.

Faulkner, D. (1995). Discretion in calling for pre-sentence reports. *The Magistrate* 51 (1): 12.

Flood-Page, C., Campbell, S., Harrington, V., Mayhew, P., & Miller, J. (2000). *Youth crime: Findings from the 1998/99 youth lifestyles survey.* Home Office Research Study. London: HMSO.

Gibson, B., Cavadino, P., Rutherford, A., Ashworth, A., & Harding, J. (1994). *The youth court: One year onwards.* Winchester: Waterside Press.

Graham, J., & Bowling, B. (1995). *Young people and crime.* Home Office Research Study, No. 145. London: HMSO.

Greenwood, P.W., Model, K.E., Rydell, C.P., & Chiesa, J. (1996). *Diverting children from a life of crime: Measuring costs and benefits.* Santa Monica, California: Rand Corporation.

Hindelang, M., Hirschi, T., & Weis, J.G. (1981). *Measuring delinquency.* Beverly Hills, California: Sage.

Home Affairs Select Committee. (1993). *Report on juvenile offenders.* London: HMSO.

Home Office Statistical Bulletin. (1987). *Criminal careers of those born in 1953: Persistent offenders and desistance.* London: Home Office.

Home Office Statistical Bulletin. (1994). *The criminal histories of those cautioned in 1985, 1988, and 1991.* London: Home Office.

Home Office. (1995). *Digest 3: Information on the criminal justice system in England and Wales.* London: Home Office Research and Statistics Department.

Home Office. (1996). *Annual report 1996: The government expenditure plans 1996-1997 to 1998-1999.* London: HMSO.

Home Office. (1997a). *No more excuses — a new approach to tackling youth crime in England and Wales.* Home Office: London.

Home Office. (1997b). *Getting to grips with crime: A new framework for local action.* London: Home Office.

Home Office. (2000). *Criminal statistics, England and Wales, 1998* (CM 4649).

Joutsen, M. (1997). Recent trends in crime in Western Europe. *European Journal on Criminal Policy and Research* 5 (1): 15-39.

Maguire, M. (1997). Crime statistics, patterns and trends: Changing perceptions and their implications. In M. Maguire, R. Morgan, & R. Reiner (Eds.), *The oxford handbook of criminology.* Oxford: Oxford University Press.

Mirrlees-Black, C., Mayhew, P., & Percy, A. (1996). *The 1996 British crime survey: England and Wales.* Home Office Statistical Bulletin. London: Government Statistical Service.

Mirrlees-Black, C., Budd, T., Partridge, S., & Mayhew, P. (1998). *The 1998 British crime survey: England and Wales.* Home Office Statistical Bulletin. London: Government Statistical Service.

Morrison, B. (1997). *As if.* London: Granta Books.

Moser, C. (1999). *Improving Literacy and Numeracy.* Report of a Working Group, Chaired by Sir Clause Moser. London: Department for Education and Employment.

NACRO. (1998). *Wasted lives: Counting the cost of juvenile offending.* London: NACRO.

Newburn T. (1997). Youth, crime and justice. In M. Maguire, R. Morgan, & R. Reiner (Eds.), *The Oxford handbook of criminology.* Oxford: Oxford University Press.

Office for National Statistics (1996). *Social focus on ethnic minorities*. London: Office for National Statistics.

Office for National Statistics. (1998). *Social Trends 28: A biography of the nation*. London: Government Statistical Service.

Payne, J. (1999). *Routes at sixteen: Trends and choices in the nineties*. London: Department for Education and Employment.

Penal Affairs Consortium. (1995). *The doctrine of doli incapax*. London: Penal Affairs Consortium.

Renshaw, J. (1998). *Follow-up report to misspent youth*. London: Audit Commission.

Social Exclusion Unit. (1998). *Truancy and school exclusion*. London: The Stationery Office.

Social Exclusion Unit. (1999). *Bridging the gap: New opportunities for 16-18 year olds not in education, employment or training*. London: The Stationery Office.

Social Exclusion Unit. (2000). *National strategy for neighbourhood renewal – report of policy action team 12: Young people*. London: The Social Exclusion Unit.

Sherman, L.W. (1997). Family-based crime prevention. In L.W. Sherman et al., *Preventing crime: What works, what doesn't, what's promising*. Washington: US Department of Justice.

Walker, M.A. (ed.) (1995). *Interpreting crime statistics*. Oxford: Clarendon Press.

Wilkinson, T. (1995). New rules for juvenile offenders. *Solicitors Journal* 10 (February): 110-111.

Notes

1 Mirrlees-Black, Mayhew, and Percy (1996) estimate that approximately 50% of "crimes" reported to the police in England and Wales are not subsequently recorded.

2 The first national self-report study was undertaken in 1993 and a second survey was undertaken in 1999.

3 Notifiable offences are those that are recorded in the annual publication of criminal statistics. They include nearly all indictable offences, which are offences that are triable in the Crown Court or triable either way (i.e., either in the magistrates' court or the Crown Court). They also include a few summary offences, such as unauthorized taking of a motor vehicle, but not other summary offences that might be considered more serious than some of those that are included (e.g., common assault, assault of a police officer, and driving after consuming alcohol).

4 Although international comparisons of recorded crime *rates* are of little value, given the different definitions of recorded crimes and different classification systems, comparisons of *trends* are more valid. Given the widespread consistency in recorded crime trends across Europe, any differences in trends between countries are unlikely to be due to changes in recording practices.

5 The counting rules for violent offences changed in 1998, but to ensure comparability, the figures presented here are calculated on a pre-1998 basis.

6 This is the latest year for which data using the old (and hence comparable) counting rules are available.

7   Victim surveys also have their limitations and tend to produce underestimates of crime levels for various reasons (see Coleman & Moynihan, 1996, for a full discussion of the limitations of victim surveys).

8   The rise in domestic and acquaintance violence is likely to be partly due to an increased willingness to report such incidents to a third party. The British Crime Survey shows that the reporting of such incidents to the police has increased since 1981 and this may reflect a greater willingness to mention such incidents to interviewers.

9   Juveniles are those who are aged from 10 to 17 at the time of sentencing. Prior to 1 October 1992, those aged 17 were not treated as juveniles in the English criminal justice system.

10 The same list of offences was used in the second survey as was used in the first.

11 The small reduction in last year offending rates for young women in the second survey is likely to be due to the wider age range in the second survey. Those aged 12 and 13 and those aged 25 to 30 were found to have lower last year offending rates than those in their mid- to late teens and early twenties.

12 The preventive focus of the government's strategy actually goes beyond the youth justice system, including the provision of a statutory responsibility to local child welfare authorities and the police to develop a community safety and crime reduction strategy (Home Office, 1997b).

13 The age was raised to 15 in August 2001.

14 The same Act also introduced drug treatment and testing orders for those aged 16 and over, which requires an offender known to be misusing drugs to agree to comply with a program of drug testing and treatment.

15 Reprimands and Final Warnings recently replaced cautioning for juvenile offenders.

16 Although in 1998 legislation was enacted to replace the statutory concept of "cautioning" with a more nuanced system of police Reprimands and Final Warnings for juvenile offenders, as yet the only available data on pre-court disposals is for cautioning.

17 Between April 2000 and March 2001, approximately 5,700 reparation orders were passed.

18 Although cautions have now been replaced by Final Warnings, there is no data yet on the latter's effectiveness.

19 Standard list offences are those that are included in the Offenders Index, which is a large data base containing the criminal records of all those convicted of such an offence since 1963. They include all indictable offences, together with some of the more serious summary offences, such as assaulting a police officer. Standard list offences are therefore very similar to notifiable offences (see note 3).

20 Between April 2000 and March 2001, 128 child safety orders were passed.

CHAPTER 5

Juvenile Crime and Justice in Scotland

Maureen Buist and Stewart Asquith

Although part of the United Kingdom (UK), Scotland has its own education system, legal system, and very distinct system of juvenile justice, the Children's Hearing System, which came into operation in 1971. This innovative juvenile justice system was based on the recommendations of a review committee on children and young persons chaired by the High Court Judge, Lord Kilbrandon. The Kilbrandon Committee was established in 1961 to review the operation of the Scottish juvenile justice system, since it was generally felt that the system did not adequately respond to either the needs of the young people it dealt with or issues of financial restraint. The Kilbrandon Report, published in 1964, made a number of recommendations to substantially overhaul the existing juvenile justice system, including the recommendation for the introduction of the Children's Hearing System.

The philosophy behind the Kilbrandon Report and the recommendation to replace juvenile courts with the Children's Hearing System was based on the premise that the focus of the juvenile justice system should be on "the needs and not the deeds of the child." The Committee felt that there was very little difference between those children coming to the attention of the authorities for committing an offence, and those coming to the attention of the authorities for child abuse, neglect, and other welfare concerns. The Committee concluded that offending was in many cases a reflection of other problems normally related to family environment. Successfully addressing the problem of child offenders, therefore, meant that an emphasis must be placed on intervening on a voluntary or, if necessary, compulsory basis where the problem begins – in the home.

Maureen Buist is formerly a research fellow with a number of Scottish Universities and is currently working for the newly established Criminal Justice Social Work Development Centre for Scotland at the University of Edinburgh.

Stewart Asquith is Head of the Department of Social Policy and Social Work at University of Glasgow, Scotland.

The emphasis of the new Children's Hearing System is, therefore, on promoting parental responsibility in bringing up their own children, and on providing services and making decisions with a primary view to strengthening the family. The aim of the Hearings is to involve the family in the decision-making process and to arrive at a decision that has the best interests of the child in mind.

In terms of decision-making authority, the Kilbrandon Committee felt that the court system was inappropriate for determining the needs of children in trouble, in that the focus was on legal requirements and procedure rather than the interests of the child. The Committee, therefore, recommended that the authority to order dispositions should rest with a body of people with a special interest in the child, and not the law. It is with this in mind that the Children's Hearing System, made up of a broad range of volunteer members from the community, was established.

In 1968, *The Social Work (Scotland) Act* received Royal Assent. Parts I and II of the Act dealt with the reorganization of social services. Part III of the Act set up the Children's Hearing System, which came into effect in 1971. The Children's Hearing System was innovative and unique in many ways, not the least of which was that it fully integrated the juvenile justice system and the child welfare system. The system has now been in place for 30 years and in that time has changed remarkably little.

The definition of a "child" in Scotland is a person under the age of 16, and Scottish criminal law provides that no child under the age of 8 years can be guilty of an offence. Children between the ages of 8 and 15 who offend are dealt with by the Children's Hearing System. There is also some provision for 16- and 17-year-olds to be dealt with by the Hearing System, but the majority of young people in this age group are dealt with by the adult criminal justice system. In certain situations children under 16 years of age may be presented in adult court on the instruction of the Lord Advocate, Scotland's principal law officer, but this seldom happens.

The collection of data for this chapter occurred at a period of considerable change in Scotland. First was the re-organization in 1995 from a system of regional government based on a two-tier system of 9 regional and 53 district councils and 3 island authorities, to 32 unitary regional administration authorities. Second was the introduction of new child welfare legislation in 1997. Third was the change of government from Conservative to Labor, which not only brought major shifts in policy and the frameworks within which these would operate, but also set in trend major consultation exercises on the way in which policy should develop. Fourth was the establishment in 1999 of a Scottish Parliament with devolved powers in respect to Health, Education, Transport and Environment, and Crime and Justice. Fifth was the reorganization of the health boards and trusts that administer the National Health Service. And finally there was the reorganization of the administration of the system of juvenile justice.

These administrative changes have had some impact on data collection as systems have altered and have sometimes led to gaps in the data available.

PART I: PROFILE OF SCOTLAND

Demographic Characteristics

In 1998, Scotland had a population of just over five million (5,120,000), approximately 10% of the total population of the UK. The birth rate has continued to decline since 1991, and in 1998 there were 1,014,194 children aged 0-15 years (General Register Office, 1999). There were 515,774 children aged 8-15 years, the ages within the jurisdiction of the juvenile justice system.

Unfortunately we still have to rely upon the 1991 Census for information on ethnic minority distribution. At that point, Scotland's black and visible minority population made up 1.3% of the total population. The largest single black and minority ethnic group was Pakistani, followed by Chinese and then Indian (General Register Office, 1993). The majority of the minority ethnic population is concentrated in the more densely populated urban areas around Glasgow and Edinburgh. The population density in Scotland is 66 people per square kilometer, compared to 238 people per square kilometer for the UK as a whole.

Family Structures

The rate of marriage declined somewhat in the decade 1986/96 from an annual rate of 7 per 1,000 population in 1986 to 5.9 in 1996 and 5.8 in 1998. In 1999, there were 11,864 divorces in Scotland resulting in a divorce rate of 2.3 per 1,000 population. The divorce rate has been relatively stable since 1986 when the rate was 2.5 per 1,000 population. The highest point during this time period was in 1994 when the rate was 2.6 per 1,000 population.

The trend towards more children being born to unmarried parents continued in 1998 so that they represented 38.9% of all live births compared to 20% in 1986. However marriage is still popular and one in four marriages in Scotland is a re-marriage. There are now around 40,000 stepfamilies in Scotland. Altogether one in eight children in Scotland will grow up in a stepfamily, and many children will experience change on more than one occasion (Stepfamily Scotland, 1998).

Information from the 1991 Census on household composition shows there were 2,020,050 households of which 609,997 (30%) contained children aged 0-15 (43% one child, 40% two children, 16.3 % three children). About one in five households with children was headed by a lone parent; the vast majority of these households (93%) are headed by women, most of whom are separated, divorced, or widowed (Tisdall & Donaghy, 1995).

Socioeconomic Characteristics

Education Levels Obtained by Youth

Compulsory schooling in Scotland begins at age 5 when children enter primary school and ends in secondary school at age 16. Prior to entering primary school children may attend some form of pre-school education.

Nursery school education has not been legally required, and until very recently, provision was at the discretion of the local authorities. The first national review of services for children under eight revealed how provision of pre-school services was extremely limited. Moreover the level and range of services in urban areas was greatly superior to that in rural areas (e.g., one rural authority had no local authority daycare or educational services for pre-school children; Buist, 1994). Since then there have been major changes in government policy as will be discussed later. Estimates of the level of pre-school provision in Scotland indicate that places exist for 95% of four-year-olds and that provision for three-year-olds is progressing.

On completion of their primary schooling (at approximately age 12), around 95% of children go on to attend public sector secondary school. The Scottish Certificate of Education (SCE) qualifications that may be acquired in the four years of compulsory education are Standard Grades, and those that may be acquired after a further two years of study are Higher Grades.[1] There has been a steady increase in the educational accomplishments of pupils in the past few years. In 1997/98, 33% of pupils in S4 (the fourth year of secondary school, a stage at which compulsory schooling may end) obtained five or more Standard Grades at level 1-2, compared to only 25% in 1992/93. The percentage of low attainers (those with no awards or awards at a poor grade) has continued to decline and in 1997/98 was 6.6% compared to a decade earlier when it was 14.9%. The rate of low educational achievement has declined more among females than among males (Scottish Executive, 2000a). There is evidence that those who have not achieved the Scottish Certificate go on to experience greater unemployment, homelessness, and deprivation (Buist & Harland, 2000).

Rates of Drop Out/Exclusion from School

The rate of pupils leaving school at the official leaving age has dropped from 46% in 1985/86 to 30% in 1997/98. Boys are more likely to leave when they reach the school leaving age than girls (34% and 26%). The proportion of pupils staying on into sixth year has also continued to increase from 21% in 1985/86 to 45.5% in 1997/98.

In terms of absences from school, each morning and afternoon of the school day counts as a possible attendance. Absence in Scottish schools is classified as authorized or unauthorized absence. Unauthorized absence includes truancy, family holidays where attendance is otherwise unsatisfactory, unexplained absence, and temporary exclusions. Unauthorized absence in primary schools is negligible and in secondary schools has remained around 1% for the past few years. However the picture varies by stage and peaks at 2% in the fourth year of secondary school (for most youth the last year of compulsory attendance; Audit Unit, 1999).

Pupils excluded from school are grouped into the two categories of permanent and temporary exclusions. Some local authorities have zero for permanent exclusions because as a matter of policy they do not permit permanent exclusions.

Employment Levels of Parents

Improvements in calculating labour market statistics were introduced in 1998 by the Office for National Statistics (Scottish Office, 2000). The overall rate of employment among adults in Scotland in 1998 (Government Statistical Services, 2000) was 71.6%, while the rate of those claiming the Job Seekers Allowance (the new name for the benefit for those who are unemployed and seeking work) was around 5.5%.

However there are variations in employment and unemployment levels according to the time of year, the age and gender of individuals, and the locality in which they live (e.g., unemployment tends to be higher than average in predominantly rural areas). Urban areas also have their "black spots" (e.g., in June 1994 the unemployment rate for males in one Edinburgh housing scheme was 30% and 10% for females; City of Edinburgh Research Section, 1996). There is also evidence that some sections of the workforce experience longer periods of unemployment compared to others.

Poverty Levels

In the years leading up to 1996, there were significant increases in the numbers of claimants for Income Support and other related benefits accessible to those not in employment. The 1991 Census showed that a very significant number of children, 257,634 (23.7%) lived in households where no one was economically active and therefore were totally reliant upon benefits. Some households, those with three or more children, parents with disabled children, and lone parents, were more at risk of being economically inactive than others.

Since the 1991 Census there have been a number of changes in the benefit system, which are intended to improve this situation. These include the "New Deal," training for young people, and also schemes for the long-term unemployed; the "New Deal for Lone Parents" in which Personal Advisors help single parents to identify their skills, develop confidence, and apply for jobs and provide advice on finding childcare; and the introduction of the Childcare Tax

Credit to help with childcare costs. It is not yet possible to determine how these measures are impacting upon families.

The definition of low pay by the Scottish Low Pay Unit was £241.86 per week (£1 is about $1.50 US) in 1998 when average earnings of full-time workers in Scotland were £350.30 per week (Kelly, 1998). The Unit's estimate for 1998 was that 31.7% of full-time employees in Scotland were on low pay. However, low pay is not distributed evenly across Scotland and tends to affect women more than men, and rural areas more than urban areas.

Since 1998 the government has introduced the Working Family Tax Credit, which guarantees Scottish families a minimum weekly income of £200. This new program was accompanied by the introduction of the National Minimum Wage, an increase in Child Benefit allowances, and a new lower rate for income tax for low-income individuals. Many of these initiatives have been developed under the banner of "Social Inclusion," a policy which operates on five key principles to eradicate poverty (Scottish Office, 1998a):

- integration of the poor;
- prevention of poverty;
- understanding poverty;
- inclusiveness of services; and
- empowerment of the poor.

It is difficult to establish levels of poverty among Scottish children because of the different sources of data and the system of benefits, which require complex analysis techniques. There are a number of ways of defining poverty, but one way is to base it on how many people have less than half the national income. On this basis, it was calculated (Fraser, 1994) that 38% of the children in Scotland could be classified as living in poverty in 1990/91. Other studies have since come up with similar estimates (Long, Macdonald, & Scott, 1995).

Another indicator of the level of poverty is based on statistics on pupils entitled to free school meals. In the years from 1993 to 1999 the statistics show that about 21% of Scottish school children were entitled to free school meals. However there were differences across the country with almost twice as many children in the City of Glasgow as the national average being entitled to free school meals (Scottish Office, 1998b).

Carstairs and Morris (1991) used Census data to produce deprivation scores for each of the Scottish postal code sectors to identify "pockets" of deprivation. They showed that 57 districts, representing 6.7% of the population of Scotland, had a deprivation score of 7 (the most deprived) and that 73% of these sectors were in the Glasgow area, the largest city. Subsequent analysis (McLoone, 1994) revealed that people living in these areas were less healthy and had higher youth mortality rates.

Social Policy Issues Related to Children and Youth

State Expenditures

During the 1990s local authorities were subject to significant reductions in spending. At that time Britain had the largest public debt ever in its history. Concerns over the debt together with the constraints upon public debt associated with the entry into the European Union led the government to impose severe financial cuts on spending for government services. For example, Edinburgh had to cut about one-quarter of its budget. Edinburgh was not unusual in the amount of reduction it had to make and these cuts undoubtedly affected services throughout Scotland. As the deficit has come under control, the budgets have stabilized and even begun to increase, albeit starting from a lower level of spending than in the past. The present government has provided additional money for specific initiatives related to their policy of social inclusion.

An analysis of identifiable expenditure (Scottish Executive, 2000b) shows that Scotland obtains 10.2% of governmental spending in the UK. It reveals that identifiable spending per head at £4,722 in 1997/98 was significantly above that of the UK average, when it was compared to £3,897 in England.

Scotland's needs for health services are greater than the rest of the United Kingdom for a number of reasons, including high mortality rates from circulatory diseases and cancer. Scotland's Health Boards do not maintain records of spending on children's health services. Identifiable governmental expenditure in Scotland in 1997/98 on health and personal social services was £5,545 million, which was 22.7% of total government spending in Scotland.

Scotland's expenditures on education are higher than the rest of the UK. This can be partly accounted for by the fact that a higher proportion of Scotland's degree courses are of four years' duration and by the net inflow of students from the rest of the UK that Scotland traditionally experiences. Spending in Scotland on education in the year 1997/98 was £3,980 million, which accounted for 16.3% of total governmental expenditure in Scotland.

Publicly funded daycare, generally known as children's and/or family centres, is the main type of service for vulnerable families with children below school age. The centres provide care for the children together with support and advice to parents. The types of problems that children may have include: disturbed behaviour, developmental delays, and physical and learning disabilities. Parental problems include mental illness, social isolation, drug and/ or solvent problems, and emotional stress (Buist, 1999).

The number of positions available in the children's and/or family centres has traditionally been extremely low, with some 6,452 places provided in Scotland as a whole in 1994 (Scottish Office, 1998c) when the under-five population was 324,319.

Since 1994 central government initiatives to promote social inclusion have been specifically targeted at vulnerable families (Scottish Office, 1998d) with the aim of providing a positive start in young children's lives. It is expected that much of the "new" money available to local authorities will be spent on the provision of family centres. However there are as yet no statistics on the level of this provision.

Child Welfare and Childcare Policies

The *Children (Scotland) Act 1995* is the new child welfare legislation for Scotland (Scottish Office, 1995). It is premised on meeting the needs of children and their families and complying with the United Nations *Convention on the Rights of the Child*. It is founded on three main principles:

- the welfare of the child is the paramount consideration when his or her needs are being considered by courts and Children's Hearings;

- no court should make an order relating to a child and no Children's Hearing should impose a supervision requirement unless the court or Hearing considers that to do so would be better for the child than making no order at all; and

- the child's views should be taken into account when major decisions are to be made about his or her future.

The Act ensures that children have a right to be heard. The emphasis is on public authorities (including social work services, education, housing, and any other relevant services) providing support to families, as they have a duty to promote the upbringing of children by their own families.

Local authorities must work in partnership with children and families as required by the Scottish Office Guidelines (Scottish Office, 1996a) (e.g., families should be given sufficient information and have access to a complaints procedure). Social workers in conjunction with families must prepare individual Care Plans for children for whom they are responsible.

Local authorities are required to set out their policies and intended arrangements for children's services and publish Children's Services Plans. All local authority departments have a duty to collaborate and consult the community for their views of the services to offer and their priorities for future development. These Plans should cover three financial years and deal with all aspects of provision for children in the authority's area.

The Act also sets out parental responsibilities and rights in relation to children. In cases of divorce or separation, children must be consulted for their views as to where they will live. Legal aid is available to children to allow them to instruct a solicitor to participate in hearings on their behalf.

In 1997 the Green Paper, "Meeting the Childcare Challenge: A Childcare Strategy for Scotland" (Scottish Office, 1997b), confirmed the government's commitment to improving the provision of nursery education and childcare across Scotland. The strategy made a fundamental contribution towards the government's objectives of addressing social exclusion and promoting economic development. The Childcare Strategy advocated a more holistic approach to childcare provision. Each local authority now has in place a Childcare Strategy that deals with issues in respect to provision of services for children aged 0-14 years (including after-school care), access to training for those who work with children, and the supply of childcare workers.

Central government funding now provides a free, part-time pre-school education place for every child in their pre-school years. Funding has been committed for the provision of places in nursery education for all three-year-olds by 2002. It is now accepted that childcare services may be provided through partnership with other sector providers. The aim of reducing class sizes in the first few years of primary schooling was also stated in the Green Paper. The most recently available figures show that, in Scotland as a whole, class sizes in publicly funded primary schools are at 24.9 students (Scottish Executive, 1999). These measures to improve early childhood education reflect the government's acknowledgement that many Scots are disadvantaged by virtue of unemployment, low skills levels, poverty, bad health, poor housing and high crime environments.

A wide-reaching review of children, young people, and offending in Scotland examined the findings of studies of delinquency together with the policies and practices (Asquith et al., 1998). The review concluded that early intervention should be recognized as a key guiding principle on which to devise a strategy for preventing crime by children and young people. The report's conclusions were heavily influenced by research (Farrington, 1994a, 1994b) linking poor parenting, early antisocial behaviour, poverty, and school failure with delinquency, and also by studies that highlighted the effectiveness of good pre-school education in preventing later delinquency (Farrington, 1994c). Allied to this was the awareness of the existence of a small group of children who were referred repeatedly on offence grounds to the Reporter (the senior official in the juvenile justice system). This report confirmed the need to develop resources to address the needs of this relatively small group of persistent offenders.

PART II:
TRENDS IN OFFENDING BEHAVIOUR BY JUVENILES

Victimization Rates

The 1996 Scottish Crime Survey (SCS) was the fourth in a series of national surveys carried out in Scotland (MVA Consultancy, 1997). This large-scale household survey of public experiences and perceptions of crime was based on interviews with 5,045 adults aged 16 and over throughout Scotland.

Estimates derived from the study suggest that in 1995 just over one million crimes were committed against individuals and private households. This was 8% less than the number of crimes estimated in the 1993 SCS (Scottish Office, 1996b). Approximately 70% of crimes were against property, and of these about half involved motor vehicles. Survey estimates suggest that the number of violent crimes decreased slightly between 1992 and 1995. There was a sharp drop in acquisitive crimes, but a slight increase in vandalism.

Two major surveys studied crime and offending behaviour among Scottish young people in recent years. Although there were considerable differences in the methodologies and the questions asked, both showed a higher rate of victimization among boys compared to girls, and low rates of reporting incidents to the police.

In the first study (Anderson, Kinsey, & Smith, 1991), 892 self-completion questionnaires were returned by students aged roughly 12 to 16 years of age (secondary school S1-S4) in Edinburgh schools. Despite the fact that the questionnaire excluded offences committed at school or at home, half the respondents said they had been victims of one or more offences against their person in the previous nine months.

About one in six respondents (17%) had been victims of theft (almost three times as many boys as girls). Just under half the incidents were committed by a peer, but only a small proportion of them (16%) were reported to the police. Over one-third (37%) of respondents had been victims of assault (twice as many boys as girls) and almost one-third had been threatened with violence; only 14% of these incidents were reported to the police.

The 1993 Scottish Crime Survey included, for the first time, a representative sample of 495 young people aged 12-15 years. Interviews took place in the parental home and looked at crime within the school setting as well as that committed in public places.

Respondents were asked whether in the previous 8 to 10 month period they had experienced any one of four types of victimization: theft or attempted theft, violence, being frightened or harassed by someone, and sexual pestering. Altogether 224 young people (45%) said they had been victimized in some way.

The majority of the 84 young people who reported being victims of theft had something stolen which they had left unattended. The most common item stolen was money (33% of victims). Two-thirds of all cases had taken place in school.

The main type of violence experienced by the young people was being punched (56%) and kicked (55%). Boys were significantly more likely to report being a victim of a violent incident than girls (32% and 21%). Additionally almost half of those who reported being assaulted in this way had been victimized more than once. Most incidents occurred in or near the school (60%), and most victims tended to be assaulted by perpetrators in their own age group and by people they either knew or had previously seen.

The most common type of harassment by peers reported was being shouted at (55%) and around half of the victims said it had occurred on two or more occasions. Harassment more commonly happened near the victim's home or somewhere other than at or near school.

Failure to report the incident to the police was widespread for all crimes, whether or not the young person regarded the incident as serious. In comparison, the finding of the adult survey revealed that just over half the crimes identified had been reported to the police.

Rates of All Reported and Recorded Crime

The 1996 SCS showed only 50% of incidents in the survey being reported to the police. However the Scottish crime surveys have consistently shown reporting rates to be higher in Scotland than in England and Wales.

While there was a steady downward trend in the number of crimes recorded from 1992 until 1997, there has been a steady increase from 420,642 in 1997 and 435,703 in 1999 (Scottish Executive, 2000c). Nearly two-thirds of crimes recorded by police are crimes of dishonesty (mainly house-breaking and theft), though the rate for these offences is relatively stable. However, nonsexual crimes of violence, which account for one-twentieth of all reported crimes, represent more than half of the increase in the overall number of crimes recorded. The "other crimes" group, which includes drugs crimes and crimes against public justice, also rose. The police clearance rate increased from 39% in 1997 to 41% in 1998.

Rates of Incidents Involving Juveniles

Scottish police forces do not record crime by age of the alleged offender. However it has been estimated (Scottish Office, 1993) that between 20% and 40% of all crime that comes to the attention of the police is committed by youths aged 14-20, who represent 11% of the population.

Research soon after the establishment of the Children's Hearing System in 1971 (Martin, Fox, & Murray, 1981) on children referred to the Reporter on offence grounds revealed that the majority were involved in trivial rather than serious offending, as does more recent research (McIvor & Kennedy, 1992).

We also have information from the two surveys of young people on the offending in which children are involved. The Edinburgh survey found that over two-thirds of all respondents admitted having committed at least one offence during the previous nine months, but that only a third of them had been involved in what was described as "moderately serious offences." The researchers found no significant social class differences and suggested that infrequent, nonserious offending is the norm rather than the exception.

Only a third of young people taking part in the Scottish Crime Survey reported ever doing any of the things on their list of antisocial behaviours and even fewer doing so in the last 12 months. This included not paying transit fare (11%), being in a physical fight (11%), shoplifting (5%), damaging property (4%), carrying a weapon (4%), buying or accepting stolen goods (3%), and driving without a licence (1%).

The most comprehensive police data on offending by children and young people comes from two Scottish Office bulletins, which used data from initial police reports on the crimes and offences in which children were *alleged* to have been involved (Scottish Office, 1990, 1991). Up until 1988, seven out of eight police reports were on boys, changing to eight out of nine in 1989. In that year 63%-64% of the children were aged 14 or 15, while 11%-12% of the children were aged 11 or under.

Over half of all police reports in the period were for property crimes (e.g., break and enter, and theft). The total number of reports for crimes declined in the period, but reports on nonsexual crimes of violence increased, as did reports for crimes of indecency. The rate of reports per 100,000 children dropped from 5,900 in 1986 to 5,200 in 1989.

The police have a number of options available to them when they apprehend a child or young person suspected of being involved in a crime. First, they may give an informal warning on the spot. Second, they can consider whether a formal warning is more appropriate. If so, the child and his or her parents are asked to appear before a senior police officer. There are national criteria for decisions relating to the giving of a formal warning, but while forces share agreement on the circumstances in which formal warnings are appropriate, there are differences between forces in procedures prior to the decision to give a warning. A third option is to refer the child or young person to the Children's Hearing System, which deals not only with children who are alleged to have been offending but also with those who are considered to be in need of care and protection. A final option is to report the child or young person to the Procurator Fiscal (the senior prosecutorial official in the adult system).

Of the children involved in the crimes described above, 12.6% were given a formal warning, 13.7% were reported to the Procurator Fiscal, and 73.6% were referred to the Reporter who is responsible for the operation of the Children's Hearing System.

PART III: THE JUVENILE JUSTICE SYSTEM IN SCOTLAND

Legislation

The Reporter has a key role in the Children's Hearing System. When the Children's Hearing System came into operation in 1971, Reporters were employed by individual local authorities. However, in 1996, they were united in one national organization comprising 142 Reporters headed by a Principal Reporter (Scottish Children's Reporter, 1998). The Reporter makes an initial decision about whether a child should be referred to a Hearing and then has an important role in any Hearing.

Referrals to the Reporter in 1996/97

Statistics for 1996/97 (Scottish Children's Reporter, 2000) are presented both in Figure 5.1, which provides an overview of the processing of referrals, as well as in the text following.

- There were a total of 46,497 referrals, representing 26,862 children, as children may be referred on more than one occasion.
- Referrals were at a rate of 26.13 per 1,000 population for those under 16.

- As in previous years, the majority of referrals (78.63%) were from the law enforcement agencies, primarily the police.
- In contrast to earlier years when the proportion of children referred on offence grounds greatly exceeded those referred on child welfare grounds, in 1996/97 the balance of referrals has more or less equalized with 54% of the referrals made on offence grounds.
- There was very little difference between the sexes in the numbers of referrals on child welfare grounds, but the pattern of boys being overrepresented in referrals to the Reporter on offence grounds compared to girls continued in 1996, with rates of 4,351 per 100,000 boys and 1,167 per 100,000 girls.
- Age 15 is the peak age for referrals on offence grounds for both boys and girls with rates of 10,732 and 3,209 per 100,000 population respectively.
- Very few children referred were aged 16 or older. Although legislation makes provision for adult courts to remit offenders under 18 to the Hearings for advice or disposal, only a small proportion of referrals for offending involved young people aged 16 or 17.[2]

Figure 5.1

Process Model of All Referrals to the Scottish Children's Hearing System, 1996

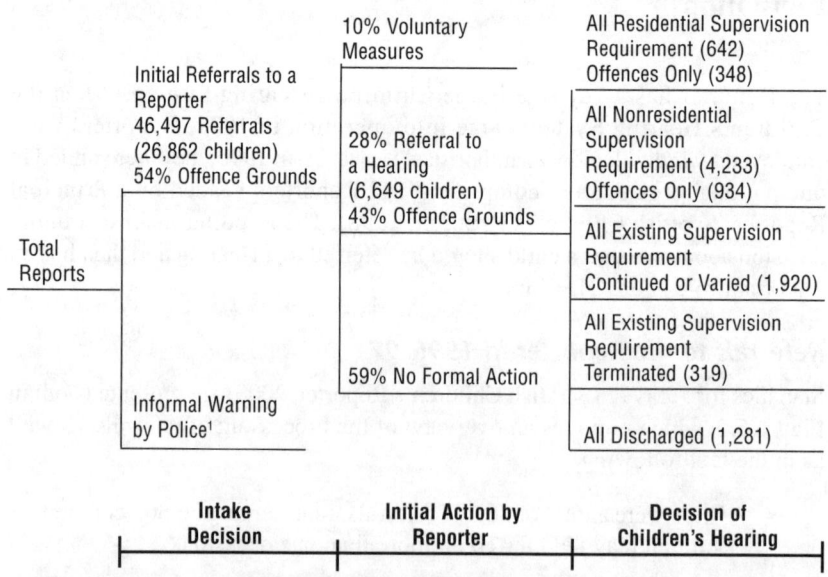

1. Centralized data concerning the total number of reports involving children or the number of children dealt with by cautioning are not maintained.

- As Table 5.1 indicates, the average number of offences per child was 2.73, but approximately half the children in all age groups had been involved in only one offence. Further, only a small percentage of children are persistent offenders.

Table 5.1

Average Number of Offences per Child by Age (%)

Age	Number of Offences						
	1	2	3	4-6	7-9	10-20	21+
8-11	65.60	16.34	5.91	7.40	2.65	1.82	0.28
12	59.50	16.83	8.55	8.88	2.43	3.02	0.79
13	55.04	17.03	8.55	10.47	3.84	3.57	1.49
14	50.66	18.07	8.90	11.64	4.14	4.65	1.93
15	54.53	19.43	8.72	10.01	3.30	3.20	0.80
16-17	47.96	20.98	12.81	13.62	3.27	1.09	0.27
All	55.29	18.06	8.48	10.18	3.45	3.41	1.14

When a Reporter receives a referral, the Reporter gathers information from the child's family and any professionals involved in order to assess the child's needs and the legal basis for intervention and support. As pictured in Figure 5.1, there are three options available at this stage as to how the child will be dealt with. The first of these options, most frequently used in 1996 and previous years, was No Formal Action. The term No Formal Action is misleading for it includes:

- referrals in which the Reporter considers formal proceedings to be unnecessary as a result of action taken by the child, the family, or other professionals;
- offence referrals in which the police may be requested to discuss the situation with the child and parents and issue a formal warning;
- a referral to the Reporter for which there is insufficient evidence of the offence to continue the proceeding; and
- referrals in which effective intervention is being provided through pre-existing supervision arrangements.

The second option open to a Reporter is where parents agree to voluntary measures, and the third option is where the Reporter decides that compulsory intervention may be necessary and the case is passed to a Children's Hearing.

In most instances the child remains in his or her own home while the Reporter is considering a referral, but the legislation does allow for the Reporter to detain the child before a Hearing takes place. There were a total of 948 pre-Hearing detentions in 1996/97; 20.89% for offences committed and 79.11% to provide a place of safety for the child for welfare concerns.

As indicated in Figure 5.1, in 1996 Reporters referred 28% of all children referred to a Hearing. This amounted to 6,649 children (4,228 boys and 2,421 girls), equating to rates per 100,000 population aged under 16 of 804 for boys and 482 for girls. As shown in Table 5.2, the grounds for referral most likely to result in the child being referred to a Children's Hearing were living in the household of an incest victim (including child subject to hearing), followed by nonattendance at school and lack of parental care.

Table 5.2
Decisions by Reporters, 1996 (%)

Grounds for Referral	No Formal Action	Voluntary Measures	Hearing
Beyond control	55	17	28
Moral danger	74	11	15
Lack of parental care	47	17	36
Victim of offence	60	16	24
At risk	43	20	37
Household of incest victim	0	33	67
Nonattendance at school	37	18	45
Solvent abuse	62	18	20
Care of local authority	80	3	16
Offence	64	6	26
All Grounds	**59**	**10**	**28**

Those referred to a Hearing on offence grounds included 2,333 boys and 530 girls – a rate of 876 per 100,000 boys and 209 per 100,000 girls in the 8-15 age group. More than half the boys had previously appeared at a Hearing as had two-thirds of the girls. Children appearing at a Hearing on offence grounds accounted for 43% of all the children referred to a Hearing. The peak age for a referral to a Hearing for boys is 14; 24% of this age group who were referred to the Reporter were subsequently referred to a Hearing compared to 17% of 15-year-olds.

The Conduct of the Children's Hearings

A Children's Hearing involves three members of a Children's Panel who are lay people recruited and trained for the task. The Reporter provides legal advice to Panel members, but does not formally take part in the proceedings.

The Hearing is attended by the parents or guardians of the child. There is provision for them to bring a representative such as a friend or legal advisor (legal aid is not available at this stage). Since the introduction of the *Children (Scotland) Act 1995*, children have the right to attend their own Hearing, and parents are provided with copies of papers circulated for the Hearing. If there is a perceived conflict of interest between the child and parents, a Hearing may appoint a Safeguarder who will prepare a report for the Hearing advising on the child's best interests.[3]

The professionals who attend may include a representative from the social work department and the child's school, each of whom is expected to provide a report for the Hearing, as will any other professional involved with the child

(e.g., psychiatrist or educational psychologist).[4]

The chairperson of the Panel is responsible for the formal aspects of the proceedings and puts the grounds of referral to the child and the family. If the child or the parents do not accept the grounds (e.g., denial of the offence), the Hearing stops. The Reporter then refers the matter to the Sheriff and a formal court hearing will be heard in chambers (without publicity) to establish if the conditions for the grounds are met (i.e., if the youth committed the offence). Legal aid is available at this stage. If the grounds are established in court, the case is remitted back to the Children's Hearing for disposal. If the grounds are not established in court, the case is discharged.

As pictured in Figure 5.1, a Hearing may discharge a youth or may impose compulsory measures of supervision considered to be required by the child. When a Hearing makes a supervision requirement in respect of a child, it sets out where the child is to live. The majority of children on whom supervision requirements are placed continue to live with their families (generally known as home supervision or non-residential supervision).

If residential supervision is considered appropriate, a child may be placed in a children's home (operated by a local authority or a nongovernmental organization), a residential school, or a residential hostel, with the latter generally reserved for older young people. There are also 88 secure accommodation places in Scotland, and there are a number of statutes under which children may be admitted. It is not clear how many children are referred to such units as a direct consequence of their offending, but in some circumstances children are admitted subsequent to a disruption of an existing residential placement.

All supervision and residential requirements are reviewed on a regular basis. The first review is held after three months and thereafter occur at regular six monthly intervals. If the supervision requirements are not being met, an immediate review by the Hearings can be requested.

Outcomes for Children Appearing at a Hearing on Offence Grounds in 1996/97

As noted above, more than half the boys referred to the Hearings on offence grounds in 1996/97 were already on a supervision requirement for offence and/or child welfare grounds. Almost a quarter of this group had the order terminated or the case discharged. The remainder had the order continued or varied.

- Over half of the boys who were not already on supervision (55.7%) had a requirement imposed upon them and the remainder had their case discharged.
- Two-thirds of the girls appearing on offence grounds were already on a supervision requirement. Just under a quarter (22.8%) of this group

had the requirement terminated or the case discharged, and the remainder had the requirement continued or varied. In the majority of the remaining cases (57%) in which the girl was not already on a supervision requirement, a supervision requirement was made, and the others had their cases discharged.

- Almost one in five of children referred to the Reporter on offence grounds was referred to a Hearing. Well over half (59%) of them were already on a supervision requirement at that point in time.

- Over two-thirds (68%) of all the children appearing at a Hearing on offence grounds either had their existing supervision requirement continued or varied, or a new requirement imposed.

- More than a quarter (27%) of the new supervision requirements or those which were varied (those which were continued as before are not counted here) were residential supervision requirements that meant the child would reside away from home.

- Children referred on offence grounds were more likely to receive a residential supervision requirement than those referred on child welfare grounds.

- In the majority of cases a placement outside of the home meant a residential school (48%) or local authority children's home (35%) and the remainder were in voluntary homes (e.g., relatives), hostels, or other residential establishments.

- In 1996, the Hearings made 110 secure accommodation authorizations, with a further 140 being continued. These cases involved 155 boys and 95 girls, and represented a decrease of 25% from 1995. It is not clear how many of these authorizations related to children who appeared before a Hearing on offence grounds.

The Effectiveness of the Children's Hearings System

A major problem in discussing the effectiveness of the system is the absence (until most recently) of research on the Hearings.

An early study (Martin, Fox, & Murray, 1981) revealed that those recruited as Panel members were predominantly middle class, with the result that greater effort was made to attract members of the local communities to serve on the Panels. Research (Buist & Mapstone, 1985; Buist & Fuller, 1997) also showed that the grounds on which children appear before a Hearing sometimes relate to pragmatic consideration of the need to have the grounds accepted by the child and parents, rather than the main cause for concern (e.g., a boy believed to have sexually abused a younger sibling appeared at a Hearing on the grounds of being without proper parental control).

Despite the fact that the philosophy of the Hearings is that children and families should feel at ease and able to discuss their difficulties, the research evidence as to whether this is occurring is conflicting. The majority of respondents in one study believed that Panel members listened to what they had to say. In contrast, another study (Freeman & Lockhart, 1994) found that a significant minority of respondents considered Panel members "snobby" and "insensitive." Yet another study (Howells et al., 1996) reported that children were anxious at Hearings.

Most worrying, there is some evidence that Panels often have a lack of options and are forced to use their second or third choice of resource (Buist & Mapstone, 1985). Some of the main criticisms to emerge from a recent research project are (Hallett & Murray, 1998):

- There are still concerns about representation in terms of the class, sex, and ethnicity of members of the Panels.
- The shortage of resources, particularly for older children, continues to be a problem.

The same research also suggests that the system does not work well for those referred for nonattendance at school, or for persistent or serious offenders.

Earlier research (McIvor & Kennedy, 1992) showed that many of the young offenders who subsequently appeared before the courts had a history of appearing at a Hearing. They found that 53% of all 16- and 17-year-olds appearing in one Sheriff's court had previously been before a Children's Hearing Panel, with all but one having been on supervision. However, their study suggested that young people who had been subject to home supervision alone were no more likely than those who had never been in contact with the Children's Hearing System to become enmeshed in a pattern of offending once they reached 16 years of age and came under the jurisdiction of the adult courts.

A new study of a cohort of young people referred to the Reporter in 1995 and followed for the next three years (Waterhouse et al., 1999) found that:

- The overwhelming majority of the 1,155 children (age 12-15) studied had already come to the attention of the Reporter with an average of eight referrals per child.
- Four hundred and sixty-five children in the cohort had been referred for offending in 1995.
- Many of the children referred for offending in February 1995 had prior referrals to the Reporter on other grounds, most commonly for truancy or risks associated with child abuse or neglect.
- One hundred and thirteen were children jointly reported (to the Reporter and the Procurator Fiscal). All had extensive histories in the Hearing System.
- Of those entering the system for the first time, two years later just over one-tenth were under supervision.

The main sanction available to a Panel is the imposition of a supervision requirement. There have been studies that have shown that home supervision (which might involve only regular meetings between the young person and a social worker) is often seen as ineffectual. One study (Triseliotis, Borland, & Lambert, 1995) reported that while some young people felt their social workers had helped them stop offending, many believed the process had had little impact upon them. Another study (Buist & Fuller, 1997) found that young people on home supervision with a condition to attend a project did not necessarily attend regularly and that there were no sanctions other than a return before a Panel to make them do so.

Since the Hearing System operates on the basis of meeting a child's needs, one must ask whether it is fair to judge the effectiveness of a system in the absence of resources identified as meeting these needs. Improvements are expected following the introduction of the new Act. The issue of resources should be addressed within the local authority's Children's Services Plan; a Panel may now specify what supervision should entail and also the part parents should play in meeting the child's needs. Social workers must consult the child and the family and draw up a Care Plan, which sets out the objectives of the supervision requirement and clarifies arrangements, and social workers must inform the Hearing as to how the objectives will be achieved and the techniques and services to be used.

Crime Prevention Initiatives

In the last decade, there have been a number of initiatives directed at the prevention of crime, many of them contained within wider strategies directed at the problems of urban deprivation. Some were partnership initiatives between the Scottish Office and the local authorities (e.g., those operating in four of Scotland's most disadvantaged housing schemes that utilized the support and energies of all agencies including community groups; Carnie, 1994).

Multi-agency strategies involving local authority departments, the police and voluntary sector have been relatively common for some time. Many local authorities have in place Youth Strategies to deal with the problems of truancy, school exclusions, and the perceived increase in levels of youth crime (Asquith et al., 1998).

One Youth Strategy that is being pilot tested is a police Recorded Warning System for first-time offenders. The police warnings are not considered an "easy option." They are described as "an uncomfortable process" (Central Police Force, 1997). The same Strategy is involved with the Freagarrach Project, which is funded by central government with additional funding from a leading nongovernmental organization and the local authority. The project works in a holistic way with groups of persistent young offenders aged 12-16 years. Offending behaviour is addressed through work on victim awareness and reparation. The young people are provided with educational support and their parents are actively involved.

The innovative Cue Ten project for persistent young offenders aimed to reduce offending by changing young people's attitudes to training and employment (Lobley & Smith, 1999). A report on the outcome for the 86 young people who took part found:

- The 26-week program proved too demanding for many of the young people. Only 40% completed the entire program.
- Those who completed the program tended to be those who were charged less frequently during the previous 12 months.
- The offending records of the group who completed the program showed more improvement in the 12 months after starting at Cue Ten than the records of the group who failed to complete the course.
- While the Cue Ten project did not deliver an overall cost saving to the criminal justice or childcare systems during the three years covered by the evaluation, it was thought to have produced modest long-term savings, through diverting young people from adult criminal careers.

Joint projects of this type, however successful, deal with very small numbers of young people (e.g., in the period from the summer of 1995 until March 1997, Freagarroch worked with 44 young people; Freaggaroch, 1998).

A recent initiative, which recognizes the social antecedents of delinquency, is the Matrix project (Barnardo's Scotland, 2000), set up to provide early special support to families whose children (aged 8-11 years) are, or are at risk of, developing antisocial and/or offending behaviour. The project works with the child, the family, and the school, and offers individual and group work programs, assistance to parents in identifying how best to support their children, and help to establish social support networks for children and families.

The Scottish Office Crime Prevention Unit was established in 1992 with the aims of developing policy, promoting national strategies, and providing support to those who wished to develop their own crime prevention strategies (Scottish Office, 1997a). The Crime Prevention Unit and the Scottish Community Education Council (a key player in strategies involving young people) established the Young People's Crime and Community Safety project, which resulted in local action projects being set up throughout Scotland (Scottish Community Education Council, 1995). It was from this initiative that the importance of involving young people in community safety projects was formalized with the establishment of a National Youth Issues Unit. Other important developments include police training, whereby frontline police officers, young people, and youth workers meet regularly to consider the relationship between young people and the police.

The principles underlying these strategies maintain the philosophy of keeping young people within their families, communities, and schools. However, the need for a valid framework for evaluating the effects of youth work on crime became obvious (Brown, 1994; Coopers & Lybrand, 1994), with the result that the Crime Prevention Unit commissioned a guide on monitoring and evaluation for those intending to establish projects (Scottish Office, 1997b) in a move to bring greater rigour and accountability to the process.

Issues and Criticisms

Much of the criticism directed at the Hearing System in recent years has been concerned with the conflict of interest between children and parents in child protection cases, with the result that a number of major enquiries into the child welfare system (Scottish Office, 1992) have taken place.

Early researchers (Morris & McIsaac, 1978) were critical of the system, arguing that it endorsed a "causal model" of deviance that they described as "Deeds imply needs which have not been met." It is true that social reports have concentrated upon the personal and family characteristics of children, thereby adopting an individual or family pathological model of deviance rather than taking account of the wider environment (Buist & Mapstone, 1985).

The 1964 Kilbrandon Report, which led to the establishment of the Children's Hearing System, did refer to the part played by the environment and the need to take a wider perspective on the development of problems. The problem is that the Reporters and Children's Panels lack the authority to ensure that appropriate services are established. Until recently they had no formal role in the development of services and policies that impact upon children and families.

The main criticism in recent years has been the failure of a system operating under a philosophy of child welfare to adequately address offending behaviour. Some critics have argued that there is a need to balance the social and personal needs of juvenile offenders against the concerns about public safety (McGhee, Waterhouse, & Whyte, 1996). However, in Scotland a punitive approach to offending by juveniles is still rejected. Instead projects for persistent offenders such as those described earlier, which address offending behaviour and operate in a holistic manner, have been established.

Another concern is the failure of the Hearing System to deal with older adolescents (aged 16-17), despite the fact that there is provision for this. Researchers (McIvor & Kennedy, 1992) noted the practice of the supervision requirements of young people approaching their 16th birthday being discharged.

Those who wish to see 16- and 17-year-olds dealt with in the juvenile system point out that the *UN Convention on the Rights of the Child*, which has been ratified by the UK government, defines a "child" as a human being below the age of 18. They argue that it is inappropriate to assume that 16- and 17-year-olds are adults, and that the criminal justice system is not suited to the needs of this age group (Save the Children, 1992).

It is also argued that the financial circumstances of 16-and 17-year-olds means they are (unlike the majority of first-time adult offenders) less likely to be fined and instead are given community sentences. Given the frequency of offending among youths, they are likely to find themselves facing custodial sentences relatively quickly once they enter the adult criminal system (e.g., in 1996 10% of young persons aged 16-20 with a charge proved against them received sentences of detention; Smith, 1997).

Criminologists (McIvor & Kennedy, 1992) point out that most offenders stop offending when they reach their late teens. It seems likely that if a significant proportion of these younger persons could be kept out of the courts, or their entry into the adult system delayed, the level of custodial sentencing for the under-21 age group would be reduced. The problem has been identified as one of lack of resources available to the Hearings (Scottish Office, 1993) in the form of projects to which young people of this age group could be referred. It is expected that these issues will be addressed following the ministerial report on young people and crime which asks local councils to conduct an audit of service provision to meet the needs of all young people who have committed offences (Scottish Executive, 2000d).

There is another way in which support might be available for young people (not all of whom will have been involved in offending) and that is also a consequence of the *Children (Scotland) Act 1995*. Under the Act, local authorities must advise, guide, and assist any young person under 19 years who was "looked after" (in Scotland the term applies to all children on supervision orders as well as those accommodated and those on other orders and warrants) by their local authority at their school leaving age (16) or thereafter. The local authority is empowered (but is not bound by law) to provide assistance to such young people who are at least 19 but not yet 21 years old, as long as it is agreed that their welfare requires such assistance. This has led to the establishment of a wide range of aftercare initiatives (Bilson et al., 1999). It remains to be seen how well these measures impact upon a group of young people who are known to fare very badly in adult life including offending (Social Services Inspectorate, 1998).

System Innovations

The Scottish system of juvenile justice has changed little in the past 25 years. The impact of the introduction of Safeguarders is one innovation that has yet to be reviewed. The move of Reporters to the status of a national organization must also be monitored.

There exists a tradition of joint approach by central government, voluntary organizations, and local authorities to crime prevention. Agencies working together in a holistic way is taken for granted in Scotland. This shows how clearly the principles enshrined within the Kilbrandon Report on which Scotland's system of juvenile justice is based have been incorporated within policies and strategies.

The links between poverty, poor health, admission to care, and risk of delinquency are recognized. Resources are being directed towards altering this situation. Scotland has a *Children Act*, which is firmly rooted in the rights of children and in the paramountcy of intervention occurring only if it is in the child's best interests. The system of juvenile justice in Scotland has "sharpened up" rather than "toughened up." All of this suggests a brighter future.

References

Anderson, S., Kinsey, R., & Smith, C. (1991). *Cautionary tales: Young people, crime and policing in Edinburgh*. Avebury, Aldershot.

Asquith, S., Buist, M., Loughran, N., & Montgomery, M. (1998). *Children, young people and offending in Scotland: A research review*. Central Research Unit, Scottish Office.

Audit Unit. (1999). *Attendance and absence in Scottish schools 1997/98 to 1998/99: Information for parents*. Scottish Office.

Barnardo's Scotland. (2000). *The Matrix Project*. Barnardo's.

Bilson, A., Buist, M., Caulfield-Dow, A., & Lindsay, M. (1999). *A safe launch: Scottish throughcare and aftercare in a European context*. Bulletin 1. Glasgow: Centre for Europe's Children.

Brown, L. (1994). *Review of urban funded youth crime projects: A feasibility study*. Scottish Office.

Buist, M. (1994). *Implementation and monitoring of the Children Act 1989 Part X and Section 19*. Central Research Unit, Scottish Office.

Buist, M. (1999) *The expectations and experiences of parents using local authority daycare*. Report to the Scottish Executive (unpublished).

Buist, M., & Fuller, R. (1997). *A chance to change: An intervention with young people who have sexually abused others*. Scottish Office.

Buist, M., & Harland, M. (2000). *Mind the gap: A study of young people making the transition from school to work*. Stirling Council.

Buist, M., & Mapstone, E. (1985). *Choosing for children: A study of interprofessional decision-making*. Social Work Services Group, Scottish Office.

Carnie, J. (1994). *The safer cities programme in Scotland: An evaluation of safe Castlemilk*. Central Research Unit, Scottish Office.

Carstairs, V., & Morris, R. (1991). *Deprivation and health in Scotland*. Aberdeen University Press.

Central Police Force. (1997). *Young offenders strategy group*. Progress Report, June. City of Edinburgh Research Section.

City of Edinburgh Research Section. (1996). *Review of social work*. GAE: Community and Residential Care for Children.

Coopers & Lybrand. (1994). *Preventative strategy for young people in trouble*. (September).

Farrington, D. (1994a). The causes and prevention of offending, with special reference to violence. In J. Shepherd (Ed.), *Violence in health care: A practical guide to coping with violence and caring for victims*. Oxford: Oxford University Press.

Farrington, D. (1994b). Delinquency prevention in the first few years of life: Part II. *Justice of the Peace and Local Government Law* 158 (34): 547.

Farrington, D. (1994c). Early developmental prevention of juvenile delinquency. *RSA Journal:* 22-23.

Fraser, N. (1994). Updated Scottish estimate of J. Culbert (University of Strathclyde) figures in 1994 for the Child Poverty Resource Unit, Glasgow.

Freaggaroch. (1998). *The Report of the Freaggaroch Project*. Barnardo's.

Freeman, I., & Lockhart, F. (1994). *The reception of children into public care: What do we really know*. Strathclyde Regional Council Social Work Department.

General Register Office. (1993). *Census report for Scotland*. HMSO.

General Register Office. (1999). *Mid-year population estimates*, Scotland.

Government Statistical Services. (2000). *Labor Market Statistics* (April).

Hallett, C. (2000). Ahead of the game or behind the times? The Scottish Children's Hearing System in the international context. *International Journal of Law, Policy and the Family, 14*: 31-44.

Hallett, C. & Murray, C. (1998). *Deciding in children's interests*. Central Research Unit. Scottish Office.

Howells, L.A., Furnell, R.G., Puckering, C., & Harris, J. (1996). Children's experiences of the Children's Hearing System: A preliminary study of anxiety. *Legal and Criminological Psychology* 1: 233-250.

Kelly, P. (1998) *Low pay in Scotland*. Scottish Low Pay Unit.

Kilbrandon, L. (1964). *Children and young persons, Scotland*. Cm 2306. Edinburgh: Scottish Home & Health Department.

Lobley, D., & Smith, D. (1999). *Working with persistent juvenile offenders: An evaluation of the Apex Cue Ten Project*. Central Research Unit, Scottish Office.

Long, G., Macdonald, S., & Scott, G. (1995). *Child and family poverty in Scotland: The facts*. Save the Children and Glasgow Caledonian University.

Martin, F., Fox, S., & Murray, K. (1981). *Children out of Court*. Edinburgh Scottish Academic Press.

Morris, A., & McIsaac, M. (1978). *Juvenile justice?* London: Heineman Educational Publishing.

McGhee, J., Waterhouse, L., & Whyte, B. (1996). Children's Hearings and children in trouble. In S. Asquith (Ed), *Children and young people in conflict with the law*. London: Jessica Kingsley.

McIvor, G., & Kennedy, R. (1992). *Young offenders in the Children's Hearing and criminal justice systems: A comparative analysis*. Dundee City Council.

McLoone, P. (1994). *Carstairs scores for Scottish post code sectors from the 1991 census*. Public Health Research Unit, University of Glasgow.

MVA Consultancy. (1997). The 1996 Scottish crime survey: First results. *Crime and criminal justice research findings no. 16*.

Salford University Business Services Limited. (1995). *Sparsity and the Scottish GAE*. Salford University.

Save the Children. (1992). *16 & 17 year olds at the interface between the Children's Hearing System and the criminal justice system.* Glasgow: Save the Children.

Scottish Children's Reporter. (1998). *Annual report 1996/97.*

Scottish Children's Reporter. (2000). *Statistical bulletin: Disposal statistics 1996/7.* Scottish Children's Reporter Administration.

Scottish Community Education Council. (1995). *Young people crime and community safety: Project report* (May).

Scottish Executive. (1999). *Statistical bulletin: Education series. School attainment and qualifications of school leavers in Scotland: 1997-98.* Scottish Office.

Scottish Executive. (2000a). *Scottish school leavers: Gender and low achievement. Scottish school leavers special report II.* Scottish Executive.

Scottish Executive. (2000b). *Government expenditure revenue in Scotland 1997-1998.* Scottish Office.

Scottish Executive. (2000c). *Recorded crime in Scotland 1999.* Scottish Office.

Scottish Executive. (2000d). *Report of the Advisory Group on Youth Crime.* Scottish Office.

Scottish Office. (1990). *Children and crime, Scotland 1988.* Government Statistical Service.

Scottish Office. (1991). *Children and crime, Scotland 1989.* Government Statistical Service.

Scottish Office. (1992). *The report of the inquiry into the removal of children from Orkney in February 1991.* HMSO.

Scottish Office. (1993). *Scotland's children: Proposals for child care policy and law.* HMSO.

Scottish Office. (1995). *Scotland's children. A brief guide to the Children (Scotland) Act 1995).* HMSO.

Scottish Office. (1996a). *Scotland's children: The Children (Scotland) Act 1995. Regulations and guidance. Vol. 1. Support and protection for children and their families.* The Stationary Office Ltd.

Scottish Office. (1996b). *Main findings from the 1993 Scottish crime survey.* The Scottish Office.

Scottish Office. (1997a). *Measure for measure: A guide to monitoring and evaluation of crime prevention initiatives.* Scottish Office.

Scottish Office. (1997b). *Meeting the childcare challenge: A childcare strategy for Scotland.* Scottish Office Green Paper.

Scottish Office. (1998a). *Social inclusion: Opening the door to a better Scotland.* Scottish Office.

Scottish Office. (1998b). Scottish education statistics. *Annual Review 3, 1998 Edition.* Scottish Office.

Scottish Office. (1998c). *Figures supplied by social work services group.* Scottish Office.

Scottish Office. (1998d). *Guidance on the expansion of support for families with very young children.* Scottish Office.

Scottish Office. (2000). *Scottish Economic Bulletin No 57.* Scottish Office.

Smith, D.J. (1997). Criminal justice sanctions as part of a wider response to crime. *The Scottish Journal of Criminal Justice Studies* 3 (August).

Social Services Inspectorate. (1998). *When leaving care is also leaving home: An inspection of services for young people leaving care.* HMSO London.

Stepfamily Scotland. (1998). *Annual report and accounts.* Edinburgh.

Tisdall, K., & Donaghy, E. (1995). *Scotland's families today.* Children in Scotland.

Triseliotis, J., Borland, M., & Lambert, L. (1995). *Teenagers and the social work services.* London, HMSO.

Waterhouse, L., McGhee, J., Loucks, N., Whyte, B., Kay, H. (1999) *The evaluation of the Children's Hearings in Scotland: Children in focus.* Central Research Unit. Scottish Office.

Notes

1. There is also an integrated modular course of studies, and pupils taking these courses may attend school and college to study for National Certificate Modules.

2. This follows a pattern of recent years, for in 1992 Scottish courts remitted only 40 cases out of 36,089 involving males aged 16-20 to the Children's Hearings. There is some evidence to indicate that this age group is disadvantaged by untimely discharge from the Hearing System.

3. Safeguarders were appointed in 5.68% of cases in 1996.

4. Where they consider it appropriate, a Panel may ask for an interdisciplinary assessment of the child prior to making a decision.

CHAPTER 6

Juvenile Crime and Justice in Northern Ireland

David O'Mahony

This chapter gives a brief outline of juvenile crime and the operation of the juvenile justice system in Northern Ireland.[1] Northern Ireland has a relatively low juvenile crime rate. Its juvenile courts deal with children 10 through 16 years of age inclusive. There is an emphasis on specialized juvenile police units dealing with child offenders, and only about 10% of cases come to court. Recently there have been efforts to further limit the use of courts and custody, as well as to increase use of determinate sentencing.

PART I: PROFILE OF NORTHERN IRELAND

Demographic Characteristics

Northern Ireland is part of the United Kingdom (UK), sharing the island of Ireland with the Republic of Ireland. It has a land mass of 14,160 square kilometres. It is a predominantly rural area with two-thirds of the population living within a 50-kilometre radius of the capital, Belfast, which is situated in the east. The only other sizeable concentration of population is in and around the city of Derry located in the northwest. Despite its small size, Northern Ireland has a rich and varied natural landscape with hills, lowlands, inland lakelands, coastal wetlands, and rocky cliff coasts. About 20% of the land area of the region, including 69% of the coastline, has been designated as of outstanding natural beauty and many areas have received international recognition as heritage sites (Geddis, 1997).

David O'Mahony is a Lecturer in Youth Justice, Institute of Criminology and Criminal Justice, School of Law, Queen's University Belfast, Northern Ireland.

In 1995, Northern Ireland's population was estimated to be 1.65 million. Although it has the fastest rate of population growth in the UK after Scotland, it is actually the most sparsely populated region in the United Kingdom with a population density of 121 persons per square kilometre in 1995. The age structure of the Northern Ireland population differs from that of the UK as a whole, as the region has proportionately more children under 16 years of age (25% of the Northern Ireland population in 1995 were under 16 years of age) and fewer people over retirement age.

Though Northern Ireland is home to people from a variety of ethnic and religious backgrounds, almost all are caucasian and there are few immigrants. Most people describe themselves in terms of being either Catholic or Protestant. For example, a Continuous Household Survey (1993/96) estimated that 42% of the Northern Ireland population were Catholic and 54% were Protestant. The perceived religious background of individuals (rather than strictly their belief) often influences a whole range of aspects of their lives, from their national identity, language, the school in which they educate their children, the political party they support, to even their names. The divisions between the two groups have also unfortunately resulted in a high degree of segregation, and Northern Ireland has been described as a divided society in which two communities live (see Cairns, 1987, and Whyte, 1990, for a good overview).

The divisions in Northern Ireland's society are linked with political differences and national identity. For example, the 1995 Northern Ireland Social Attitudes Survey revealed that 63% of Catholic respondents described themselves as "Irish" compared with only 5% of Protestants. In contrast, 64% of Protestant respondents described themselves as "British" compared with only 11% of Catholics (Breen, Devine, & Dowds, 1996). The divisions between the two communities have also led to a degree of discrimination on the basis of religious affiliation. Though the degree and extent of discrimination have been contested, arguments in the research literature have been not so much about the existence of discrimination, but about its extent (see Smith & Chambers, 1991; and Whyte, 1990). That discrimination still goes on, sadly, is sufficient to further embitter relations between the two communities.

The conflict or "troubles" that have been expressed most bluntly over the past 30 years of violence are complex, and have been described as the result of political, religious, economic and cultural divisions. These "troubles" have been referred to as a "conflict with a religious dimension." The results of the conflict are obvious. Between 1969 and 1996 (as a direct result of the conflict) 3,212 people were killed, and there were 35,233 shootings and 14,910 bombings. Between 1972 and 1996, 17,394 people were charged with terrorist and serious public order offences. However, there are glimmers of hope. At the time of writing, Northern Ireland had entered a period of relative stability following cease-fires by the main paramilitary organizations, a referendum supporting an agreement between the major political parties on its future (known as the *Good*

Friday Agreement), the establishment of an assembly to represent all sections of the community, and the gradual disarming of paramilitary groups.

Family Structure

Northern Ireland has a distinctive demography by European standards, with a high birth rate and a young age profile. It also has the largest household size (2.8 persons) of all the regions of the UK (in 1995/96). The proportion of households containing one person living alone doubled in the UK between 1961 to 1996 and more than a quarter of households now comprise a single person. Northern Ireland has mirrored these trends in household size over the last 30 years, although it still has more than double the proportion of households with five or more people.

The number of "traditional" family couples with children fell from over two-fifths of all households in Great Britain in 1971 to under a third in 1995/96. In Northern Ireland the trend has been similar, though there is still a higher proportion of households in the region comprising of the traditional family with children (under a half in 1971 to under two-fifths in 1995/96). Lone parents represent a small but growing proportion of households in Northern Ireland, and in 1995/96, one in eight households was headed by a lone parent. In 1995, 23% of births in Northern Ireland were registered outside marriage compared with 4% in 1971. The growth in lone parents mostly reflects an increase in divorce rates and live births outside marriage, and the majority of lone-parent families are headed by a woman. In 1995, 23% of all families with dependent children in Northern Ireland were headed by lone parents compared to 22% in Great Britain.

Socioeconomic Characteristics

The Economy

Gross Domestic Product (GDP) in Northern Ireland was just under £14 billion for 1995, which represents 2.3% of the UK total. (Northern Ireland shares a common currency with the United Kingdom, the pound [£]. It equals about $1.50 US.) In terms of economic activity per head of population, this represented £8,410 per person in 1995, which was the lowest among the UK regions at 83% of the UK average – marginally lower than Wales. This low rate of performance may be partially explained by two major factors. Firstly, the Northern Ireland population has the highest proportion of school-age children in the UK. More importantly, however, Northern Ireland has the highest unemployment rate among the UK regions. Placing GDP per head in a more meaningful international comparison is difficult, but a 1994 estimate suggested that Northern Ireland's GDP per head was 80% of the European average, placing it among the 25 poorest regions in the European community.

Northern Ireland has always experienced higher rates of unemployment than Great Britain. Even in the period after the Second World War, when Great Britain's unemployment rate was under 2%, the Northern Ireland rate did not fall below 5% (Northern Ireland Economic Development Office, 1993). Harmonized regional unemployment rates for the European Union in April 1995 placed Northern Ireland's unemployment rate at 13%, which is above the European average of 10.7% but lower than that of the Republic of Ireland at 14.3%. Northern Ireland's male unemployment rate is particularly high by European standards, 15.2% against a European Union average of 9.5%. Also, the proportion of unemployed who have been out of work for at least a year (the long-term unemployed rate) has been consistently higher in Northern Ireland than the rest of the UK. In January 1997, 54% of the unemployed in Northern Ireland had been out of work for at least a year, compared with only 36% in the UK.

There are a number of imbalances in the labour force in Northern Ireland. For example among the employed, the 1991 census revealed that Protestants were disproportionately represented in sales occupations, as managers and administrators, and in personal and protective service occupations, whereas Catholic representation was highest in the professional, associate professional, and technical, craft, and related occupational categories. The 1994 Labour Force Survey showed that the unemployment rate for Catholics (16%) was substantially higher than that for Protestants (9%), and the unemployment rate for Catholic males (22%) was twice that of Protestant males (11%). Two-thirds of unemployed Catholics had been looking for work for at least a year (long-term unemployed) compared with just over half of unemployed Protestants.

Education Levels

A higher proportion of pupils in Northern Ireland achieve "A" Levels (high school diploma) than their counterparts in England and Wales. Girls are generally more successful than boys in obtaining education qualifications, and among the 1994/95 school leavers, 1 in 20 boys left school with no qualifications compared with only 1 in 50 girls.

General Trends in Crime in Northern Ireland

The police recorded 68,549 notifiable offences in Northern Ireland in 1996, the vast majority (84%) of which were property-related crimes such as theft, burglary, fraud, and forgery. Theft of and theft from cars comprised almost half of all theft offences, and violent crime (offences against the person) made up a further 13% of recorded crime. In 1996 in England and Wales the proportion of recorded crime involving property was higher than that in Northern Ireland (92% as opposed to 84%). The proportion of violent offences in Northern Ireland was significantly higher than for England and Wales (13% in Northern Ireland as compared to 7% in England and Wales).

It is important to note, though, that levels of recorded crime in Northern Ireland have been consistently lower than that of England and Wales. For example, in 1996 there were 4,121 crimes per 100,000 population, which was less than half that recorded in England and Wales (Northern Ireland Office, 1997a). Further, between 1985 and 1995 Northern Ireland's overall reported crime rate increased by only 3%, compared with an increase of around 30% in England and Wales.

Although levels of crime recorded by the police give an indication of the crime rate in an area, they do not reflect the true level of offending. Many crimes may not be reported to the police, others may not be recorded, and there may be differing statistical rules used for including or excluding particular crimes. It was estimated from the Northern Ireland Crime Survey (1996) that one out of every two victims do not report crime to the police compared with about three out of five victims in England and Wales who do not report (Northern Ireland Office, 1996a, 1998).

Comparisons between jurisdictions are difficult to make, but it appears from the evidence available that Northern Ireland has generally relatively low levels of recorded crime. For example, if we consider offences defined as "crime index" offences in the United States of America, which are normally included in data from Northern Ireland, of the seven categories included, Northern Ireland has generally lower levels of crime per 100,000 population than many other jurisdictions – though more incidents of homicide and rape than other similar European jurisdictions. The International Crime Victims Survey (1996) confirmed these general findings and showed that Northern Ireland had one of the lowest victimization rates of the 11 industrialized countries surveyed, a rate considerably lower than that of Scotland, as well as England and Wales (Mayhew & Van Dijk, 1997). It is in a society with deep divisions and many problems, yet paradoxically with low levels of crime, that the juvenile justice system operates.

PART II:
TRENDS IN OFFENDING BEHAVIOUR BY JUVENILES

Juvenile Crime and Justice

The Northern Ireland juvenile justice system is responsible for children and young persons who are over 10 but under 17 years of age. The vast majority of juveniles are dealt with in special juvenile courts where a panel of three magistrates (at least one of whom should be a woman) preside over cases. The principal legislation affecting the treatment of juveniles has been the *Children and Young Persons Act (Northern Ireland) 1968* (though, note further developments below).

Considering the nature and extent of juvenile crime in Northern Ireland, there are a number of sources of information available. One source that provides broad insight is the self-report method. McQuoid (1994), for example, conducted a self-reported delinquency study in Belfast from late 1992 to early 1993 and found, like many other similar studies elsewhere, that a high proportion of young people admitted committing delinquent acts. Indeed, about 75% of 14- to 21-year-olds surveyed admitted committing at least one delinquent act at some time in their lives. A further 47% said they had done so in the past year and these figures did not include "status offences" or alcohol consumption.

McQuoid's (1994) research confirms how widespread delinquent behaviour is, particularly during adolescence and young adulthood. However, the majority of the admitted delinquent acts were relatively trivial in nature, including such things as bus-fare evasion, spraying graffiti, or minor acts of vandalism. Relatively few young people admitted committing more serious acts, such as violence against the person or drug-related offences. The research revealed that 88% of the most recent offences had gone undetected by the police, and frequent offenders tended not to be specialists but involved themselves in a range of property, violent, and drug offences. The survey also found that the peak age for offending was concentrated in the 18-19 age bracket, with proportionately more young males admitting to both offending and more serious offending than young females.

Another indication of the extent of juvenile offending is available if we consider the number of offenders found guilty in the courts according to their age, sex, and in relation to the population for their age group. However, it is important to note that if a person is found guilty on two or more separate occasions during a year, he or she is counted on each occasion, and therefore the rates are an overestimate.

The Juvenile Court statistics show that the rate of conviction peaks sharply in the late teenage years and then declines gradually with age (Northern Ireland Court Service, 1996). The statistics also reveal the extent to which offending is much more concentrated among males than females. Overall the rate of juvenile conviction in 1996 was 221 per 10,000 population. The rate for females, at 46 per 10,000, was considerably less than that for males at 407 per 10,000 – a ratio of about 9 males to each female. In 1996 the rate of conviction was highest for males aged 18 years and females aged 19 years.

PART III:
THE JUVENILE JUSTICE SYSTEM IN NORTHERN IRELAND

Police Cautioning and the Diversion of Juvenile Offenders

The police are generally the first point of contact for juveniles in the criminal justice process (see Figure 6.1). Importantly, they have considerable discretion in dealing with offenders and act as one of the main gatekeepers of the criminal justice system. In Northern Ireland the police have operated a Juvenile Liaison Scheme since 1975 as an extension of their practice of cautioning and diverting offenders away from the formal criminal justice process. The Scheme deals with juvenile offenders (10-16 inclusive) who have come to the attention of the police. Specialist officers review such cases and make decisions as to how the juveniles should be dealt with.

The police have four broad options available to them: (1) to take no further action, in which case the juvenile is not processed any further than his or her referral to the Juvenile Liaison Scheme; (2) to issue an informal warning and advice, where the juvenile is warned about the consequences of his or her behaviour and given advice about staying out of trouble (the official record of such warning and advice cannot be cited in court at a later date, but the police may keep a note of such warnings for their own records); (3) to administer a formal caution, which is officially recorded and may be cited in a court at a later date (the formal caution is usually administered by a senior officer in the presence of the juvenile and his or her parents); and (4) to process the juvenile for prosecution in the courts. The decision to prosecute in the courts is taken where the members of the Juvenile Liaison Scheme decide that a caution or less formal method of dealing with the juvenile is inappropriate. Such a decision may be taken, for example, where the offence is particularly serious and/or the juvenile has previous convictions.

For juvenile offenders, as for adults, there are a number of pre-conditions that must be met before a formal caution may be given. First, there has to be sufficient evidence to prosecute in court. It is not sufficient to simply have a *prima facie* case. Rather, there has to be a realistic prospect of conviction. Second, the juvenile must admit guilt in relation to the offence for which he or she is being cautioned. Third, the offender and his or her parents must give informed consent to the caution. The system of cautioning is not set out in legislation, but is guided by a number of Home Office Circulars that individual police forces interpret and implement in their area.

Figure 6.1
Juvenile Justice Process in Northern Ireland, 1996

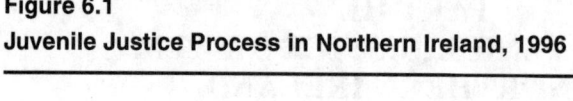

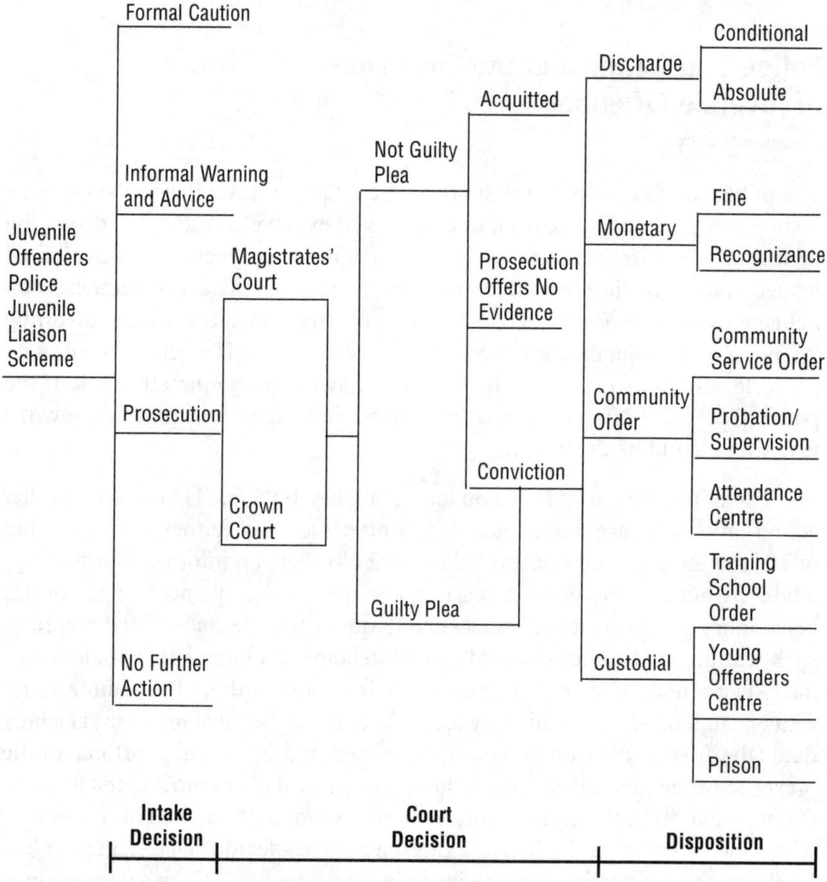

Operation of the Juvenile Liaison Scheme

In 1996, a total of 11,173 juveniles were dealt with through the police Juvenile Liaison Scheme, of whom 6,464 (58%) were given an informal warning or advice, 1,675 (15%) were formally cautioned, and 923 (8%) were prosecuted. In 2,111 cases (19%) no further action was taken (see Table 6.1). The most notable point with respect to the operation of the Juvenile Liaison Scheme is that only a small proportion (less than 1 in 10) of juveniles referred to the scheme were actually dealt with by prosecution through the courts. Further, only 15% of juveniles received an official police caution. In fact, in 1996, 77% of juveniles

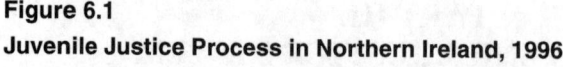

referred to the scheme were dealt with informally either by no further police action, or by being given "warnings and advice" (see Table 6.1).

Table 6.1
1996, R.U.C. Juvenile Liaison Scheme Prosecution, Cautioning, and Diversion

Action	Number	%
No Further Action	2,111	19
Informal Warning and Advice	6,464	58
Formal Caution	1,675	15
Prosecution	923	8
Number Dealt with	**11,173**	**100**

Cautioning and diverting juveniles away from the court system by the police in Northern Ireland is seen as an effective intervention for most juvenile offending. The Chief Constable's Annual Report has pointed out (from Home Office research) that the vast majority of those cautioned on a first occasion are not known to re-offend within two years (Royal Ulster Constabulary, 1996). In fact, the Scheme has been developed in a number of locations into a Juvenile Liaison Bureau Scheme. The aim of the Bureau is to promote a multi-agency approach to the reduction of juvenile crime. These Bureaus include representatives from the police, social services, probation, and the educational and welfare services. Such Bureaus meet regularly to discuss the cases of young offenders who have admitted offending. They help to decide which cases should be prosecuted or diverted, though the final decision rests with the police.

Figures from the operation of the Juvenile Liaison Scheme in Northern Ireland since 1986 show a number of trends. First, the number of juveniles dealt with by the Scheme since 1986 has generally increased. In 1986, 9,934 juveniles were dealt with, in comparison to 11,173 in 1996. Considering this change per 1,000 of the relevant population, there was a 13% increase in numbers (from 53 per 1,000 in 1996 to 59 per 1,000 population in 1996).

On the other hand, outcome patterns from the Scheme show that the rate of *prosecutions* per 1,000 population decreased over the decade from 10 per 1,000 in 1986 to 5 per 1,000 in 1996. Conversely, there has been a progressive shift towards the use of more informal methods of dealing with juvenile offenders. In 1986, 21 juveniles per 1,000 population were given "warnings and advice" and 6 per 1,000 were dealt with by "no further action." In 1996, 34 per 1,000 were given "warnings and advice" and 11 per 1,000 were dealt with by "no further action." This trend towards the increased use of informal methods of dealing with juveniles does reflect an increased willingness to divert juveniles, but may also be partly due to the larger number of juveniles being referred to the Scheme.

The majority of formal cautions are given to male offenders. Annually, between 1986 and 1996, around 80% of all juveniles cautioned were male. Females accounted for just less than 20% of all the official cautions given to juveniles. The lower number of cautions given to females corresponds generally to their lower levels of offending. However, females who do offend are more likely to receive a caution than males. When prosecutions and cautions are combined over the 1986 to 1996 period, 63% of boys were cautioned and 37% were prosecuted, while 84% of girls were cautioned and only 16% were prosecuted (Northern Ireland Office, 1997b).

Juvenile Prosecutions

The next step in the criminal justice process following police action is the prosecution of juveniles in the courts. A total of 1,181 juveniles were proceeded against in all courts in Northern Ireland in 1996, a rate of 625 juveniles per 100,000 population. The vast majority of juveniles are dealt with in Juvenile Courts, which are part of the Magistrates' Courts. In 1996, for example, 1,164 juveniles were dealt with in the Magistrates' Courts while only 17 individuals were dealt with in the Crown Court.

There are a number of stark differences between adults and juveniles brought before the courts in terms of their offending. Over half (59%) of adults proceeded against in the Magistrates' Courts in 1996 were for motoring offences, 26% were for indictable offences, and 15% for summary offences. By contrast, 75% of juveniles prosecuted were for indictable offences, 19% were summary, and only 6% were for motoring offences.

These large differences between the types of offences of juvenile and adult offenders brought before the Magistrates' Courts arise primarily because of the predominance of motoring offences among adults, whereas very few juveniles either own or drive motor vehicles. If motoring offences are removed and juveniles and adults are compared, we find a lower proportion of juveniles (20%) before the Magistrates' Courts on summary charges in comparison to adults (37%). The lower proportion of juveniles brought before the courts for summary offences may be partly a result of the operation of the Juvenile Liaison Scheme, which helps to filter out many of the petty juvenile offenders before they reach the court stage.

In terms of the nature of offences (excluding motoring and summary offences) for which juveniles are proceeded against in the Magistrates' Courts, in 1996 only 14% of indictable offences committed by youth were for violent crimes. The majority of offences by youth were property related, such as theft (44%), burglary (18%), and criminal damage to property (17%). By comparison, proportionately more adults were dealt with for violent offences such as violence against the person (21%) and sexual offences (3%) than juveniles, though more juveniles appeared to be involved in specific forms of property offences such as burglary than adults (burglary: 18% juveniles versus 10% adults). The overall pattern of offending suggests that juveniles are more involved in theft and burglary, but less involved in serious violent offences than adults.

Trends in Juvenile Prosecutions

There was a steady decrease in the rate of juvenile prosecutions from 1986 to 1992, from about 974 to 467 prosecutions per 100,000 population. However, the steady decline reversed in 1993 and prosecutions generally increased, climbing to 639 per 100,000 population in 1995 and then falling slightly to 625 per 100,000 population in 1996.

The vast majority of juvenile cases prosecuted are at the older end of the age spectrum. Sixteen-year-olds accounted for about half (46%) of all the juvenile prosecutions from 1986 to 1996 and 15-year-olds, another quarter. Almost three-quarters of cases prosecuted are in the top two age categories open to the Juvenile Court (15 to 16 years of age). In direct contrast, few juveniles under 13 are prosecuted. Only 4% of all juvenile prosecutions were children between 10 to 12 years of age. For most years from 1986 to 1996, no more than one or two 10-year-olds were prosecuted in the courts in Northern Ireland.

Juvenile prosecutions are also dominated by males. Over 90% of juvenile offenders prosecuted over the last decade have been male. Females on the whole were slightly more likely to have been prosecuted for summary offences than males, and males were more likely to have been prosecuted for motoring and indictable offences. In general terms, not only are far fewer females subject to prosecution in the Juvenile Courts, but they generally also appear for less serious offences.

Pleas and Outcomes

Moving on from prosecutions that are brought before the Juvenile Courts, the next stage is what happens to those prosecuted in the courts. In Northern Ireland the vast majority of cases are dealt with by the juvenile pleading guilty to the offence(s). In 1996 for example, 83% of juveniles who appeared in the Juvenile (Magistrates') Courts for indictable offences pled guilty, and only 17% pled not guilty. However, for those who pled not guilty, most (88%) were found to be not guilty by the courts, or had the charges dismissed without trial.

Patterns of Juvenile Convictions

There has been considerable variation in the rate of juvenile convictions. There was a drop in the rate of conviction from 855 per 100,000 in 1986 to a low of 414 per 100,000 in 1992. From 1993 there were year-by-year increases in the rate of convictions up to 1995, when there were 547 juvenile convictions per 100,000 population. The year 1996 saw the first drop in convictions since 1992. However, considering the whole 11-year period, the rate in 1996 (515 per 100,000 population) was still 40% lower than it was in 1986 (855 per 100,000 population).

There are also a number of differing patterns of sentencing according to the offences for which juveniles are convicted. In 1996, for example, the most common sentence for indictable offences was supervision in the community (39%), followed by conditional discharges (26%), and immediate custodial sentences (24%). Those indictable offences most likely to result in a custodial sentence for a juvenile were robbery (38%) and burglary (35%). For less serious types of offences, including summary and motoring offences, the most common sentences were conditional discharges or supervision in the community.

The sentencing pattern for juvenile offenders for indictable and summary offences over the past decade fluctuated considerably, especially if absolute numbers are considered. However, differences in numbers by individual sentences year to year mostly mirror the differences in the overall rate of convictions over this period. Overall, there was relative stability in the proportions of juveniles given differing sentences. For example, between about a quarter to a fifth were given custodial sentences, and around a third were given community sentences over the last decade. The more noticeable changes include a drop in the use of fines, from 18% of all sentences in 1987 to 7% in 1996, and an increase in the use of some community sentences such as the community service order.

Sentencing

In 1996 a total of 972 juveniles were sentenced by the courts across Northern Ireland. The pattern of sentencing according to the major offence classifications was similar to those proceeded against at the courts. Three-quarters (75%) of those sentenced were for indictable offences, 19% for summary offences, and 6% for motoring offences.

As far more adults were sentenced for motoring offences than juveniles, the following comparisons are made excluding motoring offences. In general terms, in 1996 (excluding motoring offences) more juveniles were sentenced for indictable and fewer for summary offences than adults (80% juveniles were sentenced for indictable offences compared to 63% of adults).

Some methods of disposal are more commonly used than others in the sentencing of juveniles. If we consider, for example, the sentencing of juveniles for indictable and summary offences in 1996, community supervision was the most common sentence. Thirty-five percent (35%) were given some form of community supervision (e.g., probation, 24%, community service, 2%, and attendance centres orders, 9%). The next most common sentence was the conditional discharge at 28%, followed by custodial sentences at 20%. The majority of custodial sentences were training school orders (15%) and only 5% were sentenced to prison establishments such as the Young Offenders Centre. The least popular sentences for juveniles in 1996 were "other" (7%), such as recognizance or absolute discharges, fines (7%), and suspended custodial sentences (3%).

When comparing adults to juveniles, there are some striking differences in terms of sentencing for indictable and summary offences. The most common sentence for adults in 1996 was the fine (33%), followed by suspended custody (18%), and immediate custodial sentences (15%). Conditional discharges (11%) and "other" (11%) were the least popular sentences for adults. The majority of adults were fined in comparison to only a very small minority of juveniles. Juveniles were also more likely to receive immediate custodial and community sentences than adults.

Custodial Sentencing

The use of custodial sentences for juveniles in Northern Ireland merits specific attention, not only because of the high proportion of juveniles given such sentences, but because the arrangements are so different here than in many other jurisdictions. The most common form of custodial sentence for juveniles in Northern Ireland has been the training school order. In 1996, 141 of the 186 juvenile custodial sentences were made to training schools. Only 45 were sentenced to prison establishments, 44 of which were to the Young Offenders Centre and 1 to adult prison.

Prior to the end of 1996, juveniles (10-16 years inclusive) could be sent to training school if they were found to be in need of care, protection, and control (welfare reasons); for persistent school truancy (education reasons); or if they were convicted of an offence that could attract a custodial sentence (justice reasons). The *Children (Northern Ireland) Order 1995* effectively removed the welfare and education cases from the training school system, which subsequently only catered to juvenile offenders.

Juvenile offenders could also be remanded to a training school while they awaited trial. The majority of training school places were in "open establishments" and operated with a welfare ethos. There were also secure placements to deal with more "difficult" children and those who had absconded from the "open establishments."

The training school order was a semi-determinate custodial sentence, providing authority for detention for a period of up to two years, but a child could be released on license after a period of six months at the discretion of the training school managers. Alternatively, a child could be released at any time if release was approved by the Northern Ireland Office. Recent statistics show that the average period of custody in the training schools for juveniles was around 10 months. However, this varied between individual training schools and many children spent considerably longer periods in custody (Northern Ireland Office, 1995).

About a quarter to a fifth of juveniles sentenced over the past decade have been placed in custody. The proportion of juveniles sentenced to custody, specifically immediate custody, is not only greater than adults (in 1996 15% of adults were sentenced to immediate custody for indictable and summary offences at all courts versus 20% of juveniles), but is also greater than that of England and Wales (where about 12% of juveniles were sent to custody in 1996, versus 20% in Northern Ireland). Moreover, on average juvenile offenders in Northern Ireland spent considerably longer time in custody than their counterparts in England and Wales.

Over the last 10 years the actual number of juveniles given custodial sentences fell from a high in 1987 of 259, to a low in 1993 of 138 juveniles. Numbers then increased nearly every year to 186 in 1996, which is equivalent to a rate of 99 per 100,000 population.

The most common offence type to attract a custodial sentence for juveniles in 1996 was theft (37% of indictable offences resulted in custody), followed by burglary (27%) and criminal damage (22%). Only a minority of juveniles sentenced to custody were for violent offences, such as "violence against the person" (5%), or "robbery" (3%). By contrast, 15% of adults were given an immediate custodial sentence for violence against the person and 26%, for theft offences. The general picture that emerges from the Northern Irish criminal statistics reveals that a higher proportion of juveniles who are sentenced are given custodial sentences (the majority of which are training school orders) than adults. Further, juveniles are more likely to receive custodial sentences for property-related crimes such as theft or criminal damage while, for adults, custodial sentences are more often imposed for violent crimes.

There were many problems with the operation of the training school system in Northern Ireland. For example, the duration of the remand of juveniles in custody while awaiting trial varied considerably, and quite often they were for lengthy periods. The period spent on remand was also not taken into account as remission, or time spent against the subsequent training school order. As noted earlier, until recently the training school system also housed children for welfare, justice, or educational reasons, and many children from the care and/or welfare side of the system ended up on the justice side after committing comparatively minor offences. As noted by the Northern Ireland Office in a policy document entitled *The Way Forward* (1996), "it is an indictment of the present system that around 50% of the current justice population were initially referred to the training schools for care or protection reasons" (Northern Ireland Office, 1996b).

Some training school orders have been made for comparatively minor offences that most probably would not result in custody for an adult. Many young people spent longer periods in custody than an adult would if convicted of a similar offence. It has been noted that some children found themselves "locked" into the system because of a lack of community facilities or poor home backgrounds. Indeed the length of time a child spent in the training school system often depended more on their behaviour in the training school system and their home circumstances than on their criminal record or the nature of the offence(s) that led to them being placed there.

Developments

There have been a number of recent developments which should help to address some of the obvious problems in the treatment of juveniles, especially those in custody and the training school system. Firstly, the *Children (Northern Ireland) Order 1995,* as mentioned earlier, was enacted recently and parallels many of the themes introduced in the *Children's Act (1989)* in England and Wales. The Order effectively separates care and education or welfare cases from juvenile offenders or justice cases in the criminal process. Custodial orders can now be made only for criminal offences, and welfare cases may not be dealt with in the criminal (juvenile or youth) court. This should help to address the problem whereby some difficult-to-manage children with welfare problems were simply passed over to the criminal justice system and help to eliminate the use of custodial orders for children with primarily welfare-based problems.

Secondly, the *Criminal Justice (Northern Ireland) Order 1996* limits the powers of the criminal courts in imposing custodial sentences on adults, and this is expected to have an effect on the approach of the Juvenile Courts of limiting the imposition of custody to more "serious" and "persistent" offenders. Certainly this is the intent of the legislation, though it remains to be seen whether it will translate into practice in the Juvenile Courts. It is hoped that custodial sentences will be restricted to the genuinely serious and more persistent offenders and not be used to deal with the petty (yet troublesome) young offenders that the childcare and criminal justice system have so often found difficult to manage.

Thirdly, and probably most importantly, the newly introduced *Criminal Justice (Children) Order (1998)* has a number of implications for the treatment of juveniles in the criminal justice system. Although the order is not a fundamental revision of the legislation, it does have significant implications for the treatment of juveniles, especially with respect to the use of custody. The Order reinforces the right to pre-bail detention for children except in the most serious cases, which it is hoped will reduce the number of juveniles remanded in custody. The Order replaces the semi-determinate training school order with a new determinate "juvenile justice order," which ranges from six months to two years duration, half of which will be spent in custody and the other half in the community under supervision. It is expected that the majority of such orders will be for the shorter six-month period, with longer sentences reserved for much more serious offenders. For the most serious and grave crimes, the indeterminate sentence of "detention during the pleasure of the Secretary of State" remains available to the courts. The legislation also now allows for time served on remand (in custody) to be remitted against a custodial sentence and for the supervision of juvenile offenders by the probation board upon their release.

The central aims of the *Criminal Justice (Children) Order (1998)* are both to reduce the numbers of juveniles sent to custody and the length of time they spend there. There is a need for reform in the juvenile justice system and in many respects this legislation is long overdue. The last major review calling for changes in the legislation was made some 20 years previously (Children and Young Persons Review Group, 1979). In many respects the plight of juveniles, especially those caught up in the training schools, had been largely ignored in Northern Ireland. This legislation, therefore, appears to be a positive step and addresses many of the difficulties and problems in the system. The legislation also appears to be progressive in light of its emphasis on reducing the use of custody and intervention except for the most serious of cases. The rhetoric is encouraging, especially given recent trends in many other jurisdictions calling for ever more punitive and tougher responses to juvenile offenders. However, it remains to be seen whether the new legislation will have all the desired outcomes. Indeed there will be a real need to objectively and independently monitor and evaluate these changes so that the desired consequences are actually achieved in the long term.

In conclusion it is worth drawing together a couple of the key points from the Northern Irish juvenile justice system. One of the major strengths of the system is its ability to deal effectively with most juvenile offending at an early stage, using the least formal and intrusive methods possible. The police are the main gate-keepers of the criminal justice process, and they are responsible for the majority of diversions away from formal prosecution. The police Juvenile Liaison Scheme diverts around 92% of juveniles away from court prosecution. Instead they are dealt with by "cautions," "warnings and advice," or "no further action." Studies suggest that the majority of juveniles can be dealt with effectively by these means and Home Office research shows the majority of such juveniles do not go on to re-offend. In fact about 85% of those cautioned in 1985 and 1988 had not been convicted of a serious offence within two years of their caution and 72% had not been convicted within five years (Home Office Statistical Bulletin, 8/94). The work of the police Juvenile Liaison Scheme (as noted earlier) is also developing, and there are currently plans to further extend the role of the police in preventing juvenile crime through education, information, and co-operation with other agencies such as education and welfare departments. There are also plans to develop restorative work with juveniles and victims of crime as part of the cautioning process and a pilot program has recently started in Belfast to explore these possibilities.

On the other hand the use of custody for juveniles in Northern Ireland could be described as one of the system's weaknesses. It has been recognized that too many juveniles have been sent to custody, sometimes for trivial offences and for lengthy periods. Generally there has been a lack of safeguards for the rights of children held in custody, despite the good intentions of most staff in the training school system. The re-conviction data makes depressing reading with one study estimating that 86% of those released from secure custody had been re-convicted within three years (Curran et al., 1995), and recent Northern Ireland Office estimates show that 97% of males given training school orders had been re-convicted within three years.

The newly introduced legislation should help address many of the difficulties experienced in the juvenile justice system. Hopefully this will build upon current good practice, emphasizing the need for preventive work, the use of effective diversionary practices away from formal prosecution, and early interventions that tackle offending while minimizing the risks of re-offending or the escalation of offending behaviour. Obviously achieving the right balance is not easy. But an emphasis that minimizes formal intervention while respecting the rights of victims, as well as the needs of the offenders, their family, and the community would appear to hold the most hope for effectively dealing with juvenile offenders in the future.

References

Breen, R., Devine, P., & Dowds, L. (1996). *Social attitudes in Northern Ireland*. Belfast: Appletree Press.

Cairns, E. (1987). *Caught in the crossfire: Children and the Northern Ireland conflict*. Belfast: Appletree Press.

Children and Young Persons Review Group (Black Report). (1979). *Legislation and services for children and young persons in Northern Ireland*. Belfast: HMSO.

Curran, D., Kilpatrick, R., Young, V., & Wilson, D. (1995). Longitudinal aspects of reconviction: Secure and open interventions with juvenile offenders in Northern Ireland. *The Howard Journal of Criminal Justice* 34 (2): 97-123.

Geddis, P. (Ed.). (1997). *Focus on Northern Ireland. A statistical profile*. London: The Stationery Office.

Mayhew, P., & Van Dijk, J. (1997). *Criminal victimisation in eleven industrialised countries. Key findings from the 1996 International Crime Victims Survey*. Netherlands: W.O.D.C.

McQuoid, J. (1994). The self-reported delinquency study in Belfast, Northern Ireland. In J. Junger-Tas et al. (Eds.), *Delinquent behaviour among young people in the Western World*. Amsterdam: Kugler Publications.

Morris, A., & Gelsthorpe, L. (1994). Juvenile justice 1945-1992. In Morgan et al. (Eds.), *The Oxford handbook of criminology*. Oxford: Clarendon Press.

Northern Ireland Court Service. (1996). *Northern Ireland judicial statistics 1996*. Belfast: Government Statistical Publication.

Northern Ireland Economic Development Office. (1993). *Demographic trends in Northern Ireland: Key findings and policy implications*. Belafast: Northern Ireland Economic Development Office.

Northern Ireland Office. (1995). *Juvenile justice arrangements in Northern Ireland*. Paper presented for the Northern Ireland Criminal Justice Conference.

Northern Ireland Office. (1996a). *A commentary on Northern Ireland criminal statistics 1995*. NIO Statistics and Research Branch. Belfast: HMSO.

Northern Ireland Office. (1996b). *Juvenile justice: The way forward*. Criminal Justice Directorate, Policy Paper.

Northern Ireland Office. (1997a). *A commentary on Northern Ireland criminal statistics 1996*. NIO Statistics and Research Branch. Belfast: HMSO.

Northern Ireland Office. (1997b). *Juveniles and the Northern Ireland criminal justice system*. NIO Statistics and Research Branch. Belfast: Government Statistical Publication.

Northern Ireland Office. (1998). *Digest of information on the Northern Ireland criminal justice system*. NIO Statistics and Research Branch. Belfast: The Stationery Office.

Royal Ulster Constabulary. (1996). *Chief Constable's annual report*. Belfast: Royal Ulster Constabulary.

Smith, D., & Chambers, G. (1991). *Inequality in Northern Ireland*. Oxford: Clarendon Press.

Whyte, J. (1990). *Interpreting Northern Ireland*. Oxford: Clarendon Press.

Notes

1   It must be said from the outset, though (as noted by Morris & Gelsthorpe, 1994), that material on the juvenile justice system in Northern Ireland is relatively thin.

CHAPTER 7

Juvenile Crime and Justice in Ireland

Kieran O'Dwyer

Ireland has a relatively large youth population. While youth crime has been a subject of media attention and there have been major recent reforms, in comparison to some other countries crime rates appear to be relatively low. Youth crime tends to be more serious among those from disadvantaged backgrounds and among early school leavers. Although gang violence is not a serious problem, drug addiction and related criminal behaviour are major concerns.

It would appear that, in comparison to other countries, victims of crime in Ireland are more likely to report to the police. Specially trained police officers deal with most juvenile offenders, and almost two-thirds of cases are dealt with informally.

The recently enacted *Children Act 2001* is the first major reform of juvenile justice legislation in Ireland since early in the twentieth century. The minimum age of juvenile court jurisdiction has been raised from 7 years to 12 years of age. The new law gives statutory recognition to principles of diversion of less serious offenders and family group conferences. The Children's Court is to use custody as a last resort, and may make orders requiring parents to participate in the supervision of their children in the community. While the new law makes a clear distinction between young offenders and children in need of protection, welfare principles remain significant for dealing with juvenile offenders.

There remain significant resource problems for the juvenile justice system, with a lack of good community programming and some antiquated juvenile custodial facilities.

Kieran O'Dwyer is Head of Research, Garda Research Unit, Garda Síochána, Ireland.

PART I:
PROFILE OF IRELAND

Demographic Characteristics

The Republic of Ireland covers just over 70,000 square kilometres and has a population of 3.7 million. The average age was 33.6 years in 1996, with a "dependency ratio"[1] of 54%. A persistent decline in the dependency ratio has occurred, attributable to a fall in birth rate and reduced emigration. Still, a high proportion of the population is concentrated in the younger age groups, with nearly a third of the population aged 18 or under, and about 42% of the population under 25 (Central Statistics Office, 1997a, 1999, 2000).

Ireland has a very homogeneous population, with 93% of its residents Irish-born and 6% born in other European Union (EU) countries, mostly in the United Kingdom (UK). Travellers (gypsies) represent a small minority group, although the notion of Irish Travellers as an ethnic group only began to gain credence in the early 1980s. Freedom of conscience and the free profession and practice of religion are constitutionally guaranteed. The majority of people belong to Christian denominations, with approximately 92% classified as Roman Catholic in the 1991 Census (Central Statistics Office, 1997a, 1992).

The population density is 52 inhabitants per square kilometre. Just over a quarter of the population lives in the Greater Dublin Area (0.95 million or 26% of the state total), with the counties around Dublin experiencing appreciable population growth in recent years. The second largest city (Cork) accounts for 5% of the national population. Between 1951 and 1996, there was an increase in the percentage of the population living in the largest centres and a decline in rural areas. The most notable increase was in towns of over 10,000 (23 centres) whose share increased from 3.6% to 10.5%. By 1996 approximately 58% of the Irish population was living in urban areas (Central Statistics Office, 1997a; National Economic and Social Council, 1997).

Family Types

Divorce rates are not a particularly useful demographic indicator in Ireland since legal divorce was only introduced in 1997. The 1996 Census enumerated 78,000 persons who categorized themselves as deserted, separated, or having had their marriage annulled. A further 9,800 declared themselves divorced, giving a separation and/or divorce rate of 65 per 1,000 married persons. Household composition provides a better indicator of family breakdown than divorce. In 1996, there were 1.1 million private households, of which 9% consisted of a lone parent with children, and 2% a lone parent with children and other persons – about 125,500 families in total, mostly headed by women.

Family size has diminished significantly in recent decades. In 1996, the average number of children per family was 1.8. Families with four or more children accounted for 13% of the total. Births outside marriage comprised over 20% of all births, with three-quarters of these to single mothers.

Socioeconomic Characteristics

Education Levels

In the 15-year period from 1980 to 1995, there were dramatic changes in the education status of school leavers in Ireland. There was rapid growth in entry to postsecondary education (from 20% to 40%), while the proportion with a secondary school Leaving Certificate qualification grew from 60% to 80%. There was a corresponding decline in those leaving with a Junior Certificate (from 30% to 15%). The proportion of those leaving before taking a Junior Certificate examination fell from around 10% to under 4% (National Economic and Social Forum, 1997). In the school year 1996/97, 98.5% of children aged 13-15 were in full-time education, as were 91.8% of 16-year-olds and 80.6% of 17-year-olds. The numbers of students aged 19 and over has increased steadily in the last 10 years (Department of Education and Science, 2000).

The Labour Force Survey of 1996 shows that of those in the labour force aged 15-24, 6% had primary education only, 25% had achieved Junior Certificate standard, 44% had acquired a Leaving Certificate or equivalent, and 25% had some postsecondary qualifications (Central Statistics Office, 1997b).

The National Economic and Social Forum (1997) identified early school leaving and youth unemployment as among the most serious social and economic problems that Ireland must address. The Forum noted that the combined effect of a fall in some traditional employment opportunities and a process of "qualification inflation" meant that the social and economic exclusion of early school leavers was becoming more acute. Early school leavers with no or low-level qualifications suffer higher levels of unemployment, more precarious job tenure, and lower pay. They are also less well positioned to avail themselves of training and progression opportunities. Recent dramatic improvements in employment levels have had an impact on youth unemployment but offer few guarantees for the longer term, especially for those without educational qualifications.

The social class distribution of early leavers is pronounced, and has become more so over time. Some 85% of early leavers come from working-class origins or small farms, where the average proportion of all school leavers from these backgrounds is around 50%. Over half (55%) of early leavers come from families where fathers are unemployed, compared to less than 20% in the total cohort (National Economic and Social Forum, 1997).

As in other countries, many of those disadvantaged in terms of education and employment end up involved in crime and substance abuse. Certainly studies of convicted prisoners and hard drug users would suggest that reductions in early school leaving and youth unemployment would have a positive impact on levels of crime and drug abuse (O'Mahony, 1993, 1997; Keogh, 1997).

Several initiatives have been taken to counter early school leaving. These include initiatives in mainstream education such as Early Start programs, home/school/community liaison schemes, guidance and psychological services, curricular reforms, and pilot projects in disadvantaged areas.

Further, second-chance education programs targeted at those who left school with no or poor qualifications have been developed. For example, the Youthreach Programme targets young people aged 15-18, trying to reach them through community workshops and out-of-school centres. Participants tend to have a variety of problems such as violence in the home, substance abuse by parents, emotional disturbance, or involvement in crime.

In addition, the Vocational Training Opportunity Scheme targets people aged over 21 who have been unemployed for six months or more, and provides free tuition and materials, as well as travel and meal allowances. Various adult and community education programs also exist. The education system has been criticized for failing to adequately meet the needs of young adults aged 18-20 who left school early.

Employment Levels

Unemployment in Ireland was very high by international standards in the late 1980s to mid-1990s, but has fallen consistently since 1993. The seasonally adjusted standardized unemployment rate was 15.6% in 1993 but had fallen to 7.7% in 1998 and was 4.5% in June 2000 (Department of Finance, 2000; Institute of Public Administration, 1999). There remain pockets of very high unemployment in several urban and rural areas, far in excess of the national average (Central Statistics Office, 1999).

The level of long-term unemployment of more than one year's duration was more resistant to improvements in economic conditions. The number peaked in 1987, fell between then and 1990 and rose again in the early 1990s. In 1995, about 10% of the potential workforce fell into this category (Department of the Tánaiste, 1995). The number finally declined in response to continuing high levels of economic growth and various policy initiatives.

The rate of youth unemployment (i.e., the number of unemployed aged 15-24 as a percentage of the labour force of that age) was 19% in 1995, below the European Union average of 21%. Between 1992 and 1995, the number of youth unemployed fell from 10,700 to 8,200, although the number aged 15-17 increased by 21% to 2,300. At 9.7%, the long-term unemployment rate for youths was 2.5 percentage points higher than for adults, according to the Labour Force Survey (National Economic and Social Forum, 1997).

The Irish economy experienced a period of unprecedented growth during the 1990s. Between 1990 and 1995, Gross Domestic Product (GDP) growth averaged 4.9% per annum. The economy expanded by 7.7% in 1996, 10.7% in 1997, 8.6% in 1998, and 9.8% in 1999. Gross National Product (GNP) growth was only slightly less (Department of Finance, 2000). Between 1995 and 1998, GDP per capita is estimated to have progressed from 92% of the European Union average to 109.5%.[2] At the same time, inflation remained consistently low until 2000. The annual percentage change in consumer prices ranged from 1.5% to 2.5% in the years 1993/96 but had risen to 5.5 in the year to June 2000 as a result of higher oil prices and a weaker European currency.

Poverty Levels

According to the Living in Ireland Survey of the Economic and Social Research Institute (Callan et al., 1999), 22% of persons fell below the poverty line (of 50% of average household income), and 35% below the 60% line. When income poverty was combined with nonmonetary deprivation indicators, such as not having a warm winter coat or a substantial daily meal, the numbers experiencing poverty were better, with 7% of households classified as below the 50% line *and* experiencing basic deprivation, and 10% classified as below the 60% equivalent. These figures could be said to represent those in long-term poverty or the consistently poor. Households headed by an unemployed person were the largest group living in poverty, representing about one-third of all households living in poverty at the 50% income line. Children faced a slightly higher risk of poverty than adults. Their risk was 24% at the 50% line, and 38% at the 60% line.

The principal changes since a similar study in 1994 were a decrease in the number experiencing consistent poverty, a 1 percentage point increase in the number below income poverty lines, a rapid increase in the risk of poverty for single-person households, and a narrowing of the gap between the poverty risk for adults and children (Combat Poverty Agency, 2000).

Social Policy Issues Related to Children and Youth

Education

Children and young people are a high priority group in all areas of government policy and in all action areas of statutory and voluntary service delivery.

Education is compulsory for children aged 6 to 15. Although not obliged to attend school, 65% of 4-year-olds and almost all 5-year-olds are enrolled in the preschool programs of primary schools. A small number of state-funded programs are in place for 3-year-olds in disadvantaged areas, in addition to preschool programs for children with special education needs. The Early Start Pre-School Programme established in 1994 is targeted at areas of particular disadvantage. Education is free at elementary and secondary level schools. Since 1996/97, undergraduate tuition fees have been abolished in publicly funded colleges and universities. Living expenses while studying remain a barrier to more equal participation at the postsecondary level although various means-tested support schemes operate.

Health

Health policy and the overall planning of health services are the responsibility of the Department of Health and Children. Administration of health services is the responsibility of Health Boards in eight regions. Services are provided in three main programs: community care, general hospital, and special hospitals. The community care program includes child health services, community nursing, infant care, and welfare services.

The Department's Health Promotion Unit has targeted young people as one of the priority population groups and has developed numerous programs for them, often in cooperation with other state agencies and voluntary bodies. Substance abuse prevention is a key theme. Programs address drug, tobacco, solvent, and alcohol use through increasing the awareness of students and parents. A child abuse prevention program, "Stay Safe," is available to all primary schools. The National Consultative Committee on Health Promotion has established a specific sub-committee on young people.

Gross noncapital expenditure on health was £2,873 million in 1997, 5.5% of GDP. Health accounted for 18% of gross current expenditure by government in 1998. (In this chapter, all monetary sums are expressed in Irish pounds (£), with £1 equal to about $1.10 US.)

Expenditure on social security and welfare was £4,763 million in 1998, 95% of which was current transfer payments. This represented 8.8% of GDP and 27% of gross current expenditure by government. A comprehensive figure for expenditure on children and youth is unavailable; child-related payments amounted to 9.7% of social welfare program expenditure in 1998, but youth and children would have benefited from other support programs as well. There were 854,000 direct recipients of weekly social welfare payments, involving 1.4 million beneficiaries or about 38% of the population (Institute of Public Administration, 1999).

Crime Prevention Initiatives

A number of prevention programs are in place with varying degrees of state support. In broad terms, of course, the entire criminal justice system has a crime deterrence objective, but this section focuses on initiatives that have prevention as their primary objective.

The Garda Síochána, Ireland's national police service, is involved in a number of ways with children and youth. The Juvenile Diversion Programme deserves mention here, although its role in case processing is discussed later. The Programme provides a system for cautioning juvenile offenders as an alternative to bringing them before the courts. Its primary purpose is to prevent re-offending and to educate juveniles on their responsibility to society. It operates through a network of Juvenile Liaison Officers (JLOs) throughout the country, under the direction of the National Juvenile Office in Dublin. JLOs are Garda members who receive special training and work mainly in plain clothes. They meet and cooperate with parents, teachers, probation officers, social workers, welfare officers, and many others in voluntary or statutory bodies concerned with young people. While much of their work has to do with individual young offenders, about a quarter of their time is spent on general preventive activities such as talks to youth clubs and individuals at risk (Garda National Juvenile Office, undated; Garda Research Unit, 1998). There is concern, though, that some of the preventive work will be crowded out by case work if, as expected, the Diversion Programme is put on a statutory footing.

The Gardaí also operate a Schools Programme of visits to primary schools. It is designed for fifth-class students, typically aged 11 or 12. It contains five modules: the role of the Gardaí, vandalism, personal safety, road safety, and cycling safety. It aims to teach children sensible and responsible patterns of behaviour in order to lessen their vulnerability to crime and improve their safety. It was recently expanded to address problems of bullying and drugs. An evaluation of the Programme provided evidence of a positive effect on pupils' knowledge and attitudes, but no assessment of long-term effect has been carried out (Garda Research Unit, 1997). The costs of the scheme are not readily available.

The Garda Síochána is also involved in Youth Diversion Projects targeting specific areas of relatively high youth crime. These operate in areas where there is a combination of a large youth population, a lack of basic amenities, and high unemployment. The projects are community based and involve multiple agencies. They are directed at young people aged 10-18 who are either involved in crime or thought to be at risk of becoming involved in crime, as well as early school leavers and those in need of support because of family circumstances. Funding is provided by the Department of Justice, Equality and Law Reform. The Programme has been expanded significantly in the past few years and further expansion is planned in the context of a National Development Plan to promote social inclusion. Twenty-nine projects were in operation at the time of writing, with a further 10 announced in May 2000.

The underlying theme of these schemes is crime prevention, by diverting young people away from conflict with the law and towards making a contribution to their quality of life. It is this focus that differentiates these schemes from mainstream youth work. In each scheme, a full-time coordinator is appointed. Programs involve both intervention and general prevention.

Intervention programs target small groups of those who have already been in conflict with the law and are likely to re-offend, and those identified through their lifestyle and vulnerability as being "at risk" of offending. For these, a forum is created where antisocial attitudes are challenged in the hope of changing behavioural patterns. Referrals are typically by Juvenile Liaison Officers, probation and welfare officers, and the project coordinator.

Prevention programs are broad based and directed at all young people in the target community. They are generally information-driven; various venues are used to disseminate information on personal safety, misuse of drugs, underage drinking, vandalism, and other topics. A combination of intervention and prevention programs is seen as important to avoid the labeling of participants. An evaluation of the programs has been carried out, but the results are not yet available.

"Copping On" is a joint national crime awareness initiative between the Garda Síochána and Youthreach (a program for early school leavers with a network of centres around the country). It developed from a clearly identified need to respond in a comprehensive, holistic way to the issue of offending behaviour among young people. Key aims of the program are to reduce the risk and incidence of offending, and to reduce harmful behaviour such as bullying and alcohol abuse. The program seeks to achieve these objectives by recognizing the experiences of young people without judgement. Core values include affirmation and value of youth and challenge with respect. The program seeks to enable early school leavers to develop their cognitive skills and behaviour in a safe environment. A resource package and training module have been developed for Youthreach personnel.

The Bridge Programme for offenders aged 16-25 should be mentioned under the heading of crime prevention initiatives. The Programme provides an alternative sanction to custody through a community-based program aimed at facilitating offender reintegration into the community. Referrals come from the courts and prisons, either under a supervision order of the court or on temporary release from prison. Participating offenders are assisted in reflecting on their offending behaviour, developing life skills and strategies to avoid re-offending, and exploring future options in education, training, and employment. The Programme is managed by a partnership involving, among others, the Probation and Welfare Service, the Dublin Vocational Educational Committee, and the Irish Youth Foundation. These three bodies fund the Programme. The Programme costs of about £5,000 per participant are estimated to be about 10% of the average cost of incarceration. It has an annual throughput of about 100 offenders, approximately 80% of whom complete the intensive group work phase of the program. In November 1996, 20% of former participants were known to have secured employment and had not re-offended. Results overall are seen as encouraging. Evaluation is continuing as regards to the long-term impact of the Programme.

Child Welfare Policy

The *Child Care Act 1991* updated the law relating to the care of children, particularly children who have been assaulted, ill-treated, neglected, sexually abused, or at risk. The Act places a statutory duty on Health Boards to identify and promote the welfare of children who are not receiving adequate care from their parents, and to provide a range of childcare and family support services. In performing these functions, the Boards must regard the welfare of the child as the first and paramount consideration.

Boards are empowered to receive into care orphans and abandoned children and, with parental consent, children whose parents are unable to care for them. Boards may make arrangements with voluntary bodies to provide services on their behalf, including adoption services. They are obliged to make accommodation available for homeless children, although there remains a problem of children living on the streets, particularly in Dublin, even though emergency accommodation can be provided.

Regulations under the Act require the Health Boards to visit, supervise, and review children in care on a more systematic basis than before. A statutory scheme has been introduced for the registration, inspection, and setting of standards for children's residential centres operated by voluntary bodies. The service developments that have taken place since 1993 have involved the appointment of 900 additional professional and administrative staff. Child Care Development Officers have been appointed as regional managers of childcare services. Team Leaders head up and supervise social work teams, and additional staff such as social workers, childcare workers, psychologists, child psychiatrists, and family support workers have been recruited. After initial hesitation, the government has committed itself to establishing an office of Ombudsman for Children to ensure the responsiveness of services to the needs of children and to promote and protect their rights.

There were 3,668 children in care on 31 December 1996. Of these, 76% were in foster care, either with relatives or elsewhere, reflecting a significant shift from residential care in group homes or institutions to fostering as the preferred mode of care. One in six children in care (16%) were in residential care, while 5% were at home. Most children were in care with parental consent (48%) or under court care orders (43%). The rest were explained by supervision orders (3%), interim care orders (3%), emergency care orders (1%), and other miscellaneous legal bases.

Child abuse has been a growing problem and was addressed in the 1991 Act. In 1986, the number of reports of alleged abuse received by Health Boards was 1,000; almost half were confirmed, and 274 involved sexual abuse. By 1995, the number of reports was 6,415, of which 2,276 were confirmed, including 765 cases of child sexual abuse. In 1987 child abuse guidelines were issued on the identification, investigation, and management of child abuse cases. The guidelines were amended in 1995 to clarify the circumstances in which the

Health Boards and the Gardaí must notify each other of suspected cases of child abuse and in relation to the consultations that should take place between both agencies (Department of Health and Children, 1987, 1995). New national guidelines were issued in 1999 (Department of Health and Children, 1999).

Responsibility for monitoring and coordinating the state response to child abuse cases rests with the Health Boards. Improved services are now in place in each Health Board area, provided either in hospitals or on a community basis. New residential and hostel facilities have been developed around the country, and therapeutic care has been developed for children and adolescents severely damaged by abuse. A child abuse prevention program is now in use in all primary schools and covers all forms of abuse including bullying. Protection for persons reporting abuse was enshrined in statute in 1998 (*Protections for Persons Reporting Child Abuse Act, 1998*).

The *Children Act 2001* updates offence provisions relating to cruelty to children, child begging, and child sex abuse and increases the penalties applicable. Cruelty is defined in terms of wilful neglect, ill-treatment, abandonment, assault, or exposure in a manner likely to cause unnecessary suffering or injury or seriously affect the child's well-being. Neglect is framed in terms of failure to provide or seek from the state agencies adequate food, clothing, heating, medical aid, or accommodation. Bullying, frightening, or threatening behaviour towards a child are included in the definition of ill-treatment, but the common law right of "reasonable chastisement" by parents remains. Provision is made for safeguarding the anonymity of child victims in court.

A controversial provision in the Act concerns the detention of children in need of special care and treatment. This affects children of all ages, whether or not they have committed an offence. A court, on application of a Health Board, may order the placement and detention in a special care unit of children whose behaviour poses a substantial risk to their health, safety, development, or welfare if the necessary care and protection is unlikely to be given otherwise. Under the special care order, a child is committed to the care of the Health Board for between 6 and 12 months, but the order may be renewed with the parent's consent. Members of the Garda Síochána are required to deliver such children to the custody of the local Health Board if they have reasonable grounds for believing that delaying action would put the child at risk. Special care units may be provided by the Health Board or by others, subject to inspection and certification. Concerns have been expressed about, among other things, secure accommodation becoming an easy option, available places being filled regardless of need, absence of adequate safeguards for protecting children's rights, and the lack of proper aftercare (Children's Legal Centre, 1997a).

PART II:
TRENDS IN OFFENDING BEHAVIOUR BY JUVENILES

Victimization Rates

Crime and victim surveys have not been carried out in Ireland, at least not on the same basis as in other countries. Some studies have been completed, but never as part of a regular series. They have usually had a fairly narrow focus (such as specific crimes or groups of crimes), or have been limited to sub-national areas and populations. Self-reported crime and delinquency studies are practically nonexistent. A synopsis of the principal studies is presented below.

The first national victimization study was carried out in 1982/83. This entailed a survey of the general public about victimization for six categories of crime. It found a victimization rate of 19 per 100 households, and an offence rate of 34 per 100 households. The number of incidents was somewhat in excess of levels recorded by the Gardaí (Breen & Rottman, 1984). The survey was not repeated in the following years and is therefore of limited help in establishing trends in victimization rates.

A 1994 national survey of public attitudes to the Garda Síochána asked about crime experiences in the previous three years, but only as a screening question to identify those who had had contact with the Gardaí. Overall, 14% of respondents reported that they or a member of their household had been a victim during the period and, of these, only 12% experienced more than one crime. Almost all crimes were reported to the Gardaí (91%), and for those not reported, the typical reason given was that it was not important enough (Murphy & Whelan, 1995). This is an extremely low level of unreported crime compared with international experience, but is supported by other studies. A 1994 study of crime victimization in Dublin, for example, found a reporting rate of 82.5%, somewhat lower but still high by international standards (O'Connell & Whelan, 1994). A similar 1999 survey of public attitudes to the Garda Síochána found that 7% of respondents had been a victim of a crime in the preceding year. Of those who reported being victims, 21% reported being victimized on more than one occasion. The most common crimes were burglary and car theft. The rate of reporting was 88%.

A national survey of victims of crime was carried out in 1996 by the Garda Síochána and the Economic and Social Research Institute. It was more concerned with the nature of the crime, its impact on the victim, and satisfaction with Garda service than with levels of crime experienced by the general public and reporting rates. Although restricted to victims who had reported to the Gardaí, it did ask about other crime experiences in the previous three years and whether those had been reported. Fifty-nine percent (59%) of respondents said they had been victimized on at least one other occasion, and 71% said they had reported this other offence. This rate of reporting, although lower than in earlier studies, cannot be assumed to be typical of the general population, since the sample comprised victims who had already reported at least once (Watson, 2000).

The Central Statistics Office carried out a large-scale victimization survey as part of its Quarterly National Household Survey in 1998. It found that 12% of households had been victimized in the previous 12 months, with reporting rates varying from 95% for theft of motor vehicles to 40% for vandalism. A comparison of reported crimes with those recorded in the Garda Síochána Annual Report reveals a sizeable gap, suggesting a higher rate of victimization than shown in police records. This is similar to comparisons in other countries and there are several possible explanations for the difference, including differences in the definition of what constitutes a crime and its subsequent categorization.

There have been no large-scale studies of self-reported crime and delinquency by juveniles that could complement official crime statistics. Self-report studies have tended to focus on specific, atypical groups, such as adult prisoners in Mountjoy Prison and drug users in Dublin (O'Mahony, 1997; Keogh, 1997).

Rates of Recorded Crime

Garda records are the only consistent, continuous source of crime data in Ireland that can provide trend information. The published police statistics are not, however, without their shortcomings. As with all police statistics, they do not include crimes that are not reported by the public, or reported crimes that are not recorded by the police. The available evidence would suggest that this unknown incidence of crime is not of the same proportion in Ireland as in other jurisdictions and that most serious crime is reported. No research has ever been carried out in Ireland on nonrecording by police of reported offences.

The published Garda statistics provide an incomplete picture of crime in another respect. Full information is provided for indictable crimes only; summary offences are included in the statistical tables only where prosecution proceedings have actually been initiated. Thus, indictable crimes are shown whether the offender is prosecuted or not, whereas not all detected summary offences are shown.

From 1986 to 1998, both the absolute level of indictable crime and the rate per 100,000 of the population grew fairly steadily in the first half of the 1990s, before beginning to drop in 1996. The downward trend continued in 1997 and 1998, despite a continuation in population increase. This is against a background of total indictable crime that fell in the mid-1980s from a peak of 102,000 in

1983, before beginning to increase again in the late 1980s. Rates per 100,000 of the population aged under 50 followed a broadly similar pattern, rising from 3,175 in 1986 to 3,687 in 1996, but falling to 3,087 in 1998.

Crimes against property and larcenies together account for the bulk of indictable crime and therefore most of the overall trend. The downturn in rates occurred one year earlier for property crimes as compared with larcenies. Offences against property averaged 1,102 and larceny offences, 1,449 per 100,000 of the population over the 13-year period reviewed. Offences against the person averaged 47 over the same period, decreasing between 1988 and 1992 before increasing again to 1995. The rate resumed an increasing path in 1997 and 1998. Other indictable offences such as misuse of drugs are relatively insignificant.

Juvenile Crime

There are two principal sources of data on juvenile crime: the main series of Garda crime statistics, and referrals under the Juvenile Diversion Programme, both published in the Garda Annual Reports. The Garda main series is of limited use regarding young offenders because data are not available by individual age for all crimes. The information on indictable crimes by juveniles is published only in respect to age cohorts up to age 17. Juveniles aged 17 are included in a grouping aged 17-21. Information is also limited to cases in which convictions were achieved or where the charge was held proved or where an order was made without conviction. It excludes offences by juveniles who were processed under the Juvenile Diversion Programme. On average, young people aged under 17 accounted for 15% of convictions for indictable crime in the years 1989/98. This ranged from a low of 9% in 1997 to 20% in 1989. The rate followed a decreasing trend from 1989 through 1995, with some fluctuation thereafter.

On the basis of conviction data, young people aged under 17 appear to be more involved in acquisitive crime than crime against the person. They accounted for an average of 20% of offences against property (ranging from 11% to 28%) as opposed to an average of 7% for offences against the person (ranging from 2% to 11%). They also accounted for an average of 10% of larcenies, ranging from 8% to 15%. The vast majority of young people convicted were males (92%).

For crimes against property and larcenies, the proportion of offences accounted for by juveniles was higher at the start of the period, decreased until the mid-1990s, and then remained comparatively low. This occurred at a time when the level of both crime and detections was rising. At least part of the explanation lies in a higher rate of diversion under the Juvenile Diversion Programme. The level of diversion decreased in the last two years in keeping with the overall decrease in crime.

Data from the National Juvenile Office (reported in the annual reports of the Garda Síochána) provide a better but still incomplete picture of juvenile crime. The data relate to referrals under the Juvenile Diversion Programme (JDP), whether first-time or repeat offenders. An age breakdown by type of crime is not available. The data are not directly compatible with the Garda crime series, which includes both indictable and nonindictable offences. Even for the indictable categories, direct comparison is not possible in all cases. The JDP data for criminal damage, for example, do not differentiate between the two types of offence.

It is Garda policy that all juvenile offender cases are referred automatically to the National Juvenile Office. Court proceedings should not be initiated without such referral unless an approval to prosecute has already been given (e.g., where an individual has already been cautioned, possibly on more than one occasion). In the past, a small number of prosecutions have taken place without referral, but the system has been tightened up in recent years. According to the referral data, juvenile offenders are mainly involved in property offences, larcenies, criminal damage to property, and burglary. Between them, these categories accounted for almost two out of three offences in 1996 (65%), although this was down to 59% of offences in 1998. Crimes of violence against the person accounted for 10% of juvenile offences in each of the years from 1996 to 1998, mostly less serious assaults. Serious and sexual assaults increased in each year, but overall numbers remained low. As a percentage of all juvenile referrals, burglaries and larcenies were on the decrease. Public order and criminal damage offences decreased in the last two years from a five-year peak in 1996. Licensing law offences grew in significance in the last two years.

Almost two out of three referrals to the National Juvenile Office are dealt with by means of caution rather than prosecution.[3] Cautions averaged 63% of referrals over the period from 1992 to 1998, varying between 62 and 66%, with the exception of 1993 (56%). On average, 72% of cautions were informal (administered by Juvenile Liaison Officers, usually in the offender's home) and 28% formal (typically administered by a Garda Superintendent in a police station and involving a period of Garda supervision). The proportion of cases dealt with by means of prosecution averaged 37%, 61% of which were at National Juvenile Office direction and 39% initiated directly at the local level. Most, if not all, of those prosecuted would have been cautioned at some earlier stage in their offending career. Female offenders are dealt with more often by means of informal caution (average of 61% over the period as compared with 43% of male referrals) with 25% prosecuted (compared with 40% of male referrals). This may be explained by the nature of female offending, not examined here.

The total number of juvenile offenders, aged under 18, who were referred to the National Juvenile Office during 1996 consists of those who were cautioned and those who were prosecuted. The national average of cautions per 1,000 youth under age 18 was 5.3 compared to 3.1 for prosecutions in 1996. The highest rate of cautions and prosecutions was in the Dublin region, with 7.6

cautions and 6.7 prosecutions per 1,000 juveniles. This variation may mean higher rates of more serious crime in the Dublin region, or a system bias towards prosecution in Dublin. Dublin is the largest urban area in Ireland.

Ages 15 and 16 are peak years for juvenile offenders referred to the National Juvenile Office. In 1996 nearly a quarter were aged 15 and one-fifth were aged 16. Slightly less than one-tenth were aged 17. It is not clear if the drop off after age 15/16 is due to a lower rate of offending, a lower rate of referral, or a combination of the two. The vast majority of juvenile offenders were male, with 86% of 1996 referrals being male and 14% female. This was fairly consistent through all age groups, with the percentage of males always in the range of 85%-89%.

Information about the socioeconomic background of juvenile offenders is not routinely collected. Official policy is that all juvenile offenders, regardless of background, are entitled to the benefits of the Diversion Programme once certain conditions are fulfilled. These conditions are simple: the offender must be under age 18, must admit the offence, and must not have been cautioned previously (with some exceptions). The offender's parent or guardian must also agree to cooperate with the Gardaí by accepting any help or advice about the juvenile. Some commentators have queried the extent of accessibility to the scheme, suggesting an element of selectivity as regards socioeconomic background of offender and type of offence. Unfortunately no hard evidence exists to either support or refute this. In particular, the absence of socioeconomic data is regrettable, especially at a time when the Programme is being put on a statutory basis.

It is not possible to say very much about the use of weapons by juveniles. Just under 2% of juvenile referrals in 1998 were in respect to possession of an offensive weapon, but this is where possession was the principal offence. Weapons were probably involved in several other offence categories, especially serious assaults, but only the principal offence is counted. An indication of weapon use is provided by a Garda survey of victims of crime in 1996, which found usage of weapons in only 6% of crimes covered by the survey (Watson, 2000).[4] This concerned mainly assaults, where a weapon (mostly sticks or clubs) was used in a third of incidents. The impression from both sets of data is of low weapon usage in Ireland. In particular, juvenile offenders have extremely limited access to firearms.

Information is not collected systematically about re-offending rates. However, Garda statistics show that 11% of juveniles included in the Diversion Programme (i.e., not prosecuted) go on to commit a second offence while still within the age limit for the Diversion Programme (up to 18). Until recently, no information was available about juvenile re-offending rates after age 18. A study of conviction rates for a random sample of 400 juveniles who were cautioned under the Diversion Programme in 1993 found that 23% went on to be convicted of an offence by January 1998, i.e., within a period of up to five years after the initial caution (O'Dwyer, 1998). Of these, 60% (or 14% of the 400) went on to a second or subsequent conviction. One in four of those with a conviction had more than three convictions at the time of the analysis. Little can be said about any "progression" from less serious to more serious crimes, with most offenders involved in similar types of offences or showing no particular pattern. Most re-offenders experience increasingly severe sanctions, often beginning with fines and care orders, and moving to imprisonment. To focus on re-offending is to look at things somewhat negatively; the counterpart is that 77% of those included in the program desisted from offending, or at least avoided a conviction, by the time of the analysis.

Drug abuse was undoubtedly a factor in re-offending. A study of users of so-called hard drugs (mainly heroin) in the Dublin area found that while only 25% of drug users surveyed were under 20 years of age, 73% had started using drugs before age 18, and 58% had been in trouble with the law before age 16 (Keogh, 1997). Re-offending was high among this group of hard drug users, with 46% admitting to being apprehended on more than one other occasion. It was estimated that the group as a whole accounted for 66% of all detected crimes in the Dublin Region in the 12-month period reviewed.

O'Mahony's (1997) survey of adult offenders in Mountjoy prison found that 77% had earlier served a sentence in St. Patrick's Institution, the closed prison for young adults. The average age of first conviction was 16.8, ranging from 10 to 40. A considerable proportion (22%) were imprisoned on their first conviction, down nevertheless from 36% in 1986. About a quarter of prisoners surveyed had experienced four or more alternative sanctions before imprisonment.

Youth gangs, a problem in some other countries, have not been a problem of the Irish crime scene.

PART III:
THE JUVENILE JUSTICE SYSTEM IN IRELAND

Legislation

The principal piece of legislation governing the Irish juvenile justice system was the *Children Act, 1908*. This Act pre-dated the foundation of the Irish State and remained largely unchanged since its enactment by the British Parliament. This may appear surprising, but Ireland was a fairly inward-looking and under-developed country until the 1960s, untroubled to any great extent by crime, and still subject to traditional social constraints of the Roman Catholic Church and the family. From the late 1960s can be traced the beginnings of economic and technological development, urbanization, a questioning of traditional social conventions, and a growth in crime (Ryan, 1995). Youth crime emerged as a major concern and the origin of several "moral panics," often fueled by media reporting of events.

Over the last three decades, the juvenile justice system attracted considerable criticism. Numerous reports, both government and independent, highlighted its inadequacy. The system of juvenile justice was described by some commentators as

> rooted in early 20th century conceptualization of childhood and a philosophy of justice increasingly viewed as unacceptable ... [with] an almost exclusive emphasis on the institutionalization of children deemed either at risk of offending (industrial schools) or convicted of offences (reformatory schools), with diversion schemes and community based sanctions only slowly emerging from the 1960s onwards (Children's Legal Centre, 1997b).

The *Children Act 2001* was recently enacted to replace the 1908 Act. The *Children Act 2001* represents a major reform of the laws governing the care, protection, and control of children and, in particular, to replace legal provisions relating to juvenile offenders.

A child is defined for purposes of the 2001 Act as a person under 18, in line with the UN *Convention on the Rights of the Child* and with the age of majority. There are limited exceptions where majority is achieved earlier (e.g., the age of consent to sexual intercourse is 17).

The age of criminal responsibility, previously 7, was raised to 12, bringing it into line with some other common law countries. The age of criminal responsibility determines the age at which children are deemed capable of committing an offence. Below that age, an offence is not available per se as grounds for intervention in relation to the child. It is interesting that a Government Task Force reporting in 1980 recommended retention of the age of 7 on the basis that it would lead to many helpful interventions for young children, that the numbers affected were small in any event, thanks inter alia to the *doli incapax* rule, and that, if the age limit were increased, society would see child offenders as "getting away with it" (Stationery Office, 1980).

Raising the age of criminal responsibility to 12 will impose a serious burden on the child welfare and health systems, including a need for secure units. Various provisions are made for dealing with "offending" children under the age of criminal responsibility, recognizing that small children are more in need of care and protection than punishment. The police, for example, are given powers to take such children home or, if required, to remove them to Health Board care. The Health Boards are given a duty to make a care or supervision order where the police believe the child is not receiving adequate care and protection and so notify the health authorities.

The common law rule of *doli incapax* is also being placed on a statutory basis. There will be a presumption that a child between the ages of criminal responsibility (i.e., 12) and 14 years is incapable of committing an offence by reason of incapacity to know that the act or omission was wrong. The presumption can be rebutted by the prosecution.

A significant element of the 2001 Act is to place the Juvenile Diversion Programme on a statutory basis.[5] This is intended to ensure that it is accepted as an appropriate response to juvenile offending and to ensure that additional resources are made available to it. There were many calls for a statutory recognition for the Programme, not least from the Dáil Select Committee on Crime (1992). However, while there is a general support for the move, there are concerns about the impact on the work of the Garda members who operate the scheme, including possible loss of local flexibility and discretion, as well as heavier emphasis on individual case work at the expense of general preventive work. Analysis is continuing on the likely impact in terms of overall workload, variation in tasks, administrative procedures, and resource and training requirements. The Act does not provide an absolute right to be considered for inclusion in the Diversion Programme. Current Garda policy is that all cases involving juveniles should initially be referred to the National Juvenile Office, but there are grounds for initiating prosecution proceedings directly at the local level. These arise principally in instances where the juvenile has a previous conviction or where a serious crime such as homicide, rape, or use of firearms is involved, or where the National Juvenile Office has already given approval to prosecute the individual concerned for any future offence (usually because of a previous serious offence). In these cases, referral to the National Juvenile Office will continue to be essentially for information only.

The Act gives great flexibility to the director of the National Juvenile Office in admitting offenders into the Diversion Programme and deciding on the type of caution and supervision that should apply. Factors taken into account for admission include the views of victims, but their consent is not a condition of admission. The attitudes of the parents or a responsible adult continue to be central. An innovation is a requirement for them to attend the administration of the caution after written notification, in keeping with the importance attached in the 2001 Act to parental involvement and responsibility. Participation in the Programme must be in the interests not only of the child, but also society in general.

Formal cautions will generally involve supervision by a Juvenile Liaison Officer (JLO; a Garda member) for a period of 12 months. Informal cautions will not involve supervision, except in exceptional circumstances and then only for 6 months. The level of supervision is a matter for the individual JLO having regard to the circumstances of the case. Again, there will be local flexibility, but guidelines on supervision, which have never been strictly defined up until now, are likely to be required. A restorative element is introduced in the formal caution, with provision for victim participation as well as an apology and reparation by the offender.

Juveniles are encouraged to participate in the Programme by provisions rendering inadmissible as evidence in any subsequent proceeding an admission of responsibility, the offence itself, or information about the child's involvement in the Diversion Programme. Admission to the Programme is explicitly stated as providing a bar to further proceedings related to that offence. These provisions codify protections under existing Garda practice.

A major innovation is the introduction of a family conference. The conference seeks to examine the problem in a controlled environment outside the judicial system. It is designed to make offenders more aware of their responsibilities to their family, the victim and society in general. The purpose is to understand the actions of the child, to appreciate the consequences of offending behaviour for the victim, to review behaviour since any supervision began, and to discuss how further offending behaviour can be prevented.

The initiative for convening a conference rests, subject to decision by the director, with the JLO responsible for supervision (and thus applies only to those formally cautioned). A conference requires the agreement and attendance of the parents of the juvenile. The JLO has discretion to invite other community members, including relatives, the victim, a person accompanying the victim, Health Board worker, probation officer, and any other relevant person such as teacher, clergy, or youth worker. The presence of the victim is seen as most influential in making offenders recognize their wrongdoing and responsibilities, but the conference can proceed without the victim.

The conference can be held in any venue, decided by the facilitator after discussion with the intended participants. The conference will regulate its own procedures, but the 2001 Act stipulates that the facilitator will be either a JLO or another Garda member. This has not found universal support, with some critics preferring a person with specialist skills who would not be seen to be closely associated with the police.

A function of the conference is to review the child's behaviour and progress since his or her admission to the Programme. The length and intensity of supervision is reviewed with particular regard to the child's educational circumstances, leisure time activities, and attitudes towards the offence and the victim. The conference has the authority to formulate an action plan for the child and to reconvene to discuss its implementation, although the Act is silent on the consequence of continued noncompliance with the action plan. The conference has no formal power of recommendation or decision, but its views are reported by the JLO to the director of the National Juvenile Office. Information, statements, or admissions disclosed or made during the conference are privileged unless also disclosed elsewhere. Proceedings are to be in camera.

A new element of accountability is introduced with the appointment of a four-member national committee to review the operation of the Programme, including family conferences. Two of the members will be from outside the Garda Síochána. The committee's annual report will be presented to both houses of Parliament.

The 2001 Act enshrines in law the principle that the vulnerability of children entitles them to special treatment during the course of an investigation. The Act also strengthens an existing provision that children detained in Garda stations are to be kept separate from adults to the extent that this is practicable. A new provision requires the Gardaí to explain to arrested children in simple language why they are being held, their legal entitlements, and how to exercise them. Various other protections have also been enacted, such as the immediate notification and continual briefing of a parent or guardian about the case, including notification of transfer to another place of detention and the notification of the right to consult with a solicitor. The provisions are similar to those existing under the "Treatment of Persons in Custody in Garda Stations Regulations 1987," but the age limit is increased to include 17-year-olds.

Attendance by a parent or guardian is not obligatory, and where they are unwilling to attend, there is provision for adult support by a relative or other person reasonably named by the child. The Bill also requires notification of the health (child welfare) authorities where the Gardaí feel that the child is in need of care and protection.

Questioning of child suspects may not take place unless a parent, guardian, or other adult is present except in specified circumstances, such as where parents do not attend in a reasonable time, or where delays would involve serious risk to others or their property. A criticism of this provision is that, if parents are not available, the adult is chosen by the Gardaí and may be unknown to the child. The establishment of a panel of nominees has been suggested (Ring, 2000). Adults accompanying the child can be excluded where they are seen to obstruct the course of justice or are themselves implicated in the offence. Written notification of all steps and proceedings is required, including provision of copies of charge sheets. The arrested child must be released on station bail unless there is reason to believe that release would "defeat the ends of justice."

Children's Court

A new Children's Court replaces the juvenile court, dealing with criminal matters of a summary nature.[6] The operation of the new court will not be greatly different from its predecessor, but the name change is seen as important in emphasizing the welfare of the child rather than the negative connotations of juvenile delinquency. An attempt is being made to make the court more child friendly by requiring that, where possible, court sittings be held at separate hours from normal District Court hours, or in a separate room or building, that those attending the two courts not be forced to mingle, and that delays in court be kept to a minimum. A dedicated Children's Court already exists in Dublin, but the volume of business in other parts of the country would not justify the construction of separate courthouses for hearing these cases. The president of the District Court will designate one or more judges as Children's Court judges, and establish a panel of judges for that purpose. It is intended that judges be appointed for a minimum of six months to alleviate an existing problem of lack of continuity. The jurisdiction of the court extends to most indictable offences where the child does not opt for trial by jury.

The 2001 Act is innovative in stating explicitly that children have the same rights and freedoms as an adult. It also includes the principle that criminal proceedings shall not be used solely to provide any assistance or services needed to care for or protect a child. It also recognizes the importance of the welfare of the child, providing that, if the court feels that a care or supervision order under the 1991 *Child Care Act* is appropriate, the court may adjourn its proceedings and direct the local health authorities to convene a "family welfare conference" to assess the child's circumstances.

The purpose of the family welfare conference is to decide the needs of the child as regards special care or protection, and to recommend to the Health Board that it apply for an appropriate order or otherwise make arrangements for the care or supervision of the child. Recommendations of the conference have to be unanimous, failing which the Health Board must make a determination. Those entitled to attend a conference include the child, the parents or guardians, any guardian appointed *ad litem,* other relatives as determined by the coordinator after consultation with the child and parents or guardians, officers of the Health Board, and any other persons whom it is deemed can make a positive contribution because of their knowledge of the child or their particular expertise. A coordinator appointed by the Health Board chairs the conference.

The health authorities must report back to the court. Where a childcare order is sought, the Children's Court can dismiss the charge on its merits. This recognizes that the alleged offence is symptomatic of a lack of care and seeks to balance the interests of the child with the interests of justice. Where an order is not sought, the health authorities must give reasons. It should be noted that the Health Board can initiate proceedings itself and does not have to await a request from the Children's Court before seeking an order.

The 2001 Act is also innovative in introducing the special care order. A court may make such an order where "the behaviour of the child is such that it poses a real and substantial risk to his or her health, safety, development or welfare" and the child needs special care or protection that he or she is unlikely to receive otherwise. A child found guilty of an offence cannot be placed in a special care unit. The Health Board is authorized to provide appropriate care, education, and treatment for the child in a special care unit, where reasonable steps may be taken to prevent the child from causing injury or from absconding. Orders will remain in force for between 6 and 12 months and may be extended. Interim special care orders apply for a period of up to 28 days or for longer periods with consent. A duty is placed on Garda members to deliver children to the custody of the Health Board where they have reasonable grounds for believing that this is necessary as a matter of urgency. Health Boards are authorized to provide and maintain special care units or make arrangements for their provision, after inspection and approval. An approval is valid for three years. Regulations may be made for periodic inspection, but some commentators are dissatisfied that periodic inspections are not directly provided for in the Act. O'Sullivan (2000), for example, argues that children committed to detention schools and places of detention are, legislatively at least, better protected than those placed in special care units in that they will have determinate sentences, regular inspections, and access to a visiting panel. Murphy (2000) is critical that the Act does not state how often such units are to be inspected or allow for the establishment of an independent body to monitor the units.

The 2001 Act provides for a third kind of family conference, this time convened by the Probation and Welfare Service. The Children's Court may direct the service to arrange such a conference where the child accepts responsibility for the criminal behaviour and the relevant adults agree to attend. The purpose of the conference is to formulate an action plan similar to that for young people cautioned under the Juvenile Diversion Programme. The court may order the child to comply with any agreed action plan and set a date for review of compliance. Failure to comply without reasonable cause will result in the resumption of court proceedings. Where compliance is satisfactory, the court may dismiss the charge. The court may itself formulate a plan where the conference could not agree. Other provisions relating to the family conference are similar to those under the Juvenile Diversion Programme.

Returning to court proceedings, where a child is remanded in custody, remand will be to a remand institution (16- and 17-year-olds) or to a junior remand centre (under 16s). The junior remand centres correspond at present to places of detention operated by the Minister for Education and Science. They will continue to be under the Department of Education and Science, partly because education is compulsory up to age 15. Various places can be designated as junior remand centres, including, with the managers' agreement, parts of detention schools. Children remanded in custody are, as far as practicable, to be kept apart from those detained. The capacity to remand children to junior centres is being expanded.

As regards bail, various conditions may be attached, provided the court is of the opinion that they are in the interests of the child. Otherwise they could be seen as unconstitutional interference with the freedom of the individual, who at that stage would be presumed innocent. As conditions, the child may be required to reside with a person, attend a course of education or training, report to a Garda station, stay away from a place, or not associate with a named individual. If an

offence is carried out while on bail, any noncompliance with the terms of bail can be taken into account in subsequent court hearings in respect of the offence.

The parents or guardian of a juvenile offender are required to appear in Children's Court during all proceedings, including cases where the child has failed to comply with the terms of a community sanction. Under the old law, their attendance was optional. They may be found in contempt of court if they fail to attend, unless excused explicitly by the court. They may be examined in any matter relating to the proceedings (including the type of control they exercise over the child). Where the parents or guardian cannot be located, the child may be accompanied in court by another adult.

Various restrictions will apply to reporting of court cases involving children and those entitled to be present. In general, proceedings concerning a child cannot be reported in a way that could lead to the identification of the child. Where a court decides to release information, it must explain its reasons in open court. The protection is to assist the child offender's recovery and rehabilitation. It is arguable that this is at the expense of the public's right to protect itself. Proceedings are in camera, but the presence of representatives of the press is permitted, and the court has discretion to admit others not directly concerned in the proceedings, such as researchers.

The *Children Act 2001* is also innovative, in the context of Irish legislation, in setting out general principles governing the power of courts in respect to juveniles. Courts should impose penalties that cause as little interference as possible to the child's education, training or employment, the development of stronger relationships within the family, the ability of the family to resolve offending behaviour, and continued residence in the family home. Detention will be imposed only as a last resort. The principles give effect to the provisions of the United Nations *Convention on the Rights of the Child.*

These principles are also given effect by provisions intended to encourage the use of a range of noncustodial sanctions. The sanctions that will be available, singly or in combination, are: a conditional discharge order; an order that the child pay a fine or court costs; an order that the parent or guardian be required to comply with conditions or supervise their child; a compensation order; an order that the parent or guardian be bound over; a deferment order; an order imposing a community sanction on the child; or a detention and supervision order.

The court must have regard for the ability of the child to pay a fine, compensation, or court costs. Imprisonment is specifically ruled out as a sanction for default of payment of a fine by the child. The appropriate sanction is a reduction in the amount of the fine, an extension of time for payment, or a community sanction.

A "bind-over" order may be made that requires the parent or guardian to enter into a recognizance to exercise proper and adequate control over their child. The consent of the parent is required, but unreasonable refusal may be treated as contempt. It is a matter for the courts to determine what is reasonable, as no guidelines are provided. The maximum amount of the recognizance is £250. Forfeiture arises where the child commits another offence within the period of the order (maximum of three years up to age 18) if the court is satisfied that the failure of the parents to exercise adequate control was a factor.

A parental supervision order may be imposed where the court is satisfied that a wilful failure of the child's parents to take care of or control the child contributed to the child's criminal behaviour. The order may require the parents to participate in a substance abuse program or in a parenting skills course, to control and supervise their child, or comply with any other instruction. A probation and welfare officer will be appointed to supervise, assist, and monitor the parents. Failure to comply may be interpreted as a contempt of court.

Imposition of a fine on the parents for a crime committed by their child would not be permissible under the Irish Constitution, but payment of compensation is seen as a civil consequence of a criminal conviction and is permissible. In requiring the parent or guardian to pay compensation, the court must also have regard for their ability to pay.

Deferred detention gives statutory recognition to a practice that has built up in recent years whereby the court chooses to defer sentence on condition that the offender complies with supervision from a probation and welfare officer. Deferment may arise where detention is decided, but no place of detention is immediately available. This seeks to avoid the creation of a "revolving door" phenomenon where offenders are released prematurely to make room for newcomers. It is likely, nevertheless, that there will be a need for more detention places if an unwarranted build-up of detention deferrals is not to occur.

The court may impose a variety of community sanctions and attach conditions, such as requiring regular attendance at school, limiting association with specified persons or places and prohibiting the consumption of alcohol. The child may also be required to perform community service. The existing law allows for community service orders for unpaid community work, but applies only to those aged 16 or over.

Among the new sanctions, a day centre order provides for attendance at day centres to be provided or approved by the Minister. Those provided directly by the Minister will be operated by the Probation and Welfare Service. Those provided by other bodies, such as voluntary organizations, will be approved and assisted by the Probation and Welfare Service. A maximum of 90 days attendance is stipulated, not necessarily on consecutive days. The juvenile will be under the supervision of a probation officer and, while attending, under the control of the person in charge of the centre. While attending, the offender participates in various rehabilitative programs. The accessibility of centres will be an important determinant of their usefulness.

Three orders are variations on the basic probation order but are applicable only to young offenders. Under the probation (training or activities program) order, a child can be referred to a specific program with the agreement of the program manager. The probation (Intensive Supervision) order requires close supervision and the child must attend an educational or training course (including school) or undergo treatment (e.g., for drug addiction) and reside at a specific address (normally the family home). A maximum of 60 days will apply.

The probation (residential supervision) order provides for residence outside the child's home, in hostels either in the local community or away from it. A maximum period of one year applies, but the supervising probation officer will decide on what days the offender should reside in the hostel. Hostels will be operated or approved by the Probation and Welfare Service.

Under the suitable person (care and supervision) order, the court may also assign an offender to the care of a suitable person in cases where the parent is unable to cope or provide a stable home environment for whatever reason. The parents' written consent is required. A maximum period of two years will apply. The child is placed under the supervision of a Probation and Welfare Officer.[7]

The mentor (family support) order enhances the possibility of allowing offenders to reside with their families by enabling them to receive nonfinancial help and advice from a suitable person, which can be a husband-and-wife team. The offender will meanwhile be under the supervision of a probation officer. The order might be appropriate for less serious offences and where the underlying causes of the offending behaviour seem treatable.

A more controversial provision is the proposed restriction on movement order. Much critical comment has focused on the curfew element, and it has been criticized as inappropriate to most offenders' situations and unenforceable. Apart from the curfew order, the court may also order a child not to frequent particular places or localities at specified times or on specified days. It is also only one of many options being provided to the court, not intended only where there are problems at home. The numbers subject to curfew will likely be small and local Gardaí should be able to identify most of them. Gardaí will also have the power to check on their homes. The curfew may operate at any time between the hours of 7 p.m. and 6 a.m. It is possible to combine supervision orders or day centre orders with movement restriction orders. Orders, other than community service orders that have no upper age restriction, may run for up to six months after age 18.

Detention can be ordered to a children's detention school for offenders aged 10-15 and to a place of detention for offenders aged 16 and 17. The children's detention schools are the responsibility of the Minister for Education and Science and the places of detention are provided by the Minister for Justice, Equality and Law Reform. The 2001 Act abolishes imprisonment of children or their committal to prison.[8] The detention may be deferred by the court if a place is not available for the child.

The maximum period of detention in a children's detention centre is generally three years, up to age 18. The maximum period of detention in a place of detention, since it is punitive in nature regardless of any treatment offered, is the maximum sentence that a District Court could apply (i.e., 12 months). This is effectively an extension of the old maximum of three months for 15- and 16-year-olds under the *Summary Jurisdiction over Children (Ireland) Act 1884*.

The court may also make a detention and supervision order, combining detention with subsequent supervision in the community. Such orders may be for four, eight, or twelve months' duration.

Before deciding on the appropriate sanction, the court must seek a report from a probation and welfare officer. For purposes of advising the courts, probation and welfare officers are preferred to lay assessors, although the latter were recommended by the Task Force on Child Care Services and the Dáil Select Committee on Crime. Advantages of using probation and welfare officers to prepare reports are seen to lie in their expertise and objectivity, an already established framework, and probable lower costs. Calls had also been made for panels similar to those used in the Scottish Children's Hearing System, but these were thought likely to be unconstitutional if given any powers. Reports must be provided as expeditiously as possible, but in any event within four weeks, with the possibility of just one extension of a further two weeks where the child is remanded on bail pending preparation of a report. The officer must make all reasonable endeavour to lodge the report within four sitting days of the scheduled resumption of the proceedings. Copies of the report must be provided to all parties with a legitimate interest in the matter. The parent or guardian has the opportunity to give evidence prior to the court decision.

The 2001 Act also replaces the legal framework governing the operation of reformatories and industrial schools. These have had an unhappy history in Ireland, particularly from the 1940s to 1960s. The centres are renamed children's detention schools and will change in many respects. Among the most significant changes are a unified management structure, specified objectives, a requirement to accept all referrals from the courts, an inspectorate and visiting panels, and a structured but flexible approach to temporary leave and early release ("placing out"), including supervision in the community. The 2001 Act also specifies prohibited forms of discipline, including treatment, that could reasonably be expected to be detrimental to physical, psychological, or emotional well-being. The inability to refuse admission to detention schools proved somewhat controversial initially, but the possibility to defer detention offers relief. The right under the previous law to refuse was also controversial, having led to occasional frustration of court orders, unfavourable public comment, adverse impact on the child, and bringing the system into disrepute.

A key provision in the 2001 Act concerns the establishment of a Special Residential Services Board under the responsibility of the Minister for Health and Children. The Board advises on policy relating to the remand and detention

of children and ensures the efficient, effective, and coordinated delivery of services to children who are subject to court orders. Among their areas of responsibility are liaison with courts in relation to the level and nature of services, the monitoring of residential accommodation and support services, and the coordination of development and provision of educational, childcare, and other programs and the necessary physical infrastructure.

Another welcome innovation in the *Children Act 2001* is the provision for restricting use of records of conviction. Under previous law, children found guilty of an offence ended up with a criminal record from which they could not escape. The 2001 Act rectifies this by providing for a partial sealing of the record after three years, provided no further offending has taken place. The only exclusion is where the original offence was serious and triable in the Central Criminal Court (e.g., murder or manslaughter). The relevant sentence must have been served, although exceptions are allowed in respect for more minor sanctions. The effect is as if the child had not committed or been charged with the offence. Evidence relating to the offence is not admissible in any proceedings, and the person cannot be required to answer questions that would reveal the offence. The sealing of records is not complete, to the extent that the offence will remain in Garda crime records.

Processing of Cases

As discussed earlier, the most comprehensive and up-to-date information is in respect to Garda Síochána activities, but even here it is not possible to give detailed statistical information on the flow of cases through the juvenile justice system. It is still useful to map the possible alternatives in the flow of cases as is pictured in Figure 7.1.

Summarizing the diversion data for 1998, 35% of referrals processed ended in prosecution and 60% in cautions (47% informal caution, 13% formal caution). No further action was taken in 5% of cases. Referrals, however, included both first-time and repeat offenders. For those prosecuted, the court in which proceedings took place is not revealed, but most offenders aged 16 or under would have been prosecuted in the Children's Courts.

No information is available on the outcome of juvenile court proceedings. Data available from the Probation and Welfare Service show that, in 1997, 119 probation orders were made in respect of offenders aged under 16, representing 8% of all probation orders. This included 10 orders in respect of children aged under 14. Those aged between 16 and 18 accounted for another 310 orders (16%). During 1997, 142 offenders aged under 16 were placed on supervision during deferment of penalty, 7% of the total. Two percent (2%) were aged under 14. Another 16% were aged between 16 and 18. Persons aged under 16 are not eligible for community service orders. Offenders aged between 16 and 18 accounted for 7% of such orders in 1997 (Government of Ireland, 2000).

Incarceration data are grossly inadequate for purposes of tracking case decisions and dispositions. Data for 1994, the latest available at the time of writing, show that, in that year, 24 males aged 15-16 were imprisoned, 0.5% of the total. Of these, 16 received sentences of less than one year, 5 had sentences of between one and three years, and 3 had sentences of three years or more. No females aged 15-16 were imprisoned. Unfortunately, 17- and 18-year-olds are grouped with older offenders for presentation purposes and could not be distinguished.

Figure 7.1

Juvenile Justice Process in the Republic of Ireland, 1998

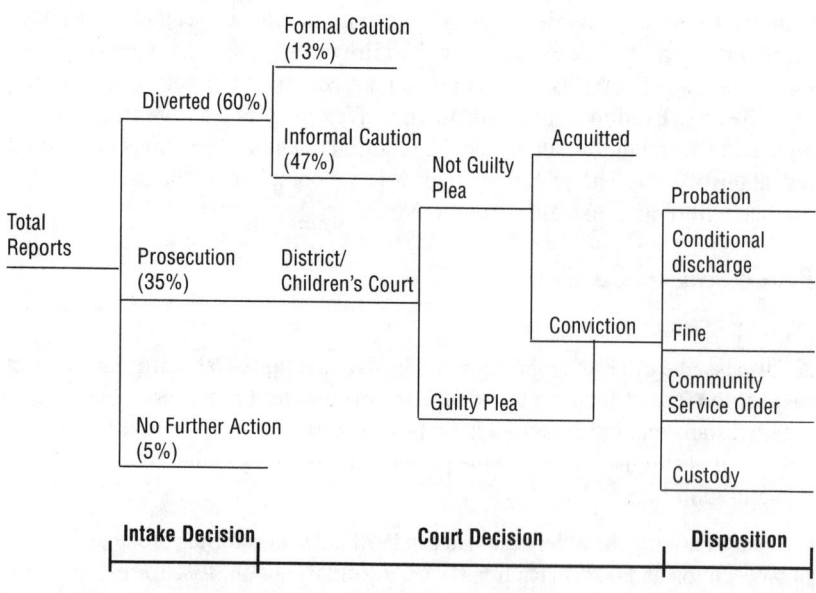

In 1994, 144 male juveniles aged 16 were sentenced to detention in St Patrick's Institution for young offenders aged 16-21. Some 60% received sentences of between six months and up to two years with a further 26% sentenced to less than six months. There were 236 offenders aged 17 and 256 aged 18, representing 21% and 23% respectively of the total sentenced to the Institution. The most common sentence was again between six months and up to two years (two out of three) with 21% to 25% sentenced to less than six months (Department of Justice, preview). A total of 1,844 persons under 21 years of age were committed to prison and places of detention in 1994. A total of 540 persons under 21 were in detention on 15 September 1996, 27% of whom were aged under 18 and 3%, female.[9]

System Effectiveness and Efficiency

Given the lack of basic data about the Irish criminal justice system, it is not possible to evaluate different types of intervention by reference to recidivism rates or processing and disposition costs. However, some information is available.

Starting with the Juvenile Diversion Programme, Garda statistics show that 11% of those included in the Programme re-offended while within the age limit (now 18, previously 17). The 1998 sample referred to earlier found a re-offending rate of 23% for first-time offenders who were cautioned, taking account of offending between four and five years after their first offence.

Is the success of the Programme due more to selectivity of intake than its efficiency and effectiveness as a deterrent? It has been argued by some that the Diversion Programme may focus on offenders who engage in minor acts of delinquency but would not progress to more serious criminal behaviour, while more serious cases, lacking the degree of parental support that the Programme requires, may be processed through court by the prosecution (O'Mahony, 1993). It has also been alleged that the Programme operates in such a way as to discriminate against first-time juvenile offenders from disadvantaged socioeconomic backgrounds.

The offences for which juveniles were cautioned are not trivial. A very small number of offences appear minor (e.g., pedal cycle offences, of which there were 33 in 1996), but these may be indicative of underlying problematic behaviour by those cautioned. The suggestion that cautioned offenders would be likely to desist from re-offending anyway cannot be refuted or supported by the present analysis, but it is somewhat speculative. To fail to respond in any way would surely encourage repeat offending. Under the Diversion Programme, offenders are left in little doubt as to the seriousness of their actions and the consequences of a recurrence. In the meantime, they avoid a criminal record. The Programme also has the advantage of being relatively quick. The delays associated with the prosecution system are avoided, with benefits to all parties involved.

The Diversion Programme is much less expensive than other criminal justice options. To process the cases through the prosecution route would entail additional police as well as court costs, not to mention the costs of overseeing any sanctions imposed.

Little information is available on the costs of other dispositions, other than community service orders and incarceration. The cost of supervising a community service order, imposed as an alternative to imprisonment, is estimated at about £2,000 per annum (Department of Justice, 1997b). The annual cost of keeping an offender in prison was approximately £46,000 in 1996. This excludes capital costs and expenditure not directly related to the running of the prison, such as services provided by the Probation and Welfare Service. This was an average across the prison system, including high security units, but the cost for prisons and places of detention used for offenders aged up to 21 was only slightly less (e.g., £39,000 for St. Patrick's Institution, £44,000 for Fort Mitchel). The average ratio of prisoners to staff is 0.75:1. The ratio for St. Patrick's Institution is 0.93:1 (Department of Justice, 1997b).

The costs of court proceedings must be added to the disposition costs. Information is not readily available, but even in their absence, the financial attraction of diversion is clear.

Issues and Criticisms

Various criticisms levied against the criminal justice system generally apply also to the juvenile justice system. These include excessive delays in court proceedings, poor court facilities, overcrowded prisons leading to the "revolving door syndrome" (early or temporary release of offenders to make way for new prisoners), inadequate opportunities for education, training, treatment, and counseling while in prison, poor integration of ex-offenders, a grossly under-resourced Probation and Welfare Service, inadequate regard for victims' needs, and a focus on retribution rather than restorative justice. The lack of even basic statistics and research has also been a regular cause of regret. Publicly available statistics are usually outdated, partial, limited, nonintegrated, and poorly explained. Research has often been descriptive rather than evaluative.

Major improvements are underway and promised, including building and refurbishment programs, institutional changes, policy development, and research support (Department of Justice, 1997a, p. 118, 1998). There is a growing interest in alternatives to prison and methods of restorative justice. There is a growing appreciation of the need to treat inequalities in society and address the underlying causes of crime. Juvenile offenders will benefit from these improvements as much as adults. It is interesting nevertheless that recent official statements on policy and plans have made scant mention of juveniles as having special needs or deserving of special attention.

Criticisms have also been raised with specific regard to the juvenile justice system. Chief among these have been the fragmentation of response by state and voluntary agencies, and the inadequacy of facilities for juveniles in courts and detention. Responsibility for children has been scattered across government departments and agencies, and gaps in service provision have been met by a variety of voluntary bodies. The appointment of a junior government minister with cross-departmental responsibility for children's affairs was a welcome initiative in this regard.

As regards the courts, facilities for juveniles are inadequate in many centres, especially outside Dublin. Juvenile courts are rarely separate from adult court, with frequent mingling of adult and juvenile offenders and an inappropriate court environment.

The lack of suitable prison places for juveniles has produced overcrowding, sharing with adults, and instances of no places being available for offenders aged under 16. Use of St. Patrick's Institution continues, despite its being described in 1985 as "an outdated, gloomy, depressing environment for any juvenile ... [where the] sense of isolation easily leads to psychological deterioration" and its closure was recommended (Stationery Office, 1985).

O'Mahony and others have also criticized the overuse of prison for young people. According to O'Mahony (1992), Ireland is distinctive in Europe as having one of the largest proportions of the prison population aged under 21 – 29.3% in 1988 (the highest of 11 countries providing comparable data in 1988). Adjusting for lower detention rates, Ireland had a detention rate of 16.1 per 100,000, second only to the UK, and was unique in experiencing an increase in the proportion of its prison population constituted by those under 21. Again according to O'Mahony (1998), "between 1987 and 1991, 243 children aged 15 and 16, who are not normally imprisonable, were classed as unruly and depraved by the courts and committed to Mountjoy Prison, an overcrowded, drug-infested adult prison."

The *Children Act 2001*, the prison building and refurbishment program, and various government programs should ensure that these criticisms are no longer justified. When it comes to dealing with juveniles, there is a need for a shift from hard, blaming attitudes to a more balanced, caring approach. The *Children Act 2001* and the recent developments in child welfare policy recognize the vulnerability and particular needs of children and represent a move from a justice model towards a welfare model.

As mentioned earlier, there was anecdotal evidence that implementation of the Juvenile Diversion Programme was not even throughout the country or for particular types of offenders. To the extent that regional inequalities existed, they are likely to be remedied when the Programme is put on a statutory basis. The enactment of the *Children Act* should ensure that all juvenile offenders are referred to the National Juvenile Office, and will effectively bring with it a requirement to monitor reasons for nonadmission to the Diversion Programme for first-time offenders.

Criticisms and Concerns about the Children Act 2001

Many criticisms and concerns have been highlighted earlier in this chapter in discussing the various provisions in the Act. While there is broad support for the Act and most of its initiatives, a major underlying concern is that, despite good intentions, the resources necessary will not be provided, and that, in particular, the Probation and Welfare Service and Health Boards will not have the capacity to handle their increased responsibilities. Many of the provisions will be meaningless if the funding for day centres, hostels, courts, and so forth is lacking. Increased staff will be required across the range of service providers, including notably health workers, Juvenile Liaison Officers, and probation and welfare officers. There is a fear that, without extra resources, the increased case load arising from the transfer of 17-year-olds to the Children's Courts will add to delays in processing juvenile cases. Extra resources are being made available, but there is concern that the emphasis will be put on physical infrastructure (e.g., secure units) rather than support services.

O'Sullivan (2000) argues for careful monitoring of the use of noncustodial sanctions. Drawing on work by Cohen (1995) and Muncie (1999), he warns that such sanctions can result in net widening, up-tariffing (use of these sentencing options rather than lighter options under the old law), confused purpose, jeopardy (accelerating routes to custody for breaches of orders), and limited visions (failure to recognize broader social context). He is pessimistic, given his perception of a prevailing punitive ethos. He is also of the view that children under the age of criminal responsibility will continue to be incarcerated in all but name, based on his presumption that the regime in a special care unit will not be very different from that of a children's detention school. He goes on to argue for a comprehensive range of measures (such as regular inspections and access of visiting panels) to ensure the safety of children while in care.

Criticisms of the proposed conference arrangements under the Juvenile Diversion Programme have been raised earlier. Some are based on a concern that Juvenile Liaison Officers may not be the ideal people to organize and run conferences, especially in families which may not be "pro-police," or that they may be lacking in skills and experience (Ring, 1997; Walsh, 1997). In their defence, however, Juvenile Liaison Officers tend to be different from other police officers. They volunteer for this police assignment and are only appointed after careful selection. They receive training and operate differently from their counterparts (wearing casual clothes, for example, and meeting juveniles on their terms and territory). The family conference furthermore takes place after a caution has been administered, so the strictly "policing" function has already been carried out. And as to a skills deficit, this is likely to arise regardless of which group is assigned the facilitation role. Perhaps a more fundamental objection is to the facilitator role being assigned to professionals (Juvenile Liaison Officer, probation and welfare officer, or social worker, as the case may be) where they have already had professional contact with the offender and/or client. O'Dea (2000) argues that the role of a facilitator is that of maintaining a balance between the power of the state and the power of families to make decisions. In this context, they must be seen to be independent. O'Dea also argues that conference procedures should be enshrined in the legislation to ensure private time for the family so that they can have ownership of any plan of action. He is also concerned that adequate finances be made available to assist participation in the conference and implementation of the plan.

Kenny (2000) has argued for a clearer and more radical approach, and has urged consideration of the concept of "child welfare boards." These would deal with all but the most serious cases of young offending, and with requests from the Health Boards for special care orders. Within such an approach, one coherent family conference system would be established, led by a designated team of childcare professionals. This would consciously take almost all youth crime out of the justice and into the welfare arena. He has also called for a fundamental shift to a sharing of power regarding planning and decision making, with agencies working with each other and with community interests.

Another issue concerns parenting skills and responsibilities. The underlying theme of parental responsibility in the Act is generally welcomed, but there is a need for support for and development of parenting skills. Some commentators are concerned that

> parental responsibility as an ethos cannot be forced on parents by fining them or by placing them in contempt of court because they are unable to control their children. It can, however, be built up if families feel they are being listened to and feel accepted, and if [care] workers are in a position to offer time, support and therapeutic skills to families. The key distinction is that between working with families and working on them (Walsh, 1997).

There is a need for greater, earlier intervention and support for families, requiring substantial funding.

There are also concerns in the case of special care orders about the absence of adequate safeguards, such as an automatic right to legal representation for the child. There is a perceived danger that the special care order will be used inappropriately simply to avail of accommodation and services not otherwise available. Some commentators doubt the institutional ability to differentiate responses to offending children and non-offending children with behavioural problems. They argue that childcare aspects should be dealt with separately as an amendment to the *Child Care Act*. Finally, the need for adequate aftercare is largely ignored in the 2001 Act.

References

Breen, R., & Rottman, D. (1984). *Crime victimization in the Republic of Ireland*. Dublin: Economic and Social Research Institute.

Callan, T., Layte, R., Nolan, B., Watson, D., Whelan, C.H., Williams, J., & Maitre, B. (1999). *Monitoring poverty trends: Data from 1997 living in Ireland survey*. Dublin: Department of Social, Community and Family Affairs.

Central Statistics Office. (1992). *Census 91: Principal demographic results*. Dublin: Central Statistics Office.

Central Statistics Office. (1997a). *Census 96: Principal demographic results*. Dublin: Central Statistics Office.

Central Statistics Office. (1997b). *Labour force survey 1996*. Dublin: Central Statistics Office.

Central Statistics Office. (1999). *Economic series extended issue covering 1987-1999*. Dublin: Central Statistics Office.

Central Statistics Office. (2000). *Vital statistics, first quarter 2000*. Dublin: Central Statistics Office.

Children's Legal Centre. (1997a). *Secure accommodation in child care*. Papers from a seminar organized by the Children's Legal Centre, comments made in respect of the *Children Bill 1996*, the relevant provisions of which are retained in the 1999 Bill.

Children's Legal Centre. (1997b). *The Children Bill, 1996: Issues and perspectives*. Dublin: Children's Legal Centre.

Cohen, S. (1995). *Visions of social control*. Cambridge: Polity.

Combat Poverty Agency. (2000). Poverty in Ireland: The current picture. Poverty Briefing No. 9, Combat Poverty Agency. From T. Callan et al. *Monitoring poverty trends, data from the 1997 living in Ireland survey*. (Dublin: Oak Tree Press, 1999), http://www.cpa.ie.

Dáil Select Committee on Crime. (1992). *First report*. Dublin: Houses of the Oireachtas.

Department of Education and Science. (2000). http://www.irl.gov.ie/educ/.

Department of Finance. (2000). *Economic background to the 1998 budget*. Monthly Economic Bulletin. Department of Finance. http://www.irlgov.ie/finance.

Department of Health and Children. (1987). *Child abuse guidelines*. Dublin: Department of Health and Children.

Department of Health and Children. (1995). *Notification of suspected cases of child abuse between health boards and Gárdaí*. Dublin: Department of Health and Children.

Department of Health and Children. (1999). *Children first, national guidelines for the protection and welfare of children*. Dublin: Department of Health and Children, Stationery Office.

Department of Justice. (1997a). *Tackling crime, discussion paper*. Dublin: Department of Justice, Equality and Law Reform.

Department of Justice. (1997b). *Report of prison service operating cost review group*. Dublin: Stationery Office.

Department of Justice. (1998). *Community security and equality: Strategy statement 1998-2000*. Dublin: Department of Justice, Equality and Law Reform.

Department of Justice. (preview). *Annual report on prisons and places of detention for the year 1994*. Dublin: Department of Justice, Equality and Law Reform.

Department of the Tánaiste. (1995). *Report of the task force on long-term unemployment*. Department of the Tánaiste, quoted in Irish National Organization of the Unemployed, Briefing Paper 1 (4) (1996).

Garda National Juvenile Office. (undated). *Information sheet by the Garda national juvenile office*.

Garda Research Unit. (1997). *Garda research unit report no. 9/97*. Templemore: Garda Síochána College.

Garda Research Unit. (1998). *Garda research unit report no. 3/98.* Templemore: Garda Síochána College.

Government of Ireland. (2000). *Probation and welfare service report 1997.* Government of Ireland.

Institute of Public Administration. (1999). *Administration yearbook and diary 2000.* Dublin: Institute of Public Administration.

Kenny, B. (2000). *Preventing youth crime: The child care context.* Discussion Paper from Barnardos and Irish Penal Reform Trust, Dublin.

Keogh, E. (1997). Illicit drug use and related crime in the Dublin metropolitan area. *Garda research unit report no. 10/97.* Dublin: Stationery Office.

Muncie, J. (1999). *Youth and crime: A critical introduction.* London: Sage.

Murphy, C. (2000). *Key features of the Children Bill, 1999 in The Children Bill, 1999.* Papers from a seminar organized by the Children's Legal Centre, Dublin.

Murphy, M., & Whelan, B.J. (1995). *Public attitudes to the Gardaí.* Communiqué. Dublin: Garda Síochána.

National Economic and Social Council. (1997). *Population distribution and policy implications: Report No. 102.* Dublin: NESC.

National Economic and Social Forum. (1997). *Early school leavers and youth unemployment.* Report No.11. Dublin: NESF.

O'Connell, M., & Whelan, A. (1994). Crime victimization in Dublin. *Irish Criminal Law Journal* 4: 85-112. Dublin: Round Hall Press.

O'Dea, P. (2000). *Family conferences in the Children Bill, 1999 in The Children Bill, 1999.* Dublin: Papers from a seminar organized by the Children's Legal Centre.

O'Dwyer, K. (1998). Juvenile diversion programme: Reoffending rates. *Garda research unit report no. 2/98.* Templemore: Garda Síochána College.

O'Mahony, P. (1992). The Irish prison system: European comparisons. *Irish Criminal Law Journal:* 47-48.

O'Mahony, P. (1993). *Crime and punishment in Ireland.* Dublin: Round Hall.

O'Mahony, P. (1997). *Mountjoy prisoners: A sociological and criminological profile.* Dublin: Stationery Office.

O'Mahony, P. (1998). *A brief overview of juvenile justice in Ireland.* Paper for conference on Children, Young People and Crime in Britain and Ireland: From Exclusion to Inclusion, Stirling University.

O'Sullivan, E. (2000). *The Children Bill, 1999: Responsibility and regulation in The Children Bill, 1999.* Papers from a seminar organized by the Children's Legal Centre, Dublin.

Ring, M.E. (1997). *The Children Bill, 1996: A legal perspective.* Dublin: Children's Legal Centre.

Ring, M.E. (2000). *Treatment of child suspects in Garda stations in The Children Bill, 1999.* Papers from a seminar organized by the Children's Legal Centre, Dublin.

Ryan, L. (1995). Policing in a changing society. *Communiqué,* Garda Síochána Management Journal.

Stationery Office. (1980). *Task force on child care services, final report.* Dublin: Stationery Office, Dublin.

Stationery Office. (1985). *Report of the commission of inquiry into the penal system*. Stationery Office. Quoted in Patrick O'Dea, *A probation and welfare perspective* (Dublin: Children's Legal Centre, 1997).

Walsh, T. (1997). *The Children Bill, 1996: A social work perspective*. Dublin: Children's Legal Centre.

Watson, D. (2000). *Victims of recorded crime in Ireland: Results from the 1996 survey*. Dublin: ESRI/Oaktree Press.

Notes

1 That is, those under 14 years of age plus those 65 or over as a percentage of those of working age.

2 Expressed in purchasing power parities.

3 This relates to cases where action is taken, in other words excluding the 4%-5% of cases where no further action is taken and excluding cases pending at year's end. No further action may arise where a complaint is withdrawn or a prosecution is statute barred or for other technical reasons.

4 The survey included 97% of indictable crimes and a number of nonindictable categories, but excluded homicides, crimes against Gardaí, and sex crimes.

5 The Diversion Programme could be said to be the most significant difference in the way juveniles and adults are treated in the Irish criminal justice system; there is no system for cautioning adults.

6 Young offenders have the right to avail themselves of the adult system of jury trial in certain serious cases.

7 The 1908 Act provided for the committal of a child to the care of a relative or other fit person, but this option was rarely exercised by a court and was probably only suitable for younger children.

8 Under the present system, young persons may be committed to prison where they are of such unruly or depraved character as to be unsuitable for detention.

9 Response by the Department of Justice, Equality and Law Reform to International Prison Watch questionnaire on Juveniles in Detention in Ireland.

CHAPTER 8

Juvenile Crime and Justice in New Zealand

Gabrielle Maxwell and Allison Morris

There have been dramatic political and economic changes in New Zealand, with major emphasis on having a more market-oriented economy, and a smaller government and a reduced debt. At the same time the country has moved to adopt innovative approaches to juvenile justice, enacting the *Children, Young Persons and Their Families Act 1989,* for those 10 through 16 years of age. The Act encourages resolution of youth crime problems outside of the formal court system. The New Zealand statute specifically encourages the process of police "street warning" of youths for minor offences, as well as more elaborate warnings or alternative diversionary actions provided to youths and their parents at police stations by members of the specialist Youth Aid Section.

The legislation also provides for family group conferences that are restorative in their goals and reflect some aspects of traditional Maori practice for resolving conflict through family and clan meetings. At these conferences, a youth and family members, the victim and a support person, a police representative, and possibly a social worker or probation officer can meet with a youth justice coordinator to discuss the offence, and arrange an appropriate (noncustodial) resolution that takes account of the concerns of the victim and the needs of the youth and family, as well as the interest of society. The youth is encouraged to be actively involved in this process and take reponsibility for his acts. Research indicates a substantial degree of victim satisfaction with family group conference outcomes, though some victims continue to feel excluded or disappointed with the process.

Only about 10% of the youth cases that police are involved with in New Zealand come to the youth court. There are some cases involving violent or

---

Gabrielle Maxwell is the Acting Director of the Crime and Justice Research Centre, Victoria University of Wellington, New Zealand.

Allison Morris is a consultant to the Crime and Justice Research Centre, Victoria University of Wellington, New Zealand.

recurrent offending, or deeply disturbed families, where court is the only appropriate response, and a custodial disposition or residential treatment is necessary. For the most serious cases, transfer to adult court is possible, and it is automatic for murder and manslaughter charges.

PART I:
PROFILE OF NEW ZEALAND

New Zealand is a small island country in the South Pacific with a population of only 3.8 million people. It has traditionally had a relatively high Gross Domestic Product (GDP) per capita of population, relatively equitable income distribution across the population, well-developed health, welfare, public housing and education systems, and enjoyed full employment. Social policies created an effective safety net for the less advantaged and were often innovative and creative in advancing and protecting their interests. These circumstances were associated with low mortality and a skilled population with relatively high levels of educational attainment compared with those in other Western countries. As will be documented in this section, these patterns have changed over the past 10 to 15 years due to a number of changes in the social support infrastructure of New Zealand.

Demographic Characteristics

The profile of the age and sex structure of New Zealand is that of a typically industrialized urbanized population that has had a relatively low birth rate and a relatively high life expectancy for many years. The 1996 census data portray a population in which a relatively high proportion (16%) are aged over 60 years and a relatively low proportion are children. In 1996, only 22% of the population were aged from 5 to 19 years.

In the 1996 census, 75% of the New Zealand population identified themselves as having European ancestry, a decrease from 82% in 1986, and 15% identified themselves as Maori, the indigenous people of New Zealand. In addition, people of Pacific Island and Asian origin make up 5% each respectively of the population. Those of Maori, Pacific Island, and Asian ethnicity are more likely to be in the 5-19 age range as compared with those of European ethnicity. The profile of the European population is of a group comprised mostly of people in their middle years, with a smaller proportion of young people. In contrast, the profiles for Maori and, to an even greater extent, Pacific Island peoples, are of high birth rate populations with a large proportion of children and a relatively low proportion of older people. The profile for Asian people is different again, with a relatively even spread among young and middle-aged but a relative lack of older people; this pattern reflects the fact that a high proportion of the Asian population are recent immigrants in their middle years.

Nearly 70% of the population of New Zealand live in major urban areas with a population of at least 30,000. Another 16% live in secondary cities and towns (with populations of at least 1,000 but less than 30,000), and only 15% of the population are classified as living in rural areas.

Family Structure

Divorce rates in New Zealand, as in other Western countries, have been gradually increasing over the last 10 years, from 11.9 per 1,000 existing marriages in 1986 to 12.3 in 1996. However, divorce rates are not necessarily an accurate reflection of the amount of break-up of intimate partnerships in New Zealand because of decreasing rates of marriage and increasing proportions of people cohabiting without entering into a legal marriage. In the 1996 Census, almost one in six couples who lived together were not married. In addition, family law in New Zealand since the early 1980s has been amended to allow people to separate and resolve issues regarding the care of children and the settlement of property without going through a formal divorce. As there is no pressure on people to divorce when a relationship ends, many of those who are legally married are in fact separated.

The stability and nature of intimate relationships in New Zealand are changing. The actual number of people moving both into and out of intimate relationships is almost certainly increasing. From the point of view of children, this means that, more often than in the past, they will experience a change in the people who are involved in parenting them and that those in the family will also change as children other than newborn babies enter and leave it.

About 40% of families in New Zealand consist of couples who do not have children living with them. Couples with dependent children account for 35% of families, and sole parents with dependent children account for 13% of families.

Socioeconomic Characteristics

Education Levels

Schooling is compulsory from age 6 to 16 years and most children enter the school system at 5 years of age. Progress through the school system is determined by the achievement of a series of qualifications that depend on the number of years that children elect to stay at school and on their ability.

In 1997, 66% of all school leavers had passed a sixth or seventh form (secondary school completion) qualification. Among ethnic groups, it was lowest for Maori, of whom only 40% had passed a sixth or seventh form qualification, and was highest for Asians (84%). The percentage who had obtained such a qualification in 1996 was higher for girls (67%) than for boys (59%).

The percentage of New Zealand school leavers passing a sixth or seventh form qualification is less than the equivalent figures for the United States, Canada, the United Kingdom, and most European countries (Organization for Economic Cooperation and Development [OECD], 1996). Information on what these figures mean in terms of attainment is provided by two OECD comparisons (OECD, 1996; OECD Canada, 1997). The figures reported in these documents show that, in New Zealand, the maths literacy score and two out of three of the literacy indices are, on average, poorer than those of most OECD countries. Thus, New Zealand is not performing as well as comparable countries in terms of school leaver qualifications or in terms of attainment.

About one-fifth of school leavers in 1996 left school without any formal qualifications and about twice this proportion of Maori leave school without further qualifications (the figure was 38% in 1997).

One way of examining schooling drop out is to look at exclusion from school as indicated by suspensions and expulsions from the education system. In New Zealand, suspensions from school can be for a specified period, and nearly two-thirds of suspensions are for a time-limited period. However, the remaining third are for an unspecified period, and these suspensions can signal the end of a school career for children below the school leaving age. In 1997, 4,076 children were indefinitely suspended. Expulsion is mainly used when the child is over the school leaving age and is intended to permanently sever the child's connection with that particular school; there were 151 expulsions in 1997. The total number of indefinite suspensions and expulsions amounted to 0.6% of the school population in 1997; this figure nearly trebles if suspensions for a specified period are added. Some of the students indefinitely suspended or expelled may later find a place in another school or finish their education by correspondence but many will not. If all the students indefinitely suspended or expelled failed to return to school, this would have comprised 8% of school leavers in 1996.

Three-quarters of the students suspended from school were boys, and about twice as many Maori pupils were suspended as would be expected on a population basis (41% of all those indefinitely suspended compared to 19% of the school population). Sixty percent (60%) of those suspended were over the age of 14 years, and a further 30% were over the age of 11 but under 14 years. Drug or substance abuse, continual disobedience, physical assaults on other students, verbal assaults on staff, and theft are the most commonly listed reasons for suspensions.

Employment Levels

For the year ending March 2000, about 61% of the total population aged 18 to 64 years were currently employed, about 50% of them full time. Employment figures are higher for men than for women; 69% of men were employed compared with 54% of women. Women are not only less likely to be employed, they are also more likely to be in part-time work.

Overall, only 4.2% of the adult population was classified as unemployed and seeking work in 2000. However, it is likely that some of those who have been unemployed over a period of time are no longer seeking work. Furthermore, official unemployment has only recently dropped this low; it generally ran at nearly 10% through 1991 to March 1993 and has gradually declined since then.

It is also important to note that the unemployment figures for young people aged 15-19 are much higher. Over the period from 1990 to March 1994 they were running at 20% or more, and in the year to March 2000, were still over 18%. Maori unemployment throughout the 1990s was consistently at least double the rate for people of European descent. These facts have important implications for young people with little education who are contemplating their future place in society.

Poverty Levels

The percentage of households living below the poverty threshold generally increased throughout the years from 1984 to 1994 and has since decreased. About twice as many of the households with children fall below poverty thresholds as compared to all households. Stephens, Frater, & Waldergrave (2000, p. 17) suggest that

> poverty increases with the number of dependent children, with the most significant increases coming for the larger families of four and five children. In part, the higher poverty incidence for the larger families is ethnically based: Maori and Pacific Islanders have on average larger families as well as lower employment rates. [Furthermore, state] assistance per child is less than the additional costs of those children.

In terms of absolute levels of poverty, after housing costs have been calculated, at least one in eight households with children and up to one in six (depending on the defining criteria) were living in poverty in New Zealand in 1994. Over the last four years the number of households with children living in poverty has declined. Stephens and his colleagues (1995) comment that families with dependent children have the highest incidence of poverty (of any group) in New Zealand and their more recent analysis has not changed this finding.

Social Policy Issues Related to Children and Youth

State expenditure on health, education, and welfare in New Zealand is channelled through three major departments of government. The amount directly related to the health and well-being of children and young people amounts to

12% of total GDP. In addition, each department contributes policy advice to government and provides other services to families that contribute to the health and well-being of children and young people either directly or through their families. A number of other departments are also involved in policy and fund services that affect the health and well-being of children, young people, and families.[1] In particular, the Ministry of Youth Affairs in 1999/2000 received $2.7 million directly from government and administered an additional $10.8 million expenditure on youth-related programs ($1NZ equals $0.40 US).

Crime Prevention Initiatives

Crime prevention initiatives became an increasing focus of government policy in the 1990s. In 1992, an interdepartmental crime prevention action group was established to develop a strategy for crime prevention. As a result of the work of this group, a Crime Prevention Unit was established within the Department of Prime Minister and Cabinet,[2] and a crime prevention strategy for New Zealand was developed (Crime Prevention Unit, 1994). This strategy focuses on seven key areas: supporting "at risk" families, reducing family violence, targeting youth "at risk" of offending, diversion, managing programs that address the misuse of alcohol and drugs, reducing white collar crime, and responding to victims.

The Crime Prevention Unit provides policy advice to government, co-ordinates the national crime prevention strategy, evaluates and monitors crime prevention activities, and disseminates information on crime prevention. Much of its work is achieved through the development of coordinated strategies with other departments and through the Safer Community Councils that exist in most cities in New Zealand. In addition, the Crime Prevention Unit has set up a number of demonstration projects that are particularly designed to meet the needs of youth at risk of offending, and in 1997 a coordinated approach was taken to establish a number of these projects in designated areas.

Other crime prevention projects have been funded and set up through other departments. Relevant activities include

- the Department of Social Welfare's response to child abuse, neglect, and youth offending;

- the Ministry of Health's responses to children and young people, particularly in relation to intentional injury, alcohol and drug abuse, and mental health;

- the New Zealand Police force's education programs, youth at risk programs for children and young people, family violence initiatives, and victim support programs;

- the Ministry of Maori Development's involvement in specific crime prevention programs for Maori children and youth;

- the Ministry of Education's development of new approaches to truancy and suspensions; and

- the Justice sector initiatives in funding services for children who have experienced or witnessed family violence and providing programs to young people who enter the correctional system.

In 1997, other specific initiatives were funded from the budgets of the New Zealand Police, the Ministry of Maori Development, the Ministry of Youth Affairs, and the Ministry of Education. The amount of funding specifically allocated to crime prevention initiatives in 1996/97 amounted to 0.02% of GDP. However, by 1999, the amount recorded as spent on crime prevention by Police, Corrections, and the Crime Prevention Unit was only $87.8 million, which represented less than .01% of GDP.

Social Services

The stated aim of social policy in New Zealand has been and continues to be to ensure a basic minimum standard of living to all families with children. A number of different social policies affect this goal. One important aspect of this is the benefits that are available to caregivers. In New Zealand, all sole parents of children who are not employed are entitled to a domestic purposes benefit that is pro-rated upon the number of dependent children in the family. Similarly, unemployment, widows', sickness, and invalids' benefits take account of the number of dependent children in the family when neither parent is in employment. Other forms of income supplements are available to assist with accommodation and special needs. Community service cards provide subsidized health services to those with low incomes. Family support through tax relief is available for all low-income families with dependent children. There are also special additional tax relief provisions for low-income families with dependent children where the income earner is employed. Childcare subsidies and student allowances are also available. Access to all these benefits, subsidies, and special provisions is dependent on income.

However, the effectiveness of the present system in assisting families to care for children has been subject to criticism in recent years because of the limited availability of support to all but those with the lowest incomes. In addition, the total amount of support for which low-income families are eligible has often been seen as insufficient. A further criticism of the system is that the income levels for tax exemption are quite low, and those with low incomes have a high effective marginal tax rate compared to those with high incomes (Shirley et al., 1997).

A second important aspect of social policy is the provision of social services and their accessibility. There have been significant changes in social service provision over the last 10 to 15 years. Public agencies have become the funders rather than the providers of services, with service provision devolved from the governmental to the nongovernmental sector, and greater reliance on volunteer services. Over the same period, the rate of youth suicide has escalated and reports of child abuse and child victimization have increased. Commentators (International Year of the Family Committee, 1994, 1995; Shirley et al., 1997) point to the reduced access to health and welfare services for children, young people, and their families.

An increasing number of women have been seeking employment. In part, this is undoubtedly due to the changed domestic arrangements that have occurred in all Western countries. Other contributing factors are the increasing number of women who are sole parents and the increasing need for two incomes in two-parent families. At the same time, the deregulation of employment contracts and the increasing proportion of casual, part-time and low-paid work has resulted in many women working in low-income positions that fail to provide an adequate standard of living for them and their family unless there is a second breadwinner.

On the economic side, the last 10 to 15 years have seen radical reform to monetary policy. As a result, there has been reduced government debt, lowered inflation, and high growth rates, but there have also been massive changes in the patterns of employment, income distribution, and social service provision that have had an adverse impact on those with lower incomes (Shirley et al., 1997). Health, welfare, educational, and public housing budgets have been reduced as a proportion of government spending. And, at the same time, the increasing numbers of sole-parent families and two-parent families in which neither parent is in paid employment have exacerbated the effects of fiscal constraint.

The poverty data quoted earlier demonstrate that targeted policies of supplementing income are no longer succeeding in ensuring equity regardless of family size. In 1995, Stephens and Bradshaw compared New Zealand with other OECD countries in terms of the structure and level of the child benefit package using the "model family method." Comparisons with services provided in other countries in terms of health, schooling, and housing reveal that, in comparison with other OECD countries, in New Zealand reducing debt and tax levels has taken precedence over reducing poverty.

Shirley et al. (1997) point to the fact that, overall, state spending on families has declined since 1986, and this is true even for low-income families. They also deliver a severe critique of social policies. They argue that the policies have failed to provide support for low-income families, have reduced the accessibility of services for children and young people in need of them, have stigmatized and blamed those who are unable to find employment, and have resulted in fragmented and inadequate systems for the support of the most needy. The fiscal reform process has ended full employment, has deregulated wages that provided for families and their economic security, and has led to the limiting of financial support for health, housing, and education to those with the lowest incomes. The result has been to abandon any coherent form of financial support that is capable of providing an effective framework for family well-being. Shirley et al. (1997) also point out that New Zealand, when compared to Canada, Great Britain, and the United States, has the least data on the outcomes of family policies.

Changing Patterns

The picture presented here of the demographic and socioeconomic characteristics of children and young people in New Zealand and of social policies of recent years is a picture of a society in which major changes are occurring. The majority European population has a relatively low birth rate and is aging. In contrast, the populations of Maori and Pacific Island peoples are for the most part composed of the young. Many of the Pacific Island peoples and members of the more recent and growing Asian population are new to the country, which provides little support for the process of adapting to a new world.

New Zealand can no longer boast of a high GDP, equitable income distribution, full employment or well-developed health, welfare, public housing, and education systems. On the contrary, social policies have failed to ensure a safety net for the most disadvantaged. The consequences of this can be seen in international comparisons that show that New Zealand contrasts unfavourably with other countries in terms of income adequacy for households with children and the educational attainment of its young people. The patterns of marital relationships and family and household structure are also changing, with increasing numbers of children growing up in families marked by parental divorce or separation or headed by single parents.

However, the election to power in late 1999 of a government dedicated to redressing social inequity has seen the introduction of policies aimed at increasing state provisions for those with the lowest incomes. Thus, benefit levels have increased and public housing costs reduced. The overall effects of these changes on children remain to be seen.

PART II:
TRENDS IN OFFENDING BEHAVIOUR BY JUVENILES

Victimization Rates

The official crime statistics do not provide information about victims in general. However, a number of offences can be identified in which either the age of the victim is a specific part of the definition of the offence (e.g., abduction of a child under 16) or the offence by definition can only involve children (e.g., infanticide). Most of these offences involve sex offences against children. An examination of data reported in the years from 1994 to 1999 shows a fairly stable rate over this period and even a slight drop over 1998/99: about 4 offences per 1,000 population under 17.[3]

The number of reported assaults on children within a family violence context can also be identified. An examination of data on the rate per 1,000 population under age 17 for the years from 1987 to 1996 shows that the number of these offences against children has increased considerably. Indeed, the rate per 1,000 population under 17 has quadrupled: from 0.3 in 1987 to 1.2 in 1996. This increase in reports is probably primarily due to policy changes in police recording practices that draw police officers' attention to the need to record assaults against children when they attend a family violence incident rather than to an increase in the commission of such acts.[4]

Finally, information is available on the number of children who were the victims of firearm offences. Walters (1997) reports, from his analysis of firearm offences known to the police in the 12 months prior to June 1996, that 3% of victims were aged under 10 and 6% were aged 10-16.

Another source of data is the number of notifications to the Department of Child, Youth and Family Services (CYF) on the basis of a child's need for "care and protection." Article 19 of the United Nations *Convention on the Rights of the Child* provides that children should be protected from all forms of physical or mental violence, injury or abuse, neglect or negligent treatment, maltreatment or exploitation, including sexual abuse. Section 14 of the *Children, Young Persons and Their Families Act 1989* is consistent with this.[5] Notifications of children under age 17 for care and protection received and accepted for investigation by CYF indicate the type of complaint established in completed investigations. In 1996/97, CYF received almost 24,000 notifications and accepted for investigation more than 18,400.[6] Most of these, however, were categorized as "behavioural or relationship difficulties" and do not obviously relate to situations of abuse or neglect. Physical and sexual abuse made up less than a quarter of the referrals established after investigation.

There are some important additions to conventional violence and abuse categories specifically mentioned in the *Domestic Violence Act 1995*. This Act defines violence as physical, sexual, or psychological violence. The latter includes intimidation, harassment, threats and, in relation to a child, "causing or allowing the child to witness the physical, sexual or psychological abuse of a person with whom the child has a domestic relationship." Over the period from June 1996 to June 1999, 33,903 applications were made for children, a rate of approximately 0.1 per 100,000 per annum.

There have been no national or representative surveys of children and young people's experience of victimization in New Zealand. A recently conducted survey of crime victims (Young et al., 1997) did include young people from the age of 15 in its sample, but the data presented grouped the ages 15-24 together. There are, however, a number of other surveys that can be referred to, although their samples are not necessarily representative.

First, 351 young people aged between 10 and 14 were interviewed by the MRL Research Group (1993) to identify young people's attitudes towards policing and these interviews provide some information about their experience of victimization.[7] Just under a third (29%) of these youngsters said that they had been the victim of a crime in the last year – mainly property stolen at school or thefts of a bicycle.

A second survey was done by Maxwell and Carroll-Lind (1996) on children's experience of violence (in the home, in the school and in the community). Questionnaires were given to 259 children aged 11-13. The first half of the questionnaire consisted of direct questions on physical, emotional, and sexual abuse, for example, "Has x ever happened to you?" or "Has x happened to you in the last 9 months?" These were followed by more open-ended questions, such as, "What were the three worst events that have ever occurred to you?"

It emerged from this survey that being hit by other children was pretty common (more than half reported this in the last 9 months), being smacked by an adult was relatively common (more than a fifth reported this in the last 9 months), as were various types of emotional abuse. Other forms of violence were less common. For example, 10% of the children reported being punched, kicked, or beaten by adults in the last 9 months, and 5% reported being sexually abused in the last 9 months.

The children were asked to rate the impact of what had happened to them. The events reported as having the most impact were sexual abuse, abuse by an adult (though children distinguished physical punishment from other forms of violence), and physical fights or being ganged up on by other children. Watching adults fight was also rated as having a relatively high impact. In response to a question about the three worst things that had ever happened to the children, the most commonly mentioned event was someone close to them dying, but this was followed by physical or emotional bullying by other children.

Saphira (1992) reviews a number of New Zealand studies of the prevalence of child sexual abuse. In one (conducted in Wellington), 38% of girls and 12% of boys reported having experienced unwelcome sexual touching. In another (the Otago Women's Health Survey, which surveyed around 2,250 women), 1 in 10 women reported being the victim of sexual abuse. Almost a third (32%) reported they had had some unwanted sexual experience before the age of 16. And in a third study (a survey of Auckland female undergraduates), over half said they had experienced some form of sexual victimization and a quarter said they had been raped or had experienced attempted rape.

The most recent New Zealand data on child sexual abuse come from the Christchurch Child Development Study (a longitudinal survey of around 1,000 children tracked since birth). These young people were surveyed at age 18 specifically about child sexual abuse (Fergusson, Lynskey, & Horwood, 1996). Seventeen percent (17%) of the girls and 3% of the boys reported experiencing sexual abuse before the age of 16. Rates of severe abuse involving intercourse or attempted intercourse were much lower, at 6% and 2% respectively. Yet this means that 1 in every 20 girls and 1 in every 70 boys reported having had this experience. Most (94%) of the offenders involved in severe abuse were said to be men and were primarily people known to the child. Almost a quarter (24%) of all the offenders were described as members of the child's family and nearly a half as nonfamily members but known to child. Less than a third (29%) of the offenders were described as strangers.

Little is known about children's victimization from official statistics in New Zealand. However, the picture that emerges from these diverse data sources is that the victimization of children is not rare, much of it is committed by persons known to the child, and the impact of this victimization on children is considerable.

Rates of All Reported and Recorded Crime

From 1878, the year in which crime records began to be kept in New Zealand, until the mid-1950s, the rate of reported crime in New Zealand was fairly stable, at just under 30 offences per 1,000 population. Since then, as in most countries, reported crime has increased. Indeed, by 1995, the rate was more than seven times the rate of 1950. The reasons for this include increased urbanization, increased opportunities for crime, changes in the age and ethnic structure of the population, and changes in reporting and recording practices by the police. There is little doubt that the changes in New Zealand's crime rates reflect trends in other Western countries.

The increase over the last 10 years has been more gradual. However, it has been somewhat greater for reported and recorded violent crime. This is due primarily to changes in police recording practices with respect to "male assault female," the principal offence under which men assaulting women with whom they have a relationship are arrested. Dishonesty offences make up the biggest proportion of reported and recorded crime. Within this category, theft is the most common offence, followed by burglary and then vehicle offences. Receiving stolen property and fraud make up only a relatively small part of dishonesty offences. Drugs and antisocial offences make up the second-largest crime group, and sexual offences make up the smallest category of reported and recorded crime.

Rates of Cleared Incidents Involving Juveniles

In the year 1998/99, police statistics recorded that over 197,000 offences had been cleared by their officers. Although there are some problems with these figures,[8] they are the "best" data source in terms of inclusiveness, and they are also the only ones available that provide information on the age of offenders. In the year 1998/99, approximately 41,500 of the offences cleared by the police were attributed to children and young people under the age of 17 years at the time of the offence. This represents 22% of all the offences cleared in that year. In other words, just over one in five cleared offences were attributed to children and young people. This percentage changed very little over the previous 10 years.

Table 8.1 shows that juvenile crime, like adult crime, primarily consists of theft (dishonesty) offences. Dishonesty offences accounted for 54% of juvenile crime, and most of the rest of the offences involve abuse or damage to property or drugs and antisocial offences. Violence accounts for 10% of juvenile crime, and sexual offences make up only about half a percent.

Table 8.1
Total Offences Attributed to Juveniles Showing Type of Offence, 1999

Offences	%
Dishonesty Offences (theft, fraud etc.)	54
Property damage	13
Drugs and antisocial offences	12
Violence	10
Property abuses	8
Administrative	3
Sexual offences	<0.5

Three points need to be made with respect to changes in the role of violent offences. First, over the period 1991/98, the number of violent offences as a whole increased and the rate of increase was greater for adults than for juveniles. Second, the increases in violent offending do not represent any significant change in the percentage of juveniles involved in violence. This percentage fluctuated over the period from 12%, down to 11%, back to 12%, and up to 13%. Third, the rate of female violent offending is increasing faster than that of males. With respect to property offences, the number of young people involved did not rise greatly and the proportion of these offences attributed to juveniles did not change much (from around 30% to 35% at most and then back to 30%).

The vast majority of juvenile offenders are over the age of 10 and, indeed, over the age of 14. Maxwell and Robertson (1995) showed that only 10 of the 109 children nominated by the police in 1994 as the most serious or recidivist child offenders had committed offences that could be classified as of "maximum seriousness." Four children had been involved in arson, five had been involved in violence towards other children, and one had committed a sexual offence.

Media headlines have sometimes focused on increases in child offending but, in fact, there was very little change at all in the proportion of offences attributed by police to children under 14 years in the years from 1989 to 1999, and offending by 10- to 13-year-olds remained a very small proportion of all offending (less than 6% of all offending). Offending by children under 10 years of age was even more uncommon (less than 1% of all offending).

A further claim in the media is that the age at which children start becoming violent is decreasing. There could be some substance to this claim. From 1991/92 to 1998/99, the number of violent offences attributed to 0- to 9-year-olds almost doubled and so did the number of those attributed to 10- to 13-year-olds – but then so too did the violent offences attributed to 31- to 50-year-olds and to those over 50. An explanation for these increases could be that society is becoming generally less tolerant of violence and that bullying, stealing from other children with threats, and family violence have all increasingly become targets for reporting to the police. Without further research, it is not possible to test such an explanation. However, police officers whom we consulted provide some support for this suggestion.

The rates of offending among young men are considerably higher than among young women in all three juvenile age groups, though the rate of offending has increased for both sexes in all juvenile age groups over the last 10 years. The rates of offending for males are much higher than for females in violent and sexual offences.

Data on the ethnicity of offenders must be treated with caution because of the ways in which the police identify and record ethnicity. However, it is clear that certain ethnic minorities are overrepresented in the young people apprehended by the police. In 1999, 48% of cleared offences were attributed to Maori juvenile offenders, although Maoris comprise about 15% of the total population. Overall, almost a quarter of all juvenile offenders are Maori males aged 14-16.

Information on socioeconomic factors is not routinely noted on police or Department of Social Welfare records. However, research consistently points to social deprivation and disadvantage in the lives of young offenders. A study in 1994 of 109 repeat or serious child offenders aged 10 to 13 years (Maxwell & Robertson, 1995) provides some information on backgrounds although, as these authors state, this information was not systematically recorded in the files they studied and the statistics that follow probably under-represent the true picture. In summary, they found that

- 21% of the children were not living with their own family;
- 65% had experienced changes of caregivers while growing up;
- 38% had other family members involved in crime;
- 48% were either already involved in alcohol or drug use or other family members were;
- 60% had at least one incident of recorded physical abuse, witnessing family violence, sexual abuse, or neglect;
- 86% were experiencing schooling problems, truanting, on correspondence, or suspended;
- 72% were already known to or in the care of the Children and Young Persons Service;

- 76% of their parents were not coping; and
- 80% of the children had at least three of the above adverse background indicators.

Two longitudinal studies have been conducted in New Zealand (Fergusson and his colleagues in Christchurch, and Silva and his colleagues in Dunedin). Both studies identify a number of background factors that have negative consequences for children. These background factors include adverse family circumstances, lack of adequate educational opportunities, lack of access to necessary health facilities, and being abused or subjected to frightening circumstances. These factors are part of what Fergusson, Horwood, and Lynskey (1992) call a broad pattern of family disadvantage that is characterized by young and uneducated parents who have few skills and supports, impoverished home circumstances, limited childhood opportunities, and a failure of supervision and nurturance. Specifically, Fergusson, Harwood, and Lynskey (1992) showed that, in a cohort of around 1,000 children aged 15 years, 10% could be classed as experiencing problems of some sort including antisocial behaviour. Of these, 3% could be classified as multi-problem children who were involved in offending, experiencing mental health problems, already involved in sexual activity, and likely to be experimenting with drugs and alcohol. Almost all of these multi-problem children were in the most disadvantaged 5% of the sample. The children in this group were characterized by having at least 19 of a list of 39 adverse background factors.

New Zealand does not record its criminal statistics by city size. They are recorded by police district, which, in terms of understanding the urban-rural distribution of juvenile offending, is not helpful.

Little information is available on the use of weapons by young people. However, Walters (1997) carried out an analysis of firearm offences known to the police during the 12 months prior to June 1996. Most of these (79%) involved aggravated robberies and threats to kill or do grievous bodily harm. Only a relatively small proportion of firearm offences can be attributed to young people. Walters (1997) also found that almost half (49%) of the firearm offences committed by young people were aggravated robberies. A further 15% were a combination of assault with intent to rob and the use of a firearm to resist arrest. These offences were mainly committed in the company of peers, usually involved airguns or imitation firearms, and targeted locations such as dairies, superettes, and petrol stations.

A claim that is commonly made in New Zealand is that there are now more juveniles who are recidivist offenders, and that the proportion of "hard core" juvenile offenders is increasing. However, there are no data that enable us to confirm or reject such claims since no records are kept in New Zealand on reconvictions. This lack of data is a concern. It should be possible to record court appearances and reappearances for young people, and to publish annual statistics on these.

Morris and Maxwell (1997) found that, in a follow-up study of about 162 young people who went to a family group conference in 1990/91, around a quarter were "persistent recidivists" four years later. Some six years later, Maxwell and Morris (1999) found that 28% of a smaller sample of 108 whom they interviewed were "persistently reconvicted."

Just over 1,700 drug offences were attributed to juveniles in 1996. This figure shows a marked increase over the figure for 10 years previously. Almost all (97%) of these offences were related to cannabis use. The majority of cannabis use offences (84%) were attributed to males and almost all (98%) were attributed to 14- to 16-year-olds. Sixty-two percent (62%) of the cannabis offences were attributed to Europeans and 35% to Maori.

Although New Zealand does have a number of quite visible gangs, information is not routinely kept on offenders' gang affiliation, except in prison records. Also, these gangs mainly involve adult offenders. However, in recent years, there have been reports of juvenile gangs in the larger cities modelled on American teenage gangs. There is also anecdotal information that young people are sometimes recruited to the adult gangs in their teenage years, but there are no hard data on this.

Self-report studies tell us that most children and young people do something illegal at least once while they are growing up. A number of New Zealand studies would certainly support this (Moffit & Silva, 1986; Fergusson, Horwood, & Lynskey, 1993; MRL Research Group, 1993; Moffit et al., 1994; Maxwell & Carroll-Lind, 1996). For example, the study for the New Zealand police by the MRL Research Group (1993) found that more than half (56%) of the children aged 10-14 knew someone who had broken the law in the past 12 months – mainly this was shoplifting. They were also asked if they had committed offences. Just under half (46%) said that they themselves had, though only 6% admitted to shoplifting and 11% admitted to drinking alcohol without their parents' permission.

Generally, self-report studies confirm the picture of crime presented in the official crime statistics. Thus, although females and younger children report that they have engaged in offending behaviour, greater proportions of males and older children report engaging in these behaviours. The issue is more complex with relation to class and ethnicity. The two largest New Zealand studies (Moffit & Silva, 1986; Fergusson, Horwood, & Lynskey, 1993), which each involved around 1,000 children, were carried out in the South Island of New Zealand, and hence both Maori and Pacific Island children are underrepresented. Both studies, however, have reported levels of self-reported offending that are much closer to the rates for Caucasian youth for Maori and Pacific Island young people than we would expect from the official crime statistics. Fergusson, Horwood, and Lynskey (1993) attribute the higher official crime figures for Maori to both social deprivation and to a greater probability of being reported to the police and dealt with "officially" by them. Moffit et al. (1994), on the other hand, did not find significant differences in terms of the young people's socio-economic status. They suggested that this was due to New Zealand's egalitarian structure. This is not a point with which we agree and we remind readers of the social deprivation and social disadvantage experienced by many young New Zealanders, as discussed at the beginning of this chapter.

Self-report information comes from the Dunedin longitudinal study (Moffit & Silva, 1986) on offending behaviour by the same cohort of children at different points in their lives. The percentages of young people admitting to delinquent acts increased with age and a greater proportion of older than younger children admitted engaging in the more serious offences. The study also confirms the "normality" of much offending behaviour. For example, almost a quarter of young people admitted to fighting over the last year. More than two-fifths admitted smoking marijuana over the past year, and almost 10% admitted stealing in the past year.

Despite concern about juvenile offending increasing rapidly over recent years, it is apparent that this increase is not out of line with increases in adult offending. Though there are increases in offending by younger children and by females, the vast majority of juvenile offenders remain older males. Overall, the proportion of crime attributed to juveniles has remained remarkably consistent over the past 10 years. Self-report data are broadly consistent with official data in terms of the characteristics of juvenile offenders, though they do indicate that, for most children and young people, offending is a phase that they go and grow through.

PART III:
THE JUVENILE JUSTICE SYSTEM IN NEW ZEALAND

Description of Legislation

Various criticisms were made of the former youth justice system in New Zealand. Doolan (1988) described it as being firmly rooted in welfare tradition and as providing too much welfare and not enough justice. Questions were raised about: the appropriateness of the frequent use of arrest and court processing, especially for young Maori; the labeling and stigmatizing of young people by dealing with minor offences in the criminal justice system, especially for young Maori; and about the impact of bringing together young people serving penalties either in institutions or in the community, especially for young Maori. Concerns were also expressed about how the welfare of children and young people who offended was being used "as a reason" in criminal proceedings for placing them in institutions for an indeterminate period (in practice this was for any time up until the age of 16) "for their own good." Questions were also raised about the value of the "training" delivered in these institutions. Maori in particular were dissatisfied, especially given the over-representation of young Maori in these institutions. They also felt alienated from and suspicious of traditional court processes.

There were also criticisms of the practice of the previous system. Research carried out by Morris and Young (1987) on the former youth justice system indicated that there were many problems in its practice: penalties were being determined by welfare factors rather than the circumstances of the offence; young people were not being diverted; police arrested young people so that they would appear in court regardless of the appropriateness of this; and communities and families were not being effectively involved through the mechanism of the Children's Boards. These Boards were intended to keep those under 14 years of age out of court, provide families with support, and encourage families to participate. In practice, families participated little, meetings were dominated by professionals, the reforms were resisted by the police, and the whole process was pretty meaningless for children and families. Morris and Young (1987), for example, found that families and young people often did not understand the proceedings, or did not participate in them because of the formality of the court. The whole event was distant and remote to them.

These various criticisms led to pressures for change and to the *Children, Young Persons and Their Families Act 1989*. This Act sets out the objects and principles that are intended to govern state intervention both with respect to children and young persons who are abused or neglected and those who commit offences. Overall, the New Zealand youth justice system attempted to move some way towards a justice approach without abandoning the desire to achieve positive outcomes for young people who offend (Maxwell & Morris, 1993). Thus it is characterized by the following:

- the separation of child welfare and juvenile offending cases;
- the endorsement of certain principles of a justice approach to youth offending – in particular, an emphasis on accountability and responsibility and on the protection of children's and young persons' rights;
- a preference for diversion from formal procedures and for deinstitutionalisation and community-based penalties; and
- the use of least restrictive alternatives.

However, the new system also reflects certain innovative strategies: being culturally sensitive and appropriate; encouraging families to be involved in all the decision-making processes involving their children; giving young persons themselves a say in how their offending should be responded to; giving victims a voice in negotiations over possible penalties for juvenile offenders; and encouraging decision making by agreement. Some of these are clearly in accord with the spirit of the United Nations *Convention on the Rights of the Child*.

CHAPTER 8 / JUVENILE CRIME AND JUSTICE IN NEW ZEALAND   207

Figure 8.1

Process Model of Crimes in the New Zealand Juvenile Justice System, 2000*

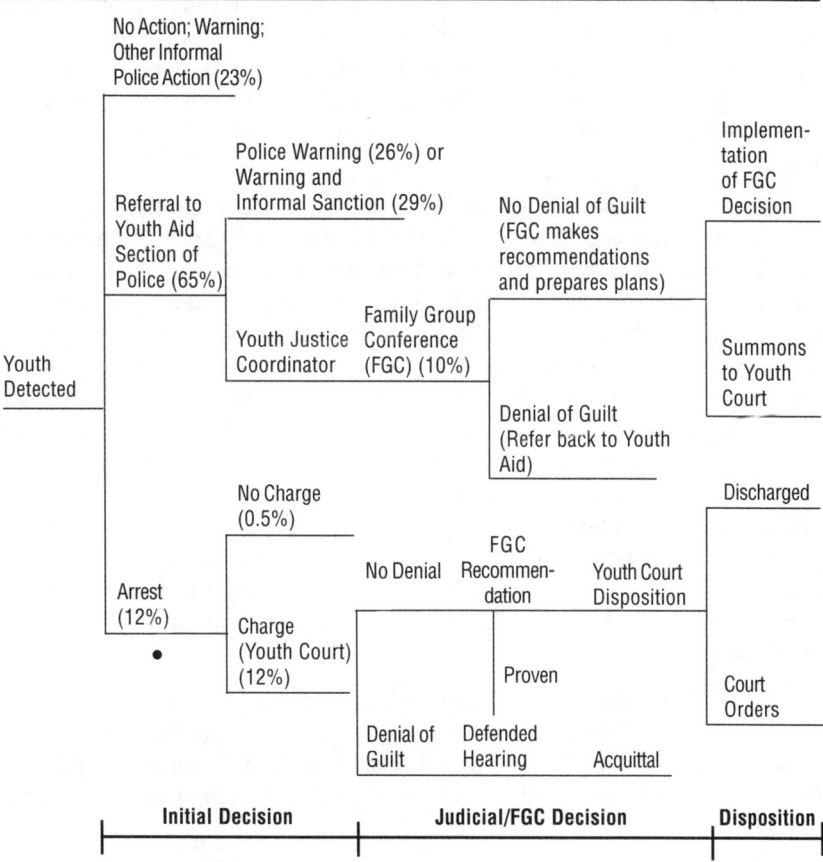

*   Data are not available for all decision points in the figure. However, denials of charges are uncommon, and the great majority of cases where a family group conference (FGC) is involved, including those that are referred to an FGC by the Youth Court, are resolved in favour of the FGC recommendations.

The intention underlying New Zealand's youth justice system is to encourage the police to adopt informal responses to juvenile offending wherever possible. The process is described in Figure 8.1. Thus, in most places in New Zealand, minor and first offenders are diverted from prosecution by means of an immediate (street) warning. Where further action is thought necessary, the police must refer the young person to the police Youth Aid Section (a specialist unit) for follow-up. The Youth Aid Section may divert the young person[9] or, when such sanctions have not been successful in the past or when the offending is more serious, refer the young person to a family group conference. During 1999/2000,

23% of offences known to the police and attributed to juveniles resulted in warnings by the investigating police officer. A further 55% were warned or diverted by Youth Aid, and another 10% were noted as being referred directly by Youth Aid for a family group conference. The police cannot refer a young person directly to court unless he or she has been arrested (discussed below). They must seek a family group conference if they wish the young person to be dealt with in court and, if the family group conference can come up with a satisfactory outcome that is acceptable to all the parties, that is the end of the matter.

Juvenile offenders can only be arrested if certain narrowly specified conditions are met and, in 1999, only 12% of young people who offended were arrested. It is usually only this arrested group who will subsequently appear in the Youth Court, which is a branch of the District Court dealing with youth justice issues only. The Youth Court is closed to the public to preserve the confidentiality of its proceedings and routinely appoints a youth advocate (a barrister or solicitor) to represent the young person where the young person does not already have a legal representative. The intention of the 1989 Act was to allow young persons, their families, and victims to be involved in the process and to influence outcomes. Thus the Youth Court judge cannot make a disposition unless a family group conference has been held, and so the young people arrested must participate in a family group conference. The Youth Court judge must take into account any plan or recommendations put forward by the family group conference.[10] The Youth Court judge has a number of dispositions available to him or her.[11]

In all, 22% of all offences known to the police and attributed to juveniles were dealt with through family group conferences. This means that around 5,000 family group conferences are held each year. Figure 8.1 sets out a description of the youth justice process and a breakdown of data gathered by us for a sample of police stations in 1999/2000.

Family group conferences are made up of the young person who has committed the offence, members of his or her family and whoever the family invites, the victim(s) or their representative, a support person for the victim(s), a representative of the police, and the mediator or manager of the process (these are called youth justice coordinators and are employees of the Department of Child, Youth and Family Services). Sometimes a social worker and/or a lawyer is present. The main goal of the conference is to formulate a plan about how best to deal with the offending. There are three principal components to this:

- ascertaining whether or not the young person admits the offence;
- information sharing among all the parties at the conference about the nature of the offence, the effects of the offence on the victim(s), the reasons for the offending, any prior offending by the young person and so on; and

- deciding the outcome or recommendation.

The family group conference is a meeting which takes place in a relatively informal setting. The room is usually arranged with comfortable chairs set in a circle. When all are present, there may be a prayer or a blessing depending on the customs of those involved. The youth justice coordinator then welcomes the participants, introduces them, and describes the purposes of the meeting. What happens next can vary, but usually the police representative reads out the summary of the offence. The young person is asked if he or she agrees with this, and any variation in the circumstances of the offending is noted. If the young person does not admit the offence, the meeting progresses no further, and the police may consider referring the case to the Youth Court for a hearing. If the young person admits the offence, the victim(s), or a spokesperson for the victim(s), is then usually asked to describe what the offences meant for him or her. A general discussion of the offence and the circumstances underlying it then occurs, and there can be a lot of emotion expressed. It is at this point that the young person and his or her family may express their remorse for what has happened and make an apology to the victim(s), although more often this occurs later (and sometimes does not happen at all).

Once everybody has discussed what the offence has meant and options for making good the damage, the professionals and the victim(s) leave the family and the young person to meet privately to discuss what plan and recommendations they wish to make to repair the damage and to prevent reoffending. The private family time can take as little as half an hour or much longer. When the family is ready, the others return and the meeting is reconvened. This is sometimes the point at which the young person and the family apologize to the victim. A spokesperson for the family outlines what they propose and all discuss the proposal. Once there is agreement among all present, the details are formally recorded and the conference concludes, sometimes with the sharing of food.

Professionals are expected to play a low-key role in the family group conference. The youth justice coordinator's task is to ensure that everyone understands what needs to be done, that all the issues that should be canvassed are, and that emotions are managed as constructively as possible. The role of the police is usually limited to describing the offence, and possibly the impact of it on the victim(s). The police may also voice their concerns if the proposals of the family seem inadequate or excessive. A youth advocate's main role is to advise on legal issues and to protect the young person's rights; they may also express an opinion about the proposed penalties if these seem excessive. The social worker, if present, will normally only provide background information on the young person and participate in supporting the plans of the family and the young person for the future. Practice can, however, vary considerably. Conferences are intended to be flexible, family centred, and responsive to victims. All these values can be breached at times, especially when professionals do not understand or accept their role.[12]

Provided the plans and decisions have been agreed to by all those attending the family group conference and, for court-referred cases, are accepted by the Youth Court judge, they are binding on all those involved. The plans are meant to take into account the views of the victim(s), the need to make the young person accountable for his or her offending, and any measure that may prevent future re-offending by enhancing the well-being of the offender or strengthening the family. The range of possible sanctions are broad (as long as they are agreed to by the parties), and can include an apology, community work, reparation, or involvement in a treatment program or custody.

Conferences devote a much longer time than the courts to dealing with a single case and reaching a resolution. Just under a third of the conferences in our research (Maxwell & Morris, 1993) took less than an hour, almost a third took between an hour and an hour and a half, and more than a quarter took between one and a half and two hours. Around 10% took more than two hours. Family group conferences can take place wherever the family wish, provided (since an amendment to the 1989 Act in 1994) the victim(s) agrees. Most commonly they are held in rooms in the Department of Social Welfare or in community rooms, and occasionally they are held on *marae* (Maori meeting houses) or in the family's home.

Processing of Cases

In 1999/2000, 10% of offences known to the police and attributed to juveniles were dealt with by referral to a family group conference, 12% resulted in prosecution in the Youth Court, 49% resulted in warnings by either frontline or Youth Aid police, and 29% were dealt with through the use of informal sanctions arranged by the Youth Aid Section of the police.

Overall, over the last 15 years, the proportion dealt with by Youth Aid has gone down slightly, the proportion prosecuted has gone up, and the proportion of young people referred to family group conferences has fluctuated (though the proportion referred to conferences directly by the police and the proportion referred by the court after referral there for prosecution has shifted so that a greater proportion now go to family group conferences after a court appearance).

Almost all family group conferences result in agreed outcomes. The figure for 1996/97 was 86%. This has hardly changed over the years since the introduction of family group conferences. It is also unusual for Youth Court judges to disagree with the recommendations made to them from family group conferences.

The intention of the *Children, Young Persons and Their Families Act 1989* was to keep young people out of courts and there was a very significant drop between 1989 and 1990, from 8,193 to 2,352. Since then, there has been a gradual increase in the number of cases going to court, but, even so, the 1998/

99 figure of 4,851 – the highest number since the Act was introduced – is still over 60% less than in 1987.

The vast majority of the cases of young people appearing in courts in 1998/99 involved property offences, about half of which involved burglary. Only a few juveniles were in court for arson or homicide. However, violent offences accounted for a greater proportion of proved cases in 1998 than in 1989, 13% as compared with 9%. The number of aggravated robberies and armed assaults also increased over this period. Correspondingly, the proportion of property offences declined, from around 47% in 1989 to 43% in 1998. Data from the Ministry of Justice (Spier, 2000) suggest also that the seriousness level of offences by young people reaching the courts has increased. The average "seriousness score"[13] in 1990, for example, was 125; in 1999 it had increased to 185.

Most (84%) of the young people dealt with in the courts in 1998 were male. Forty-two percent (42%) were Maori, and about the same percentage were New Zealand European (43%); 18% were descended from Pacific Island peoples. More than two-fifths of the young people dealt with were 16 years old; 14-year-olds accounted for less than 10%.

The most common outcome (for young people who appeared in courts in 1998) – given in more than a third of the cases – was a period of supervision. Only 8% received some kind of custodial penalty. The proportion of young people sentenced to imprisonment was small, but increased during the decade, primarily because of the increase in the seriousness of the offences resulting in the court appearances. However, at the end of 1999 there were only 13 young people under 17 years of age serving prison sentences. One of these was serving a life sentence.

Decline in Use of Residential Custody

The trend away from residential custody began in New Zealand in the early 1980s. In 1980, 23 institutions were operated by the Department of Social Welfare (DSW). A review was conducted in 1982 and resulted in new policy (Wood, 1982). The new policy envisaged a move away from institutional care, especially of young children. The effects of this policy were already apparent in 1989 when, after the introduction of the *Children, Young Persons and Their Families Act 1989*, there was a further review of residential services (Wood, 1989).

The main feature of the 1989 review was the finding of a marked decline in the use of residences which had been occurring since 1978 and had accelerated during 1989. From bed numbers of 399 in 1978, there were only 280 by 1989 to accommodate children and young people who were placed there for their welfare or as an outcome of offending. However, although there were 280 beds in 1989, occupancy was much less than half, and by December 1989, had fallen to 75 children and young people, almost all of whom were placed there because of offending. The review recommended that residential care should no longer be used for pre-teens with the exception of a small number of places for those who were seriously psychologically disturbed. It recommended that the 9 existing residences be reduced to 3 for youth justice cases and that psychologically disturbed children should be placed separately on one of these campuses or in one other residence. The remaining 5 residences were closed and 2 of the existing ones were downsized.

By 1991, the closure of 5 more institutions had been achieved. Thus within 10 years, the number of residences dropped from 23 to 4. The total number of beds had dropped from 400 to 83 of which 71 were for youth justice cases. Length of stay in the residences was limited to a maximum of three months for those sentenced to "supervision with residence" although remand cases sometimes stayed for longer periods. Substantial reductions in staff and costs were achieved over this period. From the mid 1980s to the early 1990s, staff establishments reduced from about 600 to less than 200 and costs, from $24 million to less than $10 million. Admission rates were less than a quarter of what they had been in the early 1980s.[14]

In summary, changing policies from the 1980s through to the early 1990s resulted in large reductions in the number of children and young people in residential care. Increasingly, pre-teens were placed in family homes and then in foster care. Young offenders were more likely to be cared for in the community and periods of residential care were limited to no more than three months except in cases of remands in custody. Institution numbers dropped from 23 to 4. Bed numbers were reduced to almost one-fifth of previous numbers and admission rates were reduced to less than a quarter.

System Effectiveness and Efficiency

New Zealand has very little data on which to base assessments of effectiveness or efficiency. There is no information on recidivism rates and only limited information on the costs of processing and dispositions. In 1996, there were 1,387 informations laid in the Youth Court. The total cost of these was $4,870,000 according to the Department for Courts, a cost of $3,511 per information or, put another way, a per capita cost to New Zealand of $1.35. The full cost of keeping someone in prison was $52,560 for the financial year 1998/99 or $144 per day.

Issues, Criticisms, and Future Options

Does the Youth Justice System Work?

Family group conferences were evaluated in 1990/91 by Maxwell and Morris (1993). At that time, they pointed to conferencing as a more effective and participatory system for victims, young people and families, to relatively high levels of satisfaction among everybody involved in the system (except the victims), and to major reductions in the numbers appearing in court and in the use of court orders and custodial penalties. They also noted that high rates of agreement among all parties were recorded at conferences and that victims often received apologies and other forms of recompense. At the same time, there was no evidence of net widening or the widespread use of overly severe penalties.

This is not to say that there were no problems in the early days of conferencing. Some victims were dissatisfied with outcomes, sometimes because of the outcomes themselves. More often they were dissatisfied because of the system's failure to prepare them appropriately for the meeting, the lack of support for them during the conference, and the lack of information after the conference about what was happening. Criticisms were made of many aspects of practice. For instance, only limited training was provided for many of the professionals managing the system and there was a lack of best practice guidelines.[15]

The number of youth justice coordinators and social workers managing the process of family group conferencing increased in the early years following the introduction of the new system in 1989, but from the mid-1990s, their number has remained stable or declined (Maxwell & Morris, 1996). It is not surprising, therefore, that the number of family group conferences has risen little since the mid-1990s. At the same time, the number of young people offending has risen.

Another result of limited staff resources in the youth justice sector is the questionable capacity of the system to improve those aspects of practice that have been criticized, especially with respect to the lack of preparation of victims for family group conferences, and informing victims about the outcomes of family group conferences. Further, they must monitor these outcomes to ensure that families and young people have completed those aspects of the plan involving them and that professionals have made the arrangements that they agreed to put in place. Information is not available on these issues, but many of those working in the sector feel that little has changed since the early 1990s. There has also been a lack of a planned approach to monitoring and assessing systems' issues.

Maxwell (1995) analyzed funding available for financing family group conferences and found a dramatic decline over a period when the actual number of conferences had increased. More recent information is not available due to changes in financial accounting practices.

Compounding the difficulties created by limited funding for family group conferences is the limited availability of services within New Zealand for children, young people, and their families. Despite the fact that the objects of the *Children, Young Persons and Their Families Act 1989* include the provision of accessible and culturally appropriate services for children and young people, and the strengthening of their families, since the Act there has been a decline in the public health, education, and welfare budgets. A major casualty of budgetary constraints has been the provision of services for children and young people. Even in those communities that still offer programs to deal with alcohol and drug abuse, few can provide specialized services for young people. A number of reports (Werry, 1996; McGeorge, 1995) also point to the declining availability of mental health services throughout the country, and the inadequacy of those services to meet the needs of the child and adolescent most at risk.

There are relatively few effective intervention programs for young offenders, especially those who have been involved in repeat or serious offences. In part, this reflects the general limitations on services for young people, the lack of resourcing for interventions recommended by family group conferences, and the lack of a well-developed history of service provision in this area. However, a new youth services strategy was implemented in 1999 that aims to ensure appropriate services are made available to those most at risk.

There are few alternatives in the community for vocational skills training or for a graduated return to education. Pre-employment courses are often offered only for a limited time, and few young people move on from them to employment. Some young people speak cynically of being "recycled" through several of these programs (Maxwell & Morris, 1999). Within the community there are no specialized courses that focus on preventing re-offending. *Marae* placements have been developed for Maori young people that focus on general skills and cultural knowledge, but the opportunities for placements in these programs have been limited by a lack of funds. However, with the development of the new Youth Services Strategy in 1999, a number of community sex offender and behaviour disorder programs have become available and a residential program for young sex offenders has been opened. Two youth units for offenders under the age of 20 years have also been established in adult prisons.

Even within the residential facilities, program delivery has been hampered by restricted budgets and a high turnover of residential staff. Some new initiatives are currently being introduced, but their effectiveness has not been evaluated and there has been little follow-up for young people once they return to the community.

Opposition by frontline police has been a problem for the new system from its inception. The argument has been that the *Children, Young Persons and Their Families Act 1989* is a "soft option." Some police officers are also concerned that the policing of young people has been undermined by aspects of the system that have been introduced to strengthen the protection of the rights of young people when interviewed and arrested (Maxwell & Morris, 1993). These attitudes are not shared by those in the police who are closest to the youth justice system, the Youth Aid officers (Cheer, 1998). There have been changes in general police attitudes with improved training of recruits, but the lack of support from frontline police who are gatekeepers remains a problem (Potaka, 1997).

A further criticism is that the system does not deal adequately with persistent offenders, and it has failed to reduce offending in general and re-offending in particular. This criticism is inappropriate and unrealistic. More than 80% of young people coming into the system are first offenders (Maxwell & Morris, 1993). Furthermore, it is impossible to expect a system of *processing* young people to prevent re-offending. The issue of re-offending is complex and depends on factors outside the control of the justice system.

Two papers (Morris & Maxwell, 1997; Maxwell & Morris, 1999) have examined the impact of the system on re-offending. These suggest that, of those who attend conferences, nearly a third remain conviction free six years later and nearly a third can be classified as persistently reconvicted. Factors that differentiate these two groups were identified. These included factors already identified by previous research, such as offence characteristics, childhood and family circumstances, and subsequent life events. However, they also included some important family group conference characteristics, including variables indicating that when a young person experiences a sense of remorse and makes some attempt at restitution to the victim, he or she is less likely to be reconvicted. On the other hand, when young people and their families feel ashamed by the process, the young people are more likely to be in the persistently reconvicted group.

Conclusion

The New Zealand youth justice system has been the centre of widespread international interest among professionals, policy advisers, and academics, and has been imitated by other jurisdictions. Various versions of conferencing have been developed or trialled in countries as diverse as Ireland, England, Belgium, Sweden, South Africa, Singapore, Canada, and the United States. Several Australian states have also experimented extensively with conferencing, and three states have incorporated the model in their legislation. Legislation to introduce conferencing has also been passed in Ireland and Sweden.

Conferences that result in remorse and repair of harm can reduce re-offending. High proportions of those actively participating are satisfied with outcomes, and victims can participate in a process that has the potential for restorative outcomes. In New Zealand, the system has influenced Youth Aid police thinking and encouraged their active participation in arranging diversionary solutions. Nationwide implementation of conferencing for relatively serious offences also provides evidence that restorative justice ideas can be incorporated effectively in modern criminal justice systems.

The social policy critique offered at the beginning of this chapter suggests that current policy in New Zealand is not effective in providing sufficient support for the families of young offenders to ameliorate the circumstances that place their children at risk. On closer inspection, the achievements of the youth justice system in New Zealand are mixed. The potential and power of conferencing to provide a new and more effective process for responding to young people who offend depends on a total system of delivery, and New Zealand has not achieved that. The message from this analysis is that it is important to focus not only on the decision-making system, but also on the provision of the services needed to ensure good outcomes for children and young people.

References

Cheer, M. (1998). Youth Aid officers' views on training. *Criminology: Aotearoa/New Zealand* (9): 12.

Crime Prevention Unit. (1994). *The New Zealand crime prevention strategy*. Wellington: Crime Prevention Unit.

Doolan, M. (1988). *From welfare to justice. (Towards new social work practice with young offenders: An overseas study tour report)*. Wellington: Department of Social Welfare.

Fergusson D.M., Lynskey M.T., & Horwood L.J. (1996). Childhood sexual abuse and psychiatric disorders in young adulthood: Part I: The prevalence of sexual abuse and the factors associated with sexual abuse. *Journal of the American Academy of Child and Adolescent Psychiatry* 35: 1355-1364.

Fergusson, D.M., Horwood, J.L., & Lynskey, M.T. (1992). *The childhoods of multiple problem adolescents: A 15 year longitudinal study*. Christchurch: Christchurch Child Health and Development Study.

Fergusson, D.M., Horwood, J.L., & Lynskey, M.T. (1993). Ethnicity, social background and young offending. *Australian and New Zealand Journal of Criminology* 26: 195-206.

International Year of the Family Committee. (1994). *Rights and responsibilities*. Wellington: International Year of the Family Committee in association with the Office of the Commissioner for Children.

International Year of the Family Committee. (1995). *Strengthening families*. Conference, Auckland, 1994. Wellington: International Year of the Family Committee.

Maxwell, G. (1995). Rights and responsibilities: Youth justice. In *Rights and responsibilities* (pp. 61-69). Wellington: International Year of the family Committee in association with the Office of the Commissioner for Children.

Maxwell, G.M., & Carroll-Lind, J. (1996). *Children's experience of violence.* Wellington: Office of the Commissioner for Children.

Maxwell, G., & Morris, A. (1999). *Understanding reoffending: The full report.* Wellington: Institute of Criminology.

Maxwell, G.M., & Morris, A. (1993). *Families victims and culture: Youth justice in New Zealand.* Wellington: Institute of Criminology, Victoria University of Wellington and Social Policy Agency.

Maxwell, G.M., & Morris, A. (1996). Research on family group conferences with young offenders. In J. Hudson, A. Morris, G. Maxwell, & B. Galaway (Eds.), *Family group conferences: Perspectives on policy and practice.* Annandale: The Federation Press.

Maxwell, G.M., & Robertson, J.P. (1995). *Child offenders: A report to the ministers of justice, police and social welfare.* Wellington: Office of the Commissioner for Children.

McGeorge, P. (1995) Unpublished report to the Ministry of Health on services needed for children and adolescents.

Moffit, T., & Silva, P. (1986). Self-reported delinquency: Results from New Zealand. *Australian and New Zealand Journal of Criminology* 21: 227-40.

Moffit, T., Silva, P., Lynam, D., & Henry, B. (1994). Self-reported delinquency at age 18: New Zealand's Dunedin multidisciplinary health and development study. In J. Junger-Tas, G-J, Terlouw, & M. Klein (Eds.), *Delinquent behaviour among young people in the western world.* New York: Kugler Publications.

Morris, A., & Maxwell, G. (1997). *Family group conferences and convictions.* Occasional paper no. 5. Wellington: Institute of Criminology, Victoria University of Wellington.

Morris, A., & Young, W. (1987). *Juvenile justice in New Zealand: Policy and practice.* Studies Series 1. Wellington: Institute of Criminology.

Morris, A., Maxwell, G., & Shepherd, P. (1997). *Being a youth advocate: An analysis of their role and responsibilities.* Wellington: Institute of Criminology for Victoria Link.

MRL Research Group. (1993). *Young people's attitude to policing.* Wellington: MRL Research Group.

National Collective of Independent Refuges. (1991). *Treasure the child: Children living without violence.* Wellington: National Collective of Independent Refuges.

Organization for Economic Cooperation and Development. (1996). *Education at a glance: OECD indicators.* Centre for Research and Innovation. Paris: OECD.

Organization for Economic Cooperation and Development Canada. (1997). *Literacy skills for the knowledge society.* Paris: OECD Canada.

Potaka, L. (1997). Police views on *The Children, Young Persons and their Families Act 1989. Criminology: Aotearoa/New Zealand* (8): 6-7.

Saphira, M. (1992). *Stopping child abuse.* Auckland: Penguin.

Shirley, I., Koopmnan-Boyden, P., Pool, I., & St John, S. (1997). Family change and family policies: New Zealand. In S. Kamerman & A. Kahn (Eds.), *Family change and family policies in Great Britain, Canada, New Zealand and the United States.* Oxford: Clarendon.

Spier, P. (2000). *Conviction and sentencing of offenders in New Zealand: 1990 to 1999.* Wellington: Ministry of Justice.

Stephens, R., & Bradshaw, J. (1995). A cross-country comparison of the extent to which parents and the state share responsibility for families. *Social Policy Journal of New Zealand* (3): 53-75.

Stephens, R., Waldegrave, C., & Frater, P. (1995). Measuring poverty in New Zealand. *Social Policy Journal of New Zealand* (5): 88-113.

Stephens, R., Frater, P., & Waldergrave, C., (2000). Working paper 2/00. *Below the line: an analysis of income poverty in New Zealand, 1984-1998*. Wellington: Graduate School of Business and Government Management.

Walters, R. (1997). *Firearm (Crimes Act) offences in New Zealand*. Unpublished paper presented to the 12th annual conference of the Australian and New Zealand Society of Criminology, July 1997, Griffith University, Brisbane.

Wood, R. (1982). *New horizons*. Unpubished report prepared for the Department of Social Welfare.

Wood, R. (1989). *Review of residential services*. Unpublished report prepared for the Department of Social Welfare.

Werry, J.S. (1996). *Mental health services for children and young people*. Wellington: Ministry of Health.

Young, W., Morris, A., Cameron, N., & Haslett, S. (1997). *The New Zealand national survey of crime victims*. Wellington: Ministry of Justice.

Notes

1   These departments include the Ministry of Maori Development, the Ministry of Pacific Island Affairs, the Ministry of Internal Affairs, the Ministry of Justice, the Department for Courts, the Department for Corrections, the Ministry of Women's Affairs, the Department of Labour, and the Department of Prime Minister and Cabinet.

2   It has since been located in the Ministry of Justice.

3   These data are based on offences reported to the police.

4   Much of this increase started in 1991. This was the year in which *Treasure the Child* (National Collective of Independent Refuges, 1991) was published. This drew attention to children's experience of family violence both as direct and indirect victims.

5   The physical punishment of children by parents in New Zealand is, however, exempt from charges of assault providing that the force used is "reasonable" (Section 59 of *The Crimes Act 1961*).

6   More recent data report only the notifications investigated. In 1998/99, this number was virtually the same as the 1996/97 number (18,300).

7   The survey also explored children's fear of crime. These data show that 41% of the young people interviewed said that they were afraid or very afraid of being a victim of crime and that 47% said that they were a bit afraid; only 11% said that they were not afraid of being a victim of crime. The rates of fear of crime were higher for younger children, girls, and Maori and Pacific Island children. Children said that they feared most the very serious and rare offences: murder, rape, kidnapping, but they also feared street violence. The people they said they most feared were gang

members and other teenagers. Some girls said that they were afraid of men in general.

8   These data are not an accurate representation of the number of offences that are actually committed, because many offences are never reported to the police, let alone cleared by them. Nor are they an accurate representation of the number of offenders. More than one offender may have been involved in some of these offences, but also more than one offence may have been committed by a particular offender. It is also important to note that these figures are from police records. The offenders responsible for these offences may not be convicted in a court, and in some cases they will never be charged because of insufficient evidence or because some of the charges in a case involving multiple charges may be withdrawn.

9   Diversion can include a warning in writing or in the presence of the young person's parents, an apology to the victim, or the imposition of an additional sanction (e.g., some community work).

10 People in other jurisdictions often ask about whether or not there are certain cases for which family group conferences are not appropriate, for instance, very serious offences. In New Zealand, all cases involving young offenders except murder and manslaughter will have a family group conference so that the views of families and victims can be heard. However, for those cases that go to the Youth Court, the judge can review the case and make a different disposition from that recommended if there are grounds for this. The Youth Court judge can refer the most serious offences on to the adult courts for sentence. The Youth Court will also decide the outcome when participants at the conference fail to agree. Cases of murder and manslaughter are dealt with in the adult courts but family group conferences may also be held for them.

11 The orders in the Youth Court that are most frequently used include discharge without further order or penalty, reparation, community work, supervision with activity (includes a plan covering all activities for up to 6 months), supervision with residence (a residential program for up to 3 months, which can be followed by up to 6 months supervision) and transfer to the District Court for sentence (if over the age of 15 years).

12 One example of the confusion that can exist about professional roles is provided in an analysis of the role of youth advocates (Morris, Maxwell, & Shepherd, 1997).

13 This seriousness scale, developed by the Ministry of Justice, calculates a score using potential lengths of custodial sentences set for offences in the adult courts.

14 Unfortunately exact figures on admissions of individuals, costs of running and staff numbers are not always clear from annual reports. Figures are also not always reported separately for welfare and youth justice admissions. However, the estimates given above are consistent with the pattern of information available.

15 In 1997, Morris, Maxwell, and Shepherd produced a report on the role of youth advocates that sets out best practice guidelines and will form the basis for a training program. It is hoped that best practice guidelines and training based on them will also be developed for youth justice coordinators and social workers but this has yet to occur.

Acknowledgments

We would like to acknowledge the help of everyone who worked with us by supplying, collating and organizing the information in this chapter. Alarna Sharrott played a major role in organizing and assembling the raw data and arranging them in a suitable form for presentation, and Tracy Anderson updated them. Sandy Taylor assisted with the figures. Many others supplied crucial information including Bob Hens on poverty, Mary Schollum and Rachel Bambery with police data, Philip Spier with Ministry of Justice data, Helene Carbonatto and Bruce Gadd on Crime Prevention information, Judith Davey on social policy issues, Don Gray on income maintenance and child care policy, the staff of the Department of Statistics with census tables and population pyramids, Terry Craig in the Department of Corrections with prison data, and Nicholas Pole in the Ministry of Education with data on school qualifications. Thank you to you all.

CHAPTER 9

Juvenile Crime and Justice in Australia

Ian O'Connor, Kathleen Daly, and Lyn Hinds

In Australia few topics generate as much public concern, comment, and often outrage as crime, and juvenile crime in particular. Indeed, juvenile crime appears to be a metaphor for societal concern over issues of social change, social threat, and social decay. The last 20 years have witnessed substantial legislative, policy, and practice changes in relation to how society deals with young people who offend. At almost every election in Australia, the government and opposition parties argue over who is going to be toughest on crime and criminals. There are continual changes in the criminal law and penalties for adults and juveniles. Despite these changes, public concern continues unabated as the media is replete with stories of the threats posed by juvenile crime and criminals.

This chapter identifies trends in juvenile crime in Australia and discusses how juvenile crime is dealt with in two of Australia's jurisdictions, the states of Queensland and South Australia.

Ian O'Connor is with the School of Social Work and Policy, University of Queensland, and is an Associate of the Australian Institute of Criminology, Canberra, Australia.

Kathleen Daly is with the School of Criminology and Criminal Justice, Griffith University, Brisbane, Queensland, and is also an Associate of the Australian Institute of Criminology, Canberra, Australia.

Lyn Hinds is with the School of Criminology and Criminal Justice, Griffith University, Brisbane, Queensland, Australia.

PART I:
PROFILE OF AUSTRALIA

Demographic Characteristics

Australia is a relatively wealthy developed nation with a population of 18 million (Australian Bureau of Statistics, 1996a). While the population continues to grow, it also continues to age. With Australians having smaller families and an increased life expectancy due to improved health care, the proportion of young persons of the total population is declining. In 1996, 21% of the population were 14 years or younger, compared with 25% in 1981. By 2021, this is projected to fall to between 17% and 18% (Australian Bureau of Statistics, 1996b). However, the total number of young people in the population will continue to increase because the total population is increasing.

In contrast to the nonindigenous population, the numbers and proportions of young indigenous Australians is increasing. Aboriginal and Torres Strait Islanders (ATSI) comprise approximately 2% of Australia's population (352,970; Australian Bureau of Statistics, 1996a). In 1996, 40% of the indigenous population was aged under 15 years, while only 4.2% was 60 years or older (Australian Bureau of Statistics, 1997a). This means that 3.8% of Australians under 15 years old are indigenous ATSI.

Australia is a multi-cultural country. In 1996, 22% of the population had been born overseas, while 14% spoke a language other than English (Australian Bureau of Statistics, 1996a). It has been estimated that there are nearly 1 million persons aged 12 to 15 years who are of ethnic-minority background (i.e., either they or their parents were born in a nonEnglish-speaking background country; Zelinka, 1995).

While Australia is a large country, there is little physical dispersal of the population. The overwhelming number of Australians live in and/or around the capital cities of the six states and two territories. In 1996, approximately 6.4 out of every 10 Australians lived in a capital city or in the area immediately surrounding them. Of Australia's estimated population growth of 1 million between 1991 to 1996, approximately two-thirds (665,085) occurred in capital cities.

Of the capital cities, Brisbane, the capital of Queensland, experienced the highest growth rate (2.3%), while Adelaide (South Australia) had the lowest annual rate of growth (0.4%; Australian Bureau of Statistics, 1996c). While the population growth was greater in the capital cities of most states and territories, Queensland was an exception. Outside Brisbane, the balance of Queensland experienced the greatest increase in population (n=215,557) and the highest annual population growth rate (2.6%) of any state. In contrast, the population growth in the balance of South Australia was one of the lowest (n=6,100 or 0.3%).

All states and territories experienced an increase in the proportion of the population aged 65 or over and a decrease in those aged under 15 years during 1991/96. South Australia has the largest proportion of its population aged 65 or over (14.1%) and the smallest proportion aged under 15 years (20.1%; Australian Bureau of Statistics, 1997a).

Family Structure

As in other Western developed countries, Australia has experienced significant social change during the past two decades that has been reflected in changing family structures. There has been a marked increase in the number and proportion of single-parent families with dependent children. The majority of Australian children continue to live in two-parent families, but the proportion of dependent children living with a single parent increased from 9% in 1974 to 19% in 1996 (Australian Institute of Health and Welfare, 1997). This increase is attributable to children being born outside continuing relationships and a rise in divorce rates. Australia's divorce rate has fluctuated between 2.4 and 2.9 divorces per 1,000 population during the last two decades. In 1996, there were approximately 12 divorces per 1,000 married couples.

Socioeconomic Characteristics

Child Poverty

The changing family structure combined with high rates of unemployment has resulted in a dramatic increase in the number of children growing up in poverty. The proportion of children living in poverty increased from 7.2% in 1973 to 17.5% in 1986 (Graycar & Jamrozik, 1993). In 1997, 16% of children aged under 15 years lived in a family with no parent employed (n=352,900 families of which 6% were couple families and 10% were single-parent families; Australian Bureau of Statistics, 1997b). Using a different definition of poverty, Birrell and Rapson (1997) assert that 43% of Australian children are growing up in poverty. This estimate was based on the number of children living in families where the adult caregiver was in receipt of government transfer payments targeted at the very poor. Somewhat surprisingly, 44% of these children were living in low-income families where the parents were in employment – they were the children of the rapidly growing working poor. A further 17% of the children were living in families where at least one parent was seeking employment. Thirty-two percent (32%) of the low-income children were living in sole-parent families. Birrell and Rapson (1997) note that the sheer number of children living in poverty will create future social problems given the dominant policy trend of increasingly requiring parents to maintain financial responsibility for children's education and training.

Another indicator of the extent of child poverty is the number of young people who are homeless. In June 1997, there were 9,547 young people in receipt of an independent homeless payment from the Department of Social Security (Birrell & Rapson, 1997, p. 242).

Education and Labour Market Participation

Like many Western countries, the Australian economy has experienced rapid economic change in the past two decades. In Australia's case, the economic changes reflect the process of transformation from a protected economy to an open, internationally competitive economy. This transformation has resulted in a fundamental restructuring of the labour market, including the downsizing of the manufacturing sector. In the 1950s and 1960s Australia enjoyed full employment. Since the 1970s, up to 10% of the labour market has been without jobs, and youth unemployment has been upwards of 30%. In October 1997, 20.5% of 15- to 19-year-olds in the labour market were unemployed (Australian Bureau of Statistics, 1997b). Many of the traditional jobs that working class young people obtained upon leaving school have disappeared. A significant number of young people leave the education system at the end of compulsory education (15 years of age) and do not find employment. They become the long-term unemployed. Long-term unemployment is not evenly distributed throughout society: socially and economically disadvantaged young people are the most likely group to be unemployed. Geographically such disadvantage is increasingly concentrated in particular geographic communities, on the urban fringes of cities (Gregory & Sheehan, 1998).

Partly in response to a changing labour market requirement for skilled workers, and partly as a response to the shrinking employment opportunities for youth, the federal government has encouraged increased participation in secondary, technical, and tertiary education. As a consequence, over the past two decades there has been a marked increase in completion of secondary education. In 1971, 34% of males and 27% of females completed Year 12. During the early 1970s, females achieved parity with males in completing secondary school and have subsequently exceeded them. By 1996, completion of secondary education for males and females had increased to 66% and 77% respectively.[1]

Currently of those aged 15-17 years, 82% are in some form of full-time education (either school or a tertiary education institution) and 14% are in the labour force. Of those youth in the labour force (n=112,500), 28% are unemployed. The early school leavers are at high risk of forming a tenuous foothold in the labour market. They are disproportionately from disadvantaged social and economic backgrounds. The recent changes to the public income security system in Australia create further jeopardy for this at-risk group. Access to income security is now strictly means tested, using parental income to determine youth eligibility, and it is dependent on participation in training or voluntary work schemes.

Government Expenditure

In 1995/96, total expenditures by all levels of government in Australia (Commonwealth, State and Territory, and Local) was $175 billion (at the time, $1 Australian equalled about $0.75 US), of which 3.3% ($5.8 billion) was directed to welfare or social services,[2] 15.6% ($27 billion) to health, and 13.6% ($23.8 billion) to education (Australian Institute of Health and Welfare, 1997, p. 18).

Total expenditure (private and public) on social services in 1995/96 was $8.9 billion, with governments providing 66% of funding (Australian Institute of Health and Welfare, 1997, p. 10). This represents per capita expenditure of $489, which is an average increase of 7% per year from 1989/90 to 1995/96. As a percentage of Gross Domestic Product (GDP), social services expenditure increased from 1.3% in 1989/90 to 1.8% in 1992/93 and remained at that level to 1995/96.

Over the period from 1989/90 to 1995/96, approximately 60% of combined government social service expenditure was directed to the aged and disabled, while 30% was directed towards family and child services. Expenditure on health and welfare services varies significantly between the states, reflecting the different social and economic priorities. During the period from 1989/90 to 1995/96, Queensland spent less per person on welfare services than any other state or territory. Compared with the national average per capita expenditure of $190 in 1995/96, Queensland spent $121 in 1995/96 (Commonwealth Grants Commission, 1997). In 1995/96 the national per capita child and family welfare expenditure was $46, and in Queensland, the lowest spending state, it was $28.[3]

Australia's expenditure on law and order significantly exceeds its expenditure on welfare. In 1995/96 the per capita national expenditure on "law, order and public safety" was $293, including $155 on police, $69 on the administration of justice, and $45 on corrective services. While crime control is a major expenditure by all Australian governments, it is surprising that beyond the level of rhetoric on crime prevention, and beyond the traditional activities of policing and corrections, it has received so little attention. Primary crime prevention has not formed the core part of any government's crime strategy.

A Federal System

In considering the juvenile justice system in Australia, it is important to understand that Australia is a federation of six states and two territories. Police, juvenile justice, and child welfare are the responsibility of the individual states. This means that Australia has eight juvenile justice systems – not one. The criminal law, the courts, the police, juvenile justice legislation, and crime statistics data gathering vary from state to state. Indeed even the answer to the question "Who is a juvenile?" differs between jurisdictions. This chapter is a national overview, together with a more detailed consideration of the states of Queensland and South Australia.

These two jurisdictions have particular interest for demographic and juvenile justice specific reasons. Their legislation, Queensland's *Juvenile Justice Act 1992* and South Australia's *Young Offenders Act 1993,* is the most recently enacted in Australia. Queensland is the fastest growing of the states in terms of economic growth and population, has the second largest indigenous population, and is the most decentralized of the states. On the other hand, South Australia has a low growth rate. Historically, it has been a pioneer in juvenile justice legislation and practice, laying claim to having established the world's first children's court. South Australia was the first Australian jurisdiction that placed family conferencing as a core component of its response to juvenile crime.

Summary

The social conditions of children and young people in Australia have deteriorated in the past two decades, especially for those from socially and economically deprived families. The number of children growing up in poverty has risen dramatically. While young people's participation in education has increased, their access to the labour market has been substantially reduced. On all social indicators young people from disadvantaged backgrounds have been particularly at risk of further social exclusion. The nature and consequences of these deteriorating social conditions have been documented in several government inquiries including the Human Rights and Equal Opportunity Commission's Inquiry into Youth Homelessness (Human Rights and Equal Opportunity Commission, 1989; O'Connor, 1989), the inquiry into the removal of indigenous children from their families ("the so-called stolen children;" Human Rights and Equal Opportunity Commission, 1997), and the Royal Commission into Aboriginal Deaths in Custody (1991/92).

These inquiries have found high levels of youth dislocation, youth disadvantage, and youth marginalization, especially for indigenous children. These factors are consistent with levels of family breakdown, youth homelessness, youth unemployment, and suicide by young people reported above. In Australia these indicators of the deteriorating conditions of a large segment of young people have occurred at the same time as the substantial hardening of community attitudes towards youth crime.

PART II:
TRENDS IN OFFENDING BEHAVIOUR BY JUVENILES

As previously noted, Australia is a federation of six states and two territories. Criminal law, juvenile justice, child welfare, and many other service delivery functions are state responsibilities under Australia's constitution. This results in each state having different criminal laws and juvenile justice systems. Each state publishes different collections of criminal justice statistics. For a number of crimes, such as sexual offences, the variation in offence definition is so significant that it is impossible to even approximate any national pattern.

In this chapter, trends in offending behaviour are briefly examined. First, the limited data on children as victims of crime is considered. Second, the limited data on self-reported offending behaviour is discussed. Third, changes in the reported crimes in Australia (and the two jurisdictions of interest) are noted. Finally, the characteristics of juvenile offenders in South Australia and Queensland will be considered in more detail, allowing consideration of variations in offending associated with age, gender, and ethnicity.

Children as Victims of Crime

In 1995/96, 5% of the 351 victims of homicide in Australia were under 10 years of age, and another 12% were between 11 and 19 years of age. Twenty percent (20%) of victims of sexual assaults were under 10 years of age, and another 6% were between 11 and 19 years of age. The most recent national Crime and Safety Survey (Australian Bureau of Statistics, 1993) found national victimization rates for all offences against the person were substantially higher for persons aged 15-19 years than for any older age group.

Self-Reported Offending Behaviour

There is very limited self-report data on offending by Australian juveniles. There have been a number of small self-report studies. There have been no national studies, and Australia did not participate in the international self-report delinquency study (Junger-Tas, Terlouw, & Klein, 1994). The most recent Australian self-report data on offending were collected in the Sibling Study, a longitudinal study of sibling pairs in Brisbane.

In a sample of 609 school children (12-18 years), more than 20% of the males in the sample reported that in the previous 12 months they had been involved in a range of minor delinquent activities (i.e., unlicensed driving, involved in a group fight, bought alcohol, truanting, avoided paying fares), and more serious activities, including "beat somebody up" (23%) and shoplifting (22%). Between 10% to 20% had engaged in a range of more serious delinquent activities, such as stealing, drug abuse, and property damage. In a broadly based population sample, the fact that 4.5% of the males reported involvement in a break and enter is indicative of the significant involvement of juveniles in offending behaviour. Female involvement was proportionately less than male involvement, but not to the same degree as is evident in court statistics (Ogilive, 1996).

Reported Crime in Australia[4]

In 1995/96, stealing or theft was the most frequent offence reported in Australia (3,259 per 100,000), followed by break and entry or burglary (1,966 per 100,000), and malicious damage to property (1,242 per 100,000). In 1995/96, 60% of all burglary offences were of private homes – resulting in 30 break and enters per 1,000 private homes. In 1995/96, 12 motor vehicles were stolen for every 1,000 registered cars in Australia (Mukherjee, Carcach, & Higgins, 1997). In terms of overall property offences, there was some indication of increases for the 10-year period (1985/86 to 95/96) in some offence categories such as burglary, stealing, and malicious damage.[5] However in the 1990s the burglary rate appeared to have peaked and was declining.

In relation to offences of violence, the murder rate in 1995/96 (1.99 per 100,000) and armed robbery rate (28.9 per 100,000) had remained relatively stable, but there were significant increases in the rates of assault from 1991/92 (36.56 per 100,000) to 1995/96 (51.23 per 100,000) and unarmed robbery assault (from 449 per 100,000 in 1991/92 to 608 per 100,000 in 1995/96).

There is considerable variation across state jurisdictions. In relation to the two jurisdictions of most concern in this chapter, Queensland had slightly lower rates in 1995/96 for all offence categories, and South Australia had higher rates than the national average. These variations may simply reflect recording and counting practices.

The reported crime statistics revealed some evidence of increases in some crimes in Australia. In the 10-year period from 1985/86 to 1995/96, there was clear evidence of increased rates of apprehension of both adult and juvenile offenders, and male and female offenders, for all offence categories.

In this section the pattern of juvenile crime is explored by examining the 1995/96 apprehensions of juveniles in South Australia and Queensland, and by specifically exploring the variations in offending by age, gender, and ethnicity. This section seeks to examine the crimes that result in juvenile court appearances. Unfortunately the reporting rules used in the two jurisdictions are significantly different and therefore rates cannot be directly compared between jurisdictions. In 1995/96, 14,138 cases involving juveniles were dealt with in South Australia (8,802 per 100,000), and in Queensland, there were 32,277 "offenders" proved (9,300 per 100,000).[6] In South Australia, 4,215 matters were dealt with by way of an informal caution (i.e., on the street). Nothing is known about the offences that received an informal caution, although legislatively they must be minor matters. In this section, therefore, discussion of South Australia juvenile offending is based on the 9,923 apprehensions that resulted in some form of formal processing (rate = 6,178 per 100,000).

In both states, juvenile crime was primarily property crime (Table 9.1). In South Australia, 51% of apprehensions were related to property crime and in Queensland, 71% were apprehended for property-related offences.

Table 9.1

Offences by Juveniles: South Australia and Queensland, 1995/96

Offences	South Australia	Queensland	South Australia	Queensland
(n)	9,923	32,277		
	%	%	Rate	Rate
Person				
Total homicide	0.04	0.03	2.49	3.16
Serious assault	1.53	2.69	94.63	249.8
Minor/other assault	7.89	2.14	487.49	198.8
Rape and attempted rape	0.29	0.1	18.05	9.22
Other sexual offences	0.42	0.62	26.14	57.91
Armed robbery	0.42	0.73	26.14	67.71
Unarmed robbery	1.76	0.63	108.95	58.49
Other offences against the person	1.37	0.33	84.67	30.54
Total offences against the person	**13.73**	**7.26**	**848.59**	**675.66**
Property and other offences				
Total breaking and entering	11.29	17.81	697.92	1,656.16
Stealing from shop	10.81	16.08	668.04	1,495.38
Other stealing	6.91	17.4	427.1	1,617.84
Motor vehicle theft	7.82	6.16	483.13	572.8
Fraud	1.44	1.55	89.03	144.35
Handling stolen goods	4.86	1.77	300.09	165.09
Property damage	8.3	12.3	513.01	1,143.58
Drug offences	13.19	9.04	814.97	841.04
Driving offences	1.88	0.9	116.42	84.13
Other public order	19.74	9.72	1,219.66	903.86
Total property and other offences	**86.26**	**92.73**	**5,329.41**	**8,624.27**

The single most common offence for which juveniles were apprehended in Queensland was stealing from shops, and in South Australia, drug offences. Break and enter, property damage, and drug offences were significant offence categories in both states.

It is notable that in both states a significant number of juveniles are apprehended for public order and street offences. The differences in offending patterns are substantially explained by the different counting rules, and the fact that South Australia includes persons of driving age (17-year-old persons) with its juvenile court jurisdiction. The apprehensions data also reflect the fact that in these jurisdictions, as elsewhere, males are far more likely than females to be apprehended for offending. In South Australia, 80% of offenders were male as were 81.5% of offenders in Queensland. Male and female offending patterns vary significantly. In Queensland in 1995/96, 36% of female juvenile offenders were apprehended for stealing from shops compared to 12% of boys (in South Australia, females, 19.9%, males, 8.9%). Males were more likely to commit the more serious property-related offences and serious offences against the person.

The pattern of offending also varies with age. In Queensland, 23% of male offenders aged 12 years or younger were apprehended for shoplifting compared to only 10.9% of 15- and 16-year-olds. Older juvenile males have a higher involvement in drug and good order offences. This pattern is similar for young women.

Ethnicity

A major concern in the Australian juvenile justice system has been the overrepresentation of indigenous young people in the criminal justice system. Other than in South Australia, there is limited longitudinal data on apprehension, but the overrepresentation of indigenous youth in custodial corrections is well documented.

The South Australian apprehension data indicate that Aboriginal youth constituted 2.3% of the state's population and 11.7% of apprehensions. This results in an apprehension rate of indigenous youth in South Australia of 31,342 per 100,000, compared to 4,444 for nonindigenous youth.

In Queensland, there are no data available on police apprehensions. However, 31% of all appearances in courts are by indigenous youth. The rate of juvenile court appearances per 100,000 indigenous children aged 10 to 16 years is 13,099, compared to 1,086 for nonindigenous children.

Summary

There have been significant increases in all crimes in Australia in the past decade, and juvenile involvement in crime has paralleled this increase. While the lack of national figures and the differences in availability of data make cross-state comparisons more difficult, there are some trends of particular interest in the data. Firstly, young people are frequently the victims of crime, as well as being the perpetrators of crime. Secondly, there is evidence of increased rates of apprehension, and presumably involvement in some crimes (e.g., assaults). There is a clear indication that young people's apprehensions for offences of personal violence (assault), drug-related offences, and crimes of property damage (e.g., graffiti) are increasing. Finally, there is significant overrepresentation of indigenous young people apprehended by police.

PART III:
THE JUVENILE JUSTICE SYSTEM IN AUSTRALIA

While attention to the Australian popular media might lead one to think that the problem of juvenile misbehaviour is relatively recent, such concern has been longstanding (O'Connor & Sweetapple, 1988). During the nineteenth century, young people were subject to the same laws, dealt with by the same courts, and subject to the same regime of punishment as adults. For example, Seymour (1988) reports that in 1896 in Victoria, two children aged five and seven years were imprisoned in Pentridge Prison when their parents failed to pay a fine resulting from their children's assault on another child. Despite this long-standing concern, it is only relatively recently that the criminal justice system has specifically and separately addressed the wrongdoings and purported wrongdoings of children and young people.

As in other Western nations, in the late nineteenth and early twentieth centuries, there emerged in each of the Australian states a separate system of laws, courts, and corrections specifically focused on children – a separate system of criminal justice for children. Due to Australia's constitutional arrangements, Australia has eight separate juvenile justice systems. While these systems differ in detail, in most cases the underlying approaches are similar, and all have been through recent transformations. From their origins in the early twentieth century, until the 1970s and 1980s, all Australian juvenile justice systems were modified versions of a welfare model.

By a "welfare model" we refer to a juvenile justice system that assumes that misbehaviour arises from a child's underlying psychosocial problems. The responsibility of the state and the court was thus to rehabilitate individual offenders. By the late 1960s, the scholarly literature and government reports became increasingly dominated by analyses of the failure and injustices of the welfare model. These detailed the harms suffered by children in child welfare and juvenile justice bureaucracies. The criticisms focused on the lack of due process rights, the application of coercive penalties for noncriminal matters, net widening, the failure of rehabilitation, indeterminate sentences and administrative discretion, and the injustices resulting from needs-based sentencing (lack of proportionality and equality of sanction). (See, for example, Australian Law Reform Commission, 1981; Child Welfare Practice and Legislation Review, 1985; O'Connor, 1997.) There were additional critiques of the welfare model that claimed that the courts and the child welfare system were too "soft" on children, allowing children to get away with misbehaviour too easily.

All Australian jurisdictions have now instituted modified versions of the justice model of juvenile justice. While all jurisdictions provide for diversion and determinate sentencing, South Australia has made a major effort to introduce family conferencing as a response to juvenile crime. Despite the use of conferencing as a form of diversion from court, South Australian law remains tied to a justice framework because of its explicit focus on deterrence. The relevant legislation in South Australia is the *Young Offenders Act 1993,* and in Queensland, the *Juvenile Justice Act 1992.* Each Act seeks to strike a balance between protecting the community, punishing the offender, and recognizing the developmental needs of children and young people. In both cases, however, the welfare of young people is framed as a secondary consideration. The primary concern in the Acts is with protecting the community and holding young people accountable. Queensland amended the *Juvenile Justice Act* in 1996 to make this preference explicit.

Summary of Legislation

Children may only be prosecuted for the same crimes as adults. Children can no longer be brought to court for being "uncontrollable" or being "in moral danger," as was once the case. Welfare matters are dealt with through the child protection system.[7] For the purposes of criminal proceedings, South Australia defines a child as a person from 10 to 17 years and Queensland, 10 to 16 years.[8] A child under 10 years cannot be held liable for a crime. All states and territories presume that a child over the age of criminal responsibility and under 14 or 15 is incapable of forming a guilty intention. This presumption is relatively easy to rebut if the prosecution can prove that the accused child has the capacity to know right from wrong.[9]

Police are responsible for the investigation of offences, and in those investigations, children have the same legal rights and protections as adults. In some areas, they have additional rights.

1. *Police questioning.* In any formal police questioning a child must be accompanied by an independent adult. In Queensland and South Australia this is required by legislation. The role of the independent person is not as advocate for the child, but as a presence to ensure that the young person is not overborne. How well this aim of preventing children from being overborne by police is achieved is debatable (O'Connor, 1994).

2. *Right to a lawyer.* South Australia requires by statute that a child has a right to legal advice before the child decides whether to accept a diversionary alternative. Legal representation is available at court by way of a duty lawyer system for children who are charged with offences.

3. *Pre-charge detention.* At common law, police have no power to detain a suspect for questioning prior to arrest and laying of a formal charge. However, in practice most persons, especially youths, "voluntarily"

answer police inquiries. South Australian statute regulates pre-charge detention by allowing police to detain persons suspected of committing certain indictable offences for up to 4 hours (renewable by a court) prior to laying of a charge. Queensland law is silent on this topic, and thus police practices here are essentially unregulated as the fiction of "voluntarily" assisting police with inquires is maintained.

4. *Notification of parents.* Queensland and South Australia both require police to take reasonable steps to notify parents when a child has been arrested. The South Australian legislation requires police to contact an adult nominated by the child when the parent cannot be contacted.

5. *Fingerprinting.* There is generally no restriction on the right of police to fingerprint a child once they have been arrested.

6. *Pre-trial detention.* In both jurisdictions children have the same bail entitlements as adults.

Diversion

In all states police have some discretion in determining the manner in which a matter should be dealt. Legislation in all states gives some preference to diverting first-time and minor offenders from court. The nature and form of diversion varies from state to state.

1. The South Australian *Young Offenders Act* provides for three forms of diversion – informal cautions, formal cautions, and conferences. In relation to minor[10] offences, all police officers are empowered to administer an informal caution. In effect this means that police warn offenders and send them on their way. No formal record of the warning is kept. At the discretion of the police officer, for more serious offences the Act allows the matter to be dealt with more formally by way of a formal caution or a family conference. Formal cautions are administered by a specialist officer, and the Act allows this caution to be administered with or without conditions. The allowable conditions are broad and include an apology, the payment of compensation (administrative limit $5000), and up to 75 hours of community service or any other condition deemed appropriate by the cautioning officer (e.g., curfew, school attendance, and so on). Failure to comply with the conditions can result in the matter being referred to a family conference or court. The formal caution is admissible in any further proceedings while the person is a child, as an aggravating factor in sentencing, but not admissible in adult proceedings.

   The third form of diversion in South Australia is the family conference. Where offenders admit guilt they may be referred by a specialist youth police officer or a magistrate to a family conference. The conference is convened by a Youth Justice Coordinator, an officer of the Youth Court. At a minimum, the conference is constituted by the offending child, the coordinator, and a specialist youth police officer. The Act encourages attendance by victims, parents, and others invited by the coordinator. Conference practice reflects the influence of the restorative justice paradigm pioneered in New Zealand, even though "restorative justice" is not explicitly mentioned in the Act. In the conference, the discussion focuses on the young person's explanation of the circumstances leading to the offence and on the consequences of the offence for those victimized. Conferences seek to facilitate a process whereby the participants agree on a negotiated response to the harm caused by the crime.

The *Young Offenders Act* provides that the conference has wide powers to impose sanctions including apologies, undertakings or conditions, community service (up to 300 hours), and restitution (up to $25,000). A youth's failure to complete the undertakings can result in the matter being returned to court.

2. The Queensland *Juvenile Justice Act* provides for children to be diverted by way of a police caution. The Act also provides for family conferences, but these have only been introduced on a pilot basis in three locations from April 1997. An innovative aspect of the cautioning approach in Queensland that has existed since 1963 is that it is possible for an Aboriginal elder to be involved in a caution when the offender is an Aboriginal. However, it would appear that this involvement rarely occurs.

Court

In cases where children are referred to court rather than diverted, the process of securing the child's appearance in court takes one of three forms. First, in all states a child may be summonsed, or given some form of court attendance notice to attend court at a particular time and date. This means that the child is not processed through the police watch-house. Second, the child may be arrested, charged, and released on bail to appear in court. Third, the child may be arrested, charged, and kept in custody until the matter is determined by the court. The latter option causes difficulties in a large, decentralized country such as Australia because in many parts of the country there are no specialized juvenile detention facilities, meaning that children are kept in police watch-houses with adults for relatively long periods, or if awaiting trial, transferred to juvenile institutions that are long distances from their families.

Children are dealt with in the first instance by a specialized court. South Australia and Queensland have a two-tiered court system. The first tier is presided over by a magistrate who has the jurisdiction to hear and determine a broad range of matters. More serious cases, in terms of the nature of the offence or the likely penalty, are presided over by a judge. Queensland Children's Courts are so named. In South Australia, the jurisdiction is known as the Youth Court.

The distinguishing features of the Children's Court or Youth Court are as follows:

- the court is a closed court and is not open to the public;
- the court operates as a modified court of summary jurisdiction and therefore determines the guilt or innocence of the child and the sentence; and
- the court is restricted in its imposition of penalties by provisions embodied in the juvenile justice legislation.

Dispositions for children differ from those available for adults. The Queensland legislation enshrines a set of sentencing principles, while the South Australian legislation offers direction in the Act's objectives. Both states' laws now give great attention to the punitive and deterrent role of sentencing. Strong statements of preference for noncustodial sentences, which existed in the 1980s legislation, have been watered down.[11]

There are five types of dispositions or sentences in Queensland and South Australia (as in all Australian jurisdictions).

1. *Unsupervised release orders.* In Queensland this includes "reprimand order" and good behaviour bonds, and in South Australia, discharges without penalties.
2. *Fines and other orders.* This includes fines, license disqualification.
3. *Restorative measures.* Both states allow restitution and compensation to be paid to victims in addition to other penalties.
4. *Supervised orders.* South Australia allows courts to impose "obligations," where the failure to perform the obligation can result in the child being charged with the offence of failing to discharge the obligation. Obligations ordered include supervision and attendance at projects or treatment programs. Both South Australia and Queensland provide for community service orders. Queensland has a specific probation order.
5. *Custodial orders.* Both states now empower the courts to order that children be committed to fixed periods of detention in juvenile detention centres or training school centres. Both states also allow the sentence to be suspended, and for the child to undertake an intensely supervised program of activities. In a recent amendment, South Australia provided for the court to directly sentence a child to a period of home detention.

Juvenile Justice Administration

The administration of juvenile justice orders in Australia was traditionally undertaken by the department responsible for child welfare. Working within the ethos of the welfare model, such departments managed community-based and custodial programs.

In recent years there have been changes in this structure of administration. In Queensland, juvenile corrections are administered by the same department as child welfare matters. In South Australia, custodial and community corrections are administered by the Department of Family and Community Services, and family conferences are organized by Youth Justice Coordinators (who are officers of the Youth Court), together with specialist police officers.

Processing of Cases (Diversion), 1995/96

This and the following section examine the processing of cases in the two states in 1995/96. We first consider the proportion of cases that were diverted, before turning to the outcomes for those cases that were processed in courts. The pathways through each system are summarized in separate flow charts for each state (see Figures 9.1 and 9.2).

Diversion – South Australia

Nearly 30% of the 14,138 cases were dealt with by way of an informal caution; 22% resulted in a formal caution, and 10% were referred to a family conference. The remaining 34% were dealt with by a court.[12] There is little data available on informal police cautions.

There were 3,121 formal cautions administered by police. The majority of cautions were for property offences (45.9%), compared to a relatively small proportion of offences against the person (7.5%). Those receiving cautions also tended to be younger, with 42.3% of persons 12 years and younger receiving a formal caution as opposed to 22.3% of persons 15 years and older.

The South Australian approach to cautioning differs from the other states in Australia in that it allows the police officer responsible for the caution to impose penalties by requiring the child to enter into undertakings. Undertakings were imposed in 83.9% of cases. The largest proportion (41.3%) of these undertakings required some form of behavioural outcomes, such as curfews and attending school. In the remainder of cases, 21.5% required an apology, 12% required direct compensation to the victim, and 9% were ordered to do community service.

Family conferences are a major diversionary measure in South Australia, and in 1995/96, 1,587 young people were dealt with in this way. Motor vehicle theft (21.9%) and break and enter (16.3%) were the most frequent offences dealt with by conferences. Between 10% and 20% of property offences were dealt with by conferences, rather than by caution or in court, and nearly 20% of assaults and sexual assaults were dealt with by conferences. Youths attending conferences tended to be younger than those cases disposed of in court, with 23.6% of children 12 years and younger being dealt with by way of a conference, as opposed to 12.8% of youths 15 years and older.

CHAPTER 9 / JUVENILE CRIME AND JUSTICE IN AUSTRALIA

Figure 9.1
Process Model of Crimes in Juvenile Justice in South Australia, 1995/96

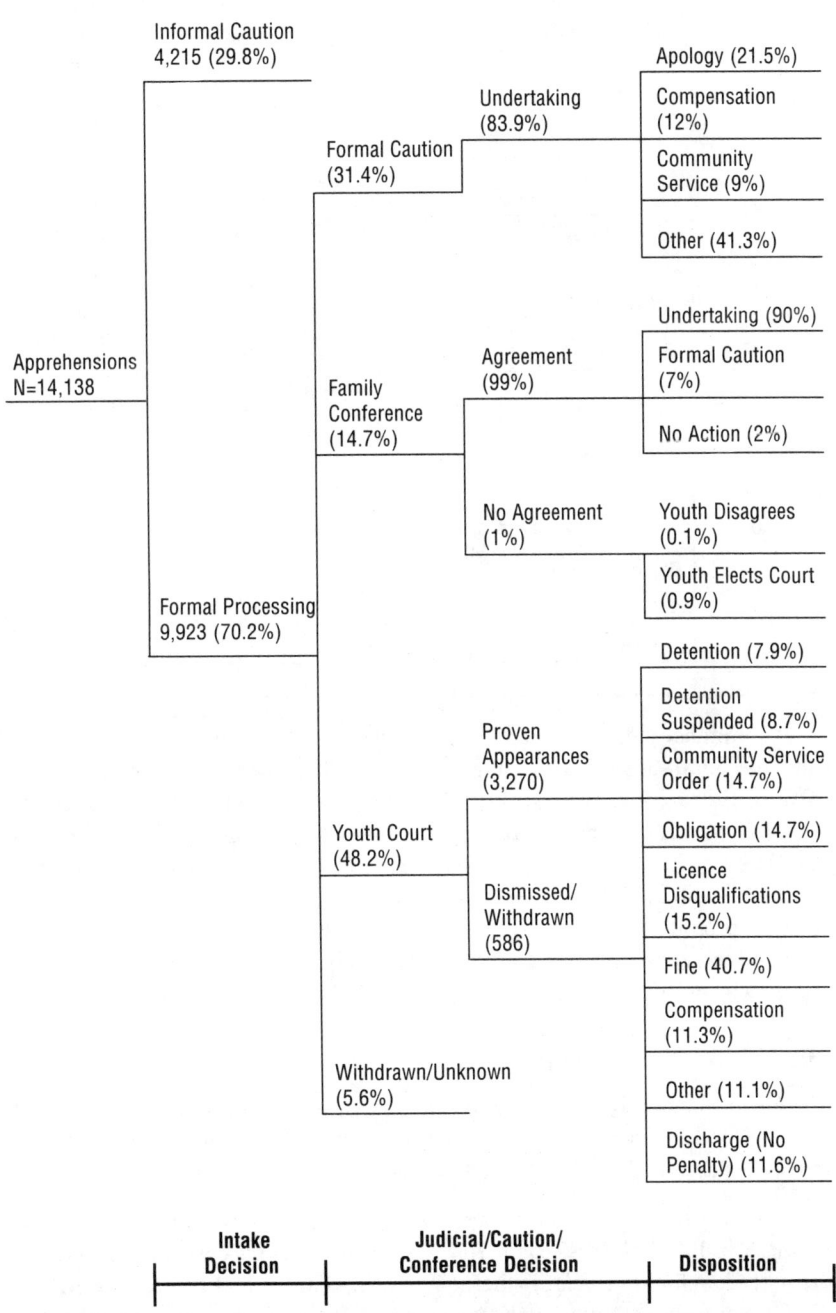

Figure 9.2
Process Model of Crimes in Juvenile Justice in Queensland, 1995/96

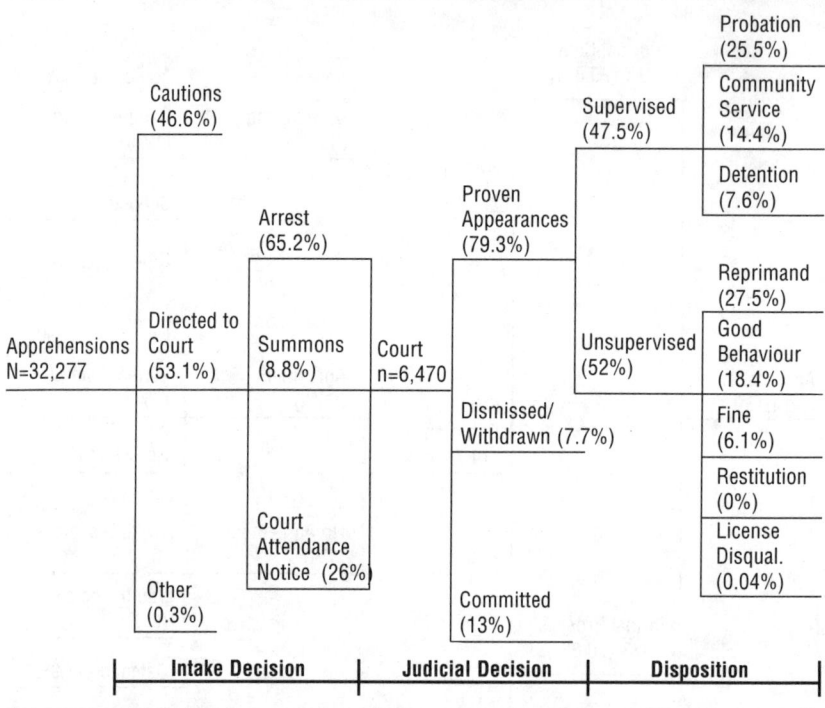

Conferences are empowered with a broad discretion to reach a satisfactory outcome. In all but 16 cases, an agreement was reached in the conference. In 90% of these conferences, the young person entered into some form of undertaking (set of conditions) as an outcome of the conference. Slightly over half the cases involved a formal apology (54.3%), 26% required the payment of restitution, and in 40% of cases, community work[13] was agreed to. While much juvenile offending involves two or more offenders, most conferences (89.3%) involved only one offender. In slightly over half the cases (54.3%) at least one victim was present.

Diversion – Queensland

The Queensland Police Service has operated a cautioning scheme for first and minor offenders since 1963. This scheme is a major response to juvenile crime in Queensland. In 1995/96, 46% of young offenders were cautioned.[14]

Some offences are more likely to result in a caution than others. For example, in 1995/96, 78.8% of offenders stealing from shops were cautioned. On the other hand, motor vehicle theft (22.3%) and break and entry of dwellings (28%) were high volume offences that had lower than average cautioning

CHAPTER 9 / JUVENILE CRIME AND JUSTICE IN AUSTRALIA 239

outcomes, as did offences for violating public orders (6.4%). A greater proportion of females are cautioned than males. In 1995/96, 62.7% of females were cautioned in comparison to 43% of males. This differential cautioning rate largely reflects the fact that most offences for which females are apprehended relate to shoplifting, an offence that has a very high cautioning rate.

Processing of Cases (Court), 1995/96

Table 9.2 details the number of final appearances,[15] proven appearances for most serious offence charged, and proven appearances dealt with by the Children's Court in Queensland at the lower tier of the system and in all Queensland courts, and the Youth Court in South Australia in 1995/96. The South Australian data show the most serious offence charged, as well as the most serious appearance that results in a finding of guilt.

Nearly five and half thousand children made appearances in Queensland before the court in 1995/96; 85% of cases were dealt with summarily by a Children's Court magistrate, and 15% were dealt with by a higher court. The great majority of children pled guilty or were found guilty of the most serious offence charged, with 6% being found not guilty or having the charge withdrawn.

Table 9.2
Appearances, Proven Appearances, Offences, and Rates per 100,000 Children, 1995/96

	Queensland		South Australia	
	Magistrate	All Courts	Most Serious	Penalty
Total appearances	5,487	6,470	3,856	3,856
Total proven appearances	4,323	5,137	3,018	3,270
Dismissed, withdrawn	334	495	838	586
Committed	830	838		
Percent dismissed/withdrawn (%)	6.10	7.70	21.70	15.20
Percent committed (%)	15.10	13.00		
Rates per 100,000 of population of relevant age				
Total appearances	1580.96	1,864.19	2,400.72	2,400.72
Total proven appearances	1,245.58	1,480.12	1,878.99	2,035.88

South Australia had much higher acquittal rates than Queensland. In over a fifth of the South Australia cases, the most serious offence charged was either withdrawn or dismissed. In a small proportion of such cases the person was found guilty of another lesser offence. However, 15% of South Australian cases did not result in a finding of guilt. It is difficult to offer an explanation for this other than that the South Australian police pursue a more aggressive charging policy and/ or that youth in South Australia have better access to legal representation.

With only minor differences in counting appearances, the rate of appearances and proven appearances may be compared across the jurisdictions. It is notable that despite South Australia having developed extensive diversion processes, with significant powers to impose penalties, it has a far higher rate of appearances before court than Queensland.

Outcomes

Because most children who appear before a court admit their guilt or are found guilty, the sentencing role is a major function of the court for the community and the offender (Naffine, Wundersitz, & Gale, 1990). Table 9.3 records the outcomes for finalized appearances in 1995/96.

In both states slightly over half of all appearances concluded with the child being placed on an unsupervised community order (reprimand or a good behaviour order). In Queensland, an increasing proportion of children have been placed under some form of supervised order (from 38% in 1988/89 to 53% in 1996/97). This trend in the use of supervised orders means that more finalized appearances are resulting in the courts imposing a specific penalty, rather than simply warning the child (as with a reprimand).

Table 9.3
Outcome for Appearance: Queensland and South Australia, 1995/96

	Queensland		South Australia	
Proven appearances (n)	5,137		3,270	
	%	Rate per 100,000	%	Rate per 100,000
Supervised order	47.49	703.03	45.96	935.76
Detention	7.65	113.23	7.92	161.25
Detention suspended			8.75	178.06
Community service order	14.35	212.35	14.68	298.84
Probation	25.49	377.44	14.62	297.60
Unsupervised order	52.00	769.59	89.97	1,831.67
Licence disqualification	0.04	0.57	15.20	309.42
Fine	6.08	89.89	40.73	829.29
Compensation/restitution	0.00	0	11.35	230.98
Other			11.07	225.37
Discharge without penalty/reprimand	27.50	407.12	11.62	236.58
Good behaviour bond	18.38	271.99		

Note: 1. Queensland based on most serious appearance and records most serious penalty. South Australia is based on most serious proven offence, but includes all penalties, and therefore totals more than 100%.

2. The population denominators for rates are 10 to 16 years for Queensland and 10 to 17 years for South Australia.

Major differences in sentencing patterns are apparent in the two jurisdictions. In Queensland, 7.7% (395) of proven offences resulted in detention orders for 319 distinct children. Section 176 of the Act allows the court, once having made a detention order, to suspend the sentence and make an immediate release order. Children so released must participate in a specified program of activities. If the child fails to satisfy the conditions of the order, he or she may be brought before the court and the order may be revoked.[16] Over half of these 319 children were released on immediate release orders. In South Australia, in 7.9% of cases a detention order was imposed, and in 8.8%, a suspended detention order resulted. Community service orders were a significant disposition in both states (Queensland, 14.4%; South Australia, 14.7%). South Australia has a higher rate of court-ordered detention than Queensland.

In the category of unsupervised orders, judges in Queensland were far more likely to discharge without penalty (i.e., reprimand) than in South Australia (27.5% vs. 11.6%). South Australian youth were far more likely to leave court with a fine to pay than their Queensland counterparts. The differences in license disqualification rates results from the South Australian jurisdiction including people of age who can hold car licenses.

Recidivism

Although recidivism is a core policy issue in juvenile justice, there is limited empirical data on the topic. The initial evaluation of the implementation of the South Australian *Young Offenders Act* gave some consideration to recidivism. Wundersitz et al. (1996) tracked the official contact that youth had with the juvenile justice system during the 18 months after the implementation of the new Act. They found that 7,162 children were the subject of at least one apprehension report. Nearly two-thirds (65.7%) had only one contact and 16.1% had two contacts. Only 7.9% had five or more contacts with the system. Wundersitz et al. also explored recidivism by examining the survival time before re-offending (within the 18-month study period). They found that, of the 4,706 persons who had been apprehended only once, 69.3% had survived for longer than six months without official police contact, and a further 14.3% had survived for between 3 and 6 months. In contrast, 56% of those with a second police contact had again come to formal notice within three months of the first appearance. Wundersitz et al. also found significant differences for Aboriginal and nonAboriginal youth. One-half (51%) of Aboriginal youth had multiple apprehensions as compared to 32.3% of nonAboriginal youth. There are no data that compare the impact of different dispositions on outcome in South Australia.

Less data on recidivism exists in Queensland. A Queensland study that followed up children who had been cautioned by the police found that, 10 years after the caution, 75% had had no further police contact (Leivesley, 1984). A cohort study of Queensland children found that 66% of children who appeared in court had only one appearance during their childhood years (O'Connor, 1992). Research consistently finds that a small proportion of offenders make multiple appearances and are responsible for a disproportionate amount of offending. The Queensland cohort study found that 1.2% of offenders were responsible for 7.3% of appearances, and 18.8% of offenders were responsible for nearly half of the cohort's appearances. As in South Australia, there are no Queensland data on the impact of particular orders on recidivism.

The most detailed Australian analysis of the relationship between recidivism and juvenile court orders was undertaken by Cain (1996), who examined the criminal histories of the 52,935 children who appeared in New South Wales' courts between 1986 and 1994. He found that 70% of offenders appeared in a children's court only once and that 30% re-offended. On the other hand, 1.6% of offenders were responsible for 9.5% of proven offences. Cain suggests that with 853 recidivists responsible for 8,657 proven criminal appearances, there is clearly a small number of offenders who "substantially drain court and juvenile resources" (Cain, 1996). Cain (1996) also finds that the harsher the initial penalty, the more likely the individual was to re-offend. Specifically, Cain (1996) found that

> for each step up the sentencing ladder there is a corresponding jump in the level of reoffending of juveniles given such orders. Noticeably this relationship exists *even* when differences in the nature of the offence committed and other factors associated with recidivism are accounted for, either statistically, or by comparing matched groups of juvenile offenders.

Juvenile Justice in Australia

The 1980s saw the widespread belief that the introduction of the justice model would remedy the problems of juvenile crime and the inequities in the juvenile justice system. However, because of flaws in the understanding of juvenile crime that underpin the justice model, it was inevitable that problems would emerge in the attempted legislative solutions to juvenile crime (O'Connor, 1997). In this section we discuss four major issues: (1) the overrepresentation of Aboriginal and Torres Strait Islander (ATSI) youth in the system, (2) the introduction of restorative justice approaches, (3) police-youth conflict, and (4) the impact of drugs.

The Overrepresentation of ATSI Youth

The overrepresentation of indigenous youth in the juvenile justice system is a cause of major concern to indigenous people, governments, and juvenile justice administrators. According to all social indicators (housing, income, health, and so on), the indigenous peoples of Australia are the most disadvantaged group in Australian society. They have suffered two centuries of cultural, economic and political domination, a concerted effort to destroy their culture, and the dispossession of much of their land (Cunneen, 1997b; Human Rights and Equal Opportunity Commission, 1997).

While the rate of incarceration of juveniles in Australia has dropped, it appears that Aboriginal and Torres Strait Islander youth have not benefited from the development of diversionary measures. The overrepresentation of ATSI young people in the juvenile justice system was highlighted as a major social problem by the Royal Commission into Aboriginal Deaths in Custody. The Commission concluded that an understanding of the disadvantage experienced by Aboriginals in Australia is critical to understanding the reasons for offending. The nature of the criminal justice system and the manner in which criminality is constructed affect relative rates of involvement in the juvenile justice system. "The exercising of the ideal of impartial justice is necessarily accompanied by the values of those who enforce the 'rule of law'" (1991/92, v.2, p. 275).

The Commission concluded that "young Aboriginals are unnecessarily, or deliberately made the subject of trivial charges or multiple charges, with the result that the appearance of a serious criminal record is built up at an early age" (1991, v.2, p. 275). Racial discrimination, poor relations between police and Aboriginal youth, and the reliance of Aboriginal youth on public space for recreation increase the likelihood of their having adverse contact with the police (see White, 1990; Youth Justice Coalition, 1990). Early and extended contact with the juvenile justice system is a predictor of adult involvement in the criminal justice system (see Royal Commission into Aboriginal Deaths, 1991/92; see also O'Connor, 1993, 1994).

The level of overrepresentation and the process of its amplification is evident in the Queensland juvenile justice system. In 1995/96, a third (31.8%) of all final proven appearances of juveniles in Queensland courts were Aboriginal and Torres Strait Islander children. Aboriginal children constitute only 3.6% of the persons aged from 10 to 16 years in Queensland.

Aboriginal and Torres Strait Islander and nonATSI children appeared before court for similar reasons – though a slightly smaller proportion of Aboriginal and Torres Strait Islander children appeared on theft and break and enter offences than other children. Conversely, the rate of assault offences was slightly higher for ATSI children.

Of those found guilty by the courts, Aboriginal children accounted for a smaller proportion of those who were reprimanded (24.9%), fined (18.5%), and placed on good behaviour orders (24.6%). That is, while a third of all appearances involved Aboriginal and Torres Strait Islander children, only about one-quarter of all children reprimanded or fined were Aboriginal and Torres Strait Islanders.

In contrast, at the higher end of the sentencing tariffs (that is, those penalties that involve deeper penetration of the criminal justice system), Aboriginal and

Torres Strait Islander children accounted for 40.6% of community service orders and 53% of detention orders. In South Australia in 1995/96, while Aboriginal youth constituted 2.3% of the youth population, they comprised 11.7% of all appearances, 14.7% of those receiving community service orders, and 11.3% of those receiving detention orders.

For nonATSI children, on the other hand, the data for Queensland shows that while they comprised 96.4% of the total population aged 10-16 years, they constituted 68.2% of all finalized proven court appearances, 75% of all reprimands, 78.5% of fines, 75.4% of good behaviour orders, 59.4% of community service orders, and 46.8% of detention orders.

The overrepresentation of Aboriginal children is starkest when the Queensland data on distinct children's appearances before courts are examined (as opposed to the appearance data discussed above). During 1995/96, for every 1,000 Aboriginal and Torres Strait Islander children in Queensland aged 10 to 17 years, 68.7 made at least one appearance before a court. In contrast, only 7.2 in 1,000 nonATSI children appeared before a court. That is, Aboriginal and Torres Strait Islander children were nearly 10 times more likely to appear in court. The extent of the overrepresentation of ATSI youth is magnified as children progress through the scale of tariffs. Aboriginal children are 26 times more likely to receive a detention order. This pattern of overrepresentation of ATSI children in the system has remained relatively stable over recent years, despite the report of the Royal Commission into Aboriginal Deaths in Custody and numerous other reports.

There is also a tendency for ATSI children to come into the system at an earlier age. For example, in Queensland, 69% of children aged 12 and under who were admitted to supervised orders were Aboriginal and Torres Strait Islanders, as were 50% of 13- and 14-year-olds. For detention orders, the situation was worse: all children 12 and under in detention were ATSI as were 81% of those aged 13 and 14 years. This grim picture is parallelled in South Australia. Research consistently demonstrates that earlier entry into the juvenile justice system, and particularly into detention centres, is a predictor of longer term contact with the criminal justice system.

The involvement of Aboriginal and Torres Strait Islander youth in the juvenile justice system is a major social problem. It precipitates the likelihood of long-term involvement in the adult criminal justice system, and causes much social disruption in their communities of residence. Problems of social order, of the relationship between juveniles, their community, and the broader society, are increasingly being defined as the responsibility of the criminal justice system. In relation to children, this is both costly and socially and politically destructive. The criminalization of juvenile misbehaviour results in the imposition of external controls and solutions. A better approach would be to support the development of local and community-based solutions. The imposition of external solutions destroys traditional modes of social control, and as a consequence, gives rise to problems that result in children coming into contact with the welfare and juvenile justice systems.

The Impact of Restorative Justice

The introduction of the justice model neither successfully addressed concerns about the general ineffectiveness of the juvenile justice system nor potential abuses of power in the justice system. Nor did the adoption of the justice model adequately respond to public concern about juvenile crime and the perceived lack of a "tough" response. Appealing to the forces of both the political left and right, there is a now increasing interest in Australia in the idea of restorative justice. This development is strongly influenced by New Zealand's *Children's, Young Persons and Their Families Act 1989* and John Braithwaite's theory of reintegrative shaming (Braithwaite, 1989). A restorative justice approach potentially marks a departure from the orthodoxy of the justice and welfare models. The New Zealand approach to juvenile justice sought specifically to avoid the pitfalls of the justice and welfare models by

- responding to the overrepresentation of poor, working-class and Maori children in the juvenile justice system;
- recognizing the needs of victims of crime;
- minimizing reliance on criminal prosecution and fostering diversionary measures to resolve crime;
- strengthening the role of family and the traditional family group for Maori children; and
- protecting children during police investigations.

In a New Zealand family group conference, the young person is encouraged to take responsibility for the offence and to make efforts to restore the harm. Family groups support the young offender (and perhaps also the victims). A coordinator runs the conference, where a police officer is also present.

In South Australia and New Zealand, the family conference represents an attempt to bring together all the parties who have been affected by an offence: the offender, his or her parents, the victim, and his or her supporters. The aim of the conference is, through a process of negotiation, to identify the damage (financial and emotional) caused by the offence and to determine an appropriate outcome – that is, to reach a negotiated solution to resolve the harm caused by the crime. It is theoretically a process that directly addresses the experience of both victim and offender and that transfers the ownership of the problem from the state to the individuals involved. Rather than conceptualizing offending behaviour as a problem solely for the state, it recognizes the participants affected by the offending and provides a radically different way of resolving harm in the criminal justice system. It may be particularly appropriate for juveniles because much of their offending occurs in their local community and deeply affects the offenders' families. It can provide an environment in which the behaviour, not the individual, can be identified as problematic and condemned, and where the individual offender can remedy the harm. It personalizes both the victim and offender, that is, the victim becomes a real person to the child, and the real harm suffered by the victim is also apparent to the child. Similarly, the child offender becomes a real person to the victim. So, rather than being the thug seen on the television news, it is the child down the road with all of his or her strengths and weaknesses. The conference process and the completion of the conference agreement provide a symbolic and actual process of reintegration and reconciliation between the offender, the victim, and community. Rather than stigmatizing the offender, it can provide a pathway to reintegration.

There is a growing literature on restorative justice and family conferencing in Australia and New Zealand (see, e.g., Alder & Wundersitz, 1994; Bargen, 1996; Blagg, 1997; Braithwaite & Daly, 1994; Braithwaite & Mugford, 1994; Cunneen, 1997b; Daly, 1996; Hudson et al., 1996; Morris & Maxwell, 1993). With the exception of an empirical study of conferencing in New Zealand (Morris & Maxwell, 1993) and several preliminary studies of conferencing in the Australian Capital Territory and South Australia (Daly, 1996; Sherman & Braithwaite, 1997; Wundersitz, 1997), there is scant empirical evidence on how conferences work in practice and their impact on the participants. The bulk of the literature has focused on debates between those who advocate conferencing and those who see its many problems. Some polarization occurred in the early 1990s when "Wagga-style" conferencing began to take hold in Australia. This model of conferencing, which has since been marketed to jurisdictions in the U.S., Canada, England, and elsewhere, was first used in the city of Wagga Wagga (New South Wales) in 1990. It was a form of "caution plus," where a police officer ran the conference. Early critiques of conferencing challenged the wisdom of empowering the police to run conferences.

Several areas of critique were consolidated during the 1990s. Some questioned whether a young person's legal rights were given adequate consideration (Warner, 1994). Others noted problems in using the conferencing strategy for Aboriginal youth (Blagg, 1997) and for some offences involving females as victims (Stubbs, 1995). Still others identified a range of problems, including net widening, the plausibility of the idea of "reintegrative shaming" within an organizationally stigmatizing criminal justice environment, and overemphasis on *individual* young offenders while ignoring wider social problems such as inequality and social vulnerability (Polk, 1994). Two major studies of conferencing are currently underway that will address these and other questions, one in the Capital Territory (RISE or Reintegrative Shaming Experiment) and the other in South Australia (for South Australia Juvenile Justice – Research on Conferencing). The progress of these studies is recorded on the web site of the Australian Institute of Criminology (www.aic.gov.au).

Police-Youth Conflict

Police are at the front end of the juvenile justice system. They have many contacts with youth, only a relatively small portion of which result in a child being apprehended for an offence. Police and young people both occupy public spaces, such as streets, entertainment venues, shops and so forth. Conflict arises between police and youth over the use of this space. The very presence of youth on the streets can be a cause of concern for the police. The targeting of youth as potential criminals undermines amicable relations between police and young people, and in consequence, respect for the law.

There is evidence in Australia that the relationship between police and youth is problematic. O'Connor and Sweetapple (1988) found that the interactions between police and youth were permeated by psychological, and sometimes physical, intimidation. Cunneen (1997a) found evidence of Aboriginal youth detained in Queensland having been subject to police violence. White (1990), the Youth Justice Coalition (1990), and Alder et al. (1992) document the poor state of police-youth relations in Western Australia, South Australia, New South Wales, Queensland, and Victoria.

Formal complaint systems respond to individual complaints. Where particular groups (e.g., youth, disadvantaged people) are reluctant to come forward, complaint mechanisms do not ensure the necessary accountability (see O'Connor, 1995). The mistreatment of youth is rarely reported by youth because of fear of retaliation by police, and because youth do not think that they will be believed.

The relationship between the police and young people is a matter of ongoing concern for the juvenile justice system. For most young people, the police will be the only point of contact with the criminal justice system. The nature of police interactions with young people can either elevate or suppress the rate of young people's formal involvement with the justice system. The Australian data reported in this chapter evidence relatively high rates of apprehension of youth for street-related offences. Police-youth relationships should be subject to increased scrutiny as jurisdictions are moving to the point where police may directly impose the penalty, as with cautioning in South Australia, or endorse the penalty, as with South Australian conferences.

The Impact of Drugs

The last 20 years have witnessed the increased penetration of drugs into the daily lives of many young people. Many young people now enter the criminal justice system as a result of being charged with a drug-related offence (see previous sections). The actual use of drugs is far higher than the rate of apprehension, as is evidenced from the self-report data presented above. This self-report data found that 18% of the school sample had used cannabis in the previous 12 months, 7% had abused prescription medication, and 2.5% had used ecstasy, acid, or speed. The rates in the at-risk and offending samples were far higher.

The increased penetration of drugs into the daily lives of young people has increased the risk of associated crime. The available Australian research continues to evidence drug and alcohol abuse as both a motivator for crime (e.g., burglaries as a source of stolen property to be exchanged directly or indirectly for drugs), and as a disinhibiting agent present at the time of the offending behaviour. The most recent Australian study of 247 juveniles in detention in New South Wales found that 30% of those detained for break and enter, and 16% of those detained for shop stealing claimed that the crime was committed to obtain money for drugs (Copeland & Howard, 1997). A second study of youth in detention found that "across all offence categories, 54% of males and 64% of females were drunk at the time of the offence. In addition, 45% of males and 59% of females reported that their current crime was committed to obtain money for alcohol or other drugs" (Copeland & Howard, 1997). Appropriate responses to juvenile offending therefore need to take account of the impact of substance abuse problems.

Conclusion

There is a growing tension in the Australian juvenile justice system. During the 1970s and 1980s, most attention was invested in re-writing juvenile justice legislation to accord with justice model principles and, at an administrative level, reducing the number of juveniles in detention. The implicit belief was that the justice model provided a legislative solution to the problem of juvenile crime. The major concern was to avoid net widening, which is a common criticism of cautioning, conforming, and other diversion programs. The noble aim of keeping children out of the juvenile justice system, of keeping welfare and criminal justice issues separate, at times became an expression of the edict "the less done the better." The focus of the system was gate-keeping and the administration of court-ordered penalties. The development of programs that responded to the needs of offenders was not a prominent policy concern. Thus effort was invested in ensuring that custodial and community-based programs were only for the serious and repeat offenders. This focus on repeat offenders, while ignoring their social context and the processes of law enforcement, in part explains why Aboriginal (and other disadvantaged youth) are so overrepresented in detention centres.

The lack of attention to the social context of juvenile crime has also resulted in major changes in those social circumstances not being fully taken into account in the development of juvenile justice programs. In the same period as the justice model emerged in Australia, the youth labour market collapsed. For many poor and disadvantaged young people, the transition from school to work has been disrupted. Those young people who are least likely to continue in post-compulsory education, and who are most likely to be unemployed, are the poor and disadvantaged – the very same young people who are most likely to have contact with the criminal justice system. For many of these young people, the pro-social effects of employment are no longer available. Yet employment has been one of the key socialization processes in the transition from childhood to adulthood.

The justice system has eschewed the welfare model's focus on the needs of the child and the often harsh coercive responses to those needs. However, many of the needs were real, even while the responses were inappropriate. Lack of income, homelessness, abuse, exploitation, and drug abuse all have detrimental effects on children. To ignore their association with crime is to engage in the process of victim blaming. The social circumstances of youth in the last two decades in Australia have worsened substantially as the pendulum has swung towards holding children totally accountable for the behaviour.

Finally, tensions in juvenile justice administration have resulted from a loss of community confidence in the system. In Australia, crime, and juvenile crime in particular, makes good "bad news." Community concern and moral panic are whipped up by the media and politicians who seek to make capital out of the problem. On the other hand, the push to minimize intervention and to exclude the victims from the equation means that the media frenzy actually resonates with the ordinary person. This is particularly the case with juvenile crime, much of which is committed locally and has high nuisance effect, even if the value of property is low. The push simply to characterize and excuse offenders as "disadvantaged youth" ignores the fact that many of their victims are also disadvantaged.

It is in this light that the move to a restorative approach to justice may offer much to the development of an effective juvenile justice system by potentially building community confidence in that system. Within social justice legislative parameters it can locate some of the solutions to the problem of juvenile crime at a local level.

References

Alder, C., O'Connor, I., Warner, K., & White, R. (1992). *Perceptions of the treatment of juveniles in the legal system.* Report to the National Youth Affairs Research Scheme: Hobart: National Clearinghouse for Youth Studies, University of Tasmania.

Alder, C., & Wundersitz, J. (Eds.). (1994). *Family conferencing and juvenile justice.* Canberra: Australian Institute of Criminology.

Australian Bureau of Statistics. (1993). *Crime and safety, Australia.* Cat no. 4509.0.

Australian Bureau of Statistics. (1996a). *Census.*

Australian Bureau of Statistics. (1996b). *Projection of the populations of Australian States and Territories.* Cat no. 3222.0.

Australian Bureau of Statistics. (1996c). *Regional population growth.* Cat no. 3218.0.

Australian Bureau of Statistics. (1997a). *Demographic statistics.* Cat no. 3101.0.

Australian Bureau of Statistics. (1997b). *Labour force.* Cat no. 6203.0.

Australian Law Reform Commission. (1981). *Child welfare.* Canberra: AGPS.

Australian Institute of Health and Welfare. (1997). *Australia's welfare.* Canberra: AGPS.

Bargen, J. (1996). Kids, cops, courts, conferencing and children's rights: A note on perspectives. *Australian Journal of Human Rights* 2 (2): 209-228.

Birrell, B., & Rapson, V. (1997). Poor families, poor children: Who cares for the next generation. *People and Place* 5 (3): 44-53.

Blagg, H. (1997). A just measure of shame? Aboriginal youth and conferencing in Australia. *British Journal of Criminology.*

Braithwaite, J. (1989). *Crime, shame and reintegration.* Sydney: Cambridge University Press.

Braithwaite, J., & Daly, K. (1994). Masculinities, violence and communitarian control. In T. Newburn and E. Stanko (Eds.), *Just boys doing business?* (pp. 189-231). London: Routledge.

Braithwaite, J., & Mugford, S. (1994). Conditions of successful reintegration ceremonies: Dealing with juvenile offenders. *British Journal of Criminology* 34 (2): 139-171.

Cain, M. (1996). *Recidivism of juvenile offenders.* Sydney: Department of Juvenile Justice.

Child Welfare Practice and Legislation Review. (1985). *Equity and social justice for children, families and communities.* Melbourne: Government Printer.

Commonwealth Grants Commission. (1997). *Report on general revenue grant relativities.* Canberra: AGPS.

Copeland, J. & Howard, J. (1997). Substance abuse and juvenile crime. In A. Borowski & I. O'Connor (Eds.), *Juvenile crime, justice and corrections.* Melbourne: Longman.

Cunneen, C. (1997a). Indigenous young people and juvenile crime. In A. Borowski & I. O'Connor (Eds.), *Juvenile crime, justice and corrections.* Melbourne: Longman.

Cunneen, C. (1997b). Community conferences and the fiction of indigenous control. *Australian and New Zealand Journal of Criminology* 30 (3): 292-311.

Daly, K. (1996). *Diversionary conferences in Australia: A reply to the optimists and skeptics.* Paper given to the American Society of Criminology, Annual Meeting, November, Chicago.

Graycar, A., & Jamrozik, A. (1993). *How Australians live: Social policy in theory and practice.* MacMillan: Melbourne.

Gregory, B., & Sheehan, P. (1998). Poverty and the collapse of full employment. In J. Fincher & J. Nieuwenhuysen (Eds.), *Australian poverty: Then and now* (pp. 103-126). Melbourne: Melbourne University Press.

Hudson, J., Morris, A., Maxwell, G., & Galaway, B. (Eds.). (1996). *Family group conferences: Perspective on policy and practice.* Monsey NY: Willow Tree Press.

Human Rights and Equal Opportunity Commission. (1989). *Our homeless children.* AGPS: Canberra.

Human Rights and Equal Opportunity Commission. (1997). *Bringing them home: Report of the national inquiry into the separation of Aboriginal and Torres Strait Islander children from their families.* Sydney: Human Rights and Equal Opportunity Commission.

Junger-Tas, J., Terlouw, G., & Klein, M.W. (1994). *Delinquent behavior among young people in the western world: First results of the international self-report delinquency study.* New York: Kugler Publications.

Juvenile Justice Advisory Committee. (1996). *Annual report for year ended 30th June 1996.* Adelaide: Juvenile Justice Advisory Committee.

Leivesley, S. (1984). *Juvenile Aid Bureau: An evaluation of police work with juveniles, 1970-1983.* Brisbane: Queensland Police Department.

Maxwell, G. M., & Morris, A. (1993). *Families, victims and culture: Youth justice in New Zealand.* Social Policy Agency and Victoria University of Wellington.

Morris, A., & Maxwell, G. (1993). Juvenile justice in New Zealand: A new paradigm. *Australian and New Zealand Journal of Criminology* 26: 72-90.

Mukherjee, S., Carcach, C., & Higgins K. (1997). *Juvenile crime and justice.* Canberra: Australian Institute of Criminology.

Naffine, N., Wundersitz, J., & Gale, F. (1990). Back to justice for juveniles: The rhetoric and reality of law reform. *Australian and New Zealand Journal of Criminology* 23 (3): 192-205.

O'Connor, I. (1989). *Our homeless children: Their experiences.* Sydney: Human Rights and Equal Opportunity Commission.

O'Connor, I. (1992). *Youth crime and justice in Queensland: An information and issues paper.* Brisbane: Criminal Justice Commission.

O'Connor, I. (1993). Aboriginal child welfare law, policy and practice. *Australian Social Work* 46 (3): 11-22.

O'Connor, I. (1994). Young people and their rights. In R. White & C. Alder (Eds.), *The police and young people* (pp. 76-101). Cambridge: Cambridge University Press.

O'Connor, I. (1995). *Children, crime and justice in Queensland: An information and issues paper.* Brisbane: Criminal Justice Commission.

O'Connor, I. (1997). Models of juvenile justice. In A. Borowski & I. O'Connor (Eds.), *Juvenile crime, justice and corrections.* Melbourne: Longman.

O'Connor, I., & Sweetapple, P. (1988). *Children in justice.* Melbourne: Longman.

Ogilive, E. (1996). Masculine obsessions: an examination of criminology and gender. *Australian and New Zealand Journal of Criminology* 29 (3): 205-226.

Polk, K. (1994). Family conferencing: theoretical and evaluative concerns. In C. Alder & J. Wundersitz (Eds.), *Family conferencing and juvenile justice.* Canberra: Australian Institute of Criminology.

Royal Commission into Aboriginal Deaths in Custody. (1991/92). *National report.* Canberra: AGPS.

Seymour, J. (1988). *Dealing with juvenile offenders.* North Ryde, Sydney: Law Book Co.

Sherman, L., & Braithwaite, J. (1997). *RISE working papers #1 - #4: A series of reports on research in progress on the reintegrative shaming experiment.* (RISE) for Restorative Community Policing. Canberra: Australian National University.

Stubbs, J. (1995). Communitarian conferencing and violence against women: A cautionary note. In M. Valverde, L. MacLeon, & K. Johnson (Eds.), *Wife assault and the Canadian criminal justice system* (pp. 260-289). Toronto: Centre of Criminology, University of Toronto.

Warner, K. (1994). The rights of the offender in family conferences. In C. Alder & J. Wundersitz (Eds.), *Family conferencing and juvenile justice* (pp. 141-152). Canberra: Australian Institute of Criminology.

White, R. (1990). *No space of their own: Young people and social control in Australia.* Cambridge: Cambridge University Press.

Wundersitz, J. (1997). Pre-court diversion: The Australian experience. In A. Borowski & I. O'Connor (Eds.), *Juvenile crime, justice and corrections.* Melbourne: Longman.

Wundersitz, J., Doherty, J., Gardner, J., & Mannik, M. (1996). *The South Australian juvenile justice system: A review of its operation.* Adelaide: Office of Crime Statistics.

Youth Justice Coalition. (1990). *Kids in justice.* Sydney: Youth Justice Coalition.

Zelinka, S. (1995). Ethnic minority young people in Australia. In C. Guerra & R. White (Eds.), *Ethnic minority young people in Australia.* Hobart: National Clearinghouse for Youth Studies.

Notes

1   Australia's secondary school retention rates peaked in 1992/93 and have declined since that date.

2   Welfare services are defined as assistance to individuals with special needs, which have been categorized into (1) family and child welfare services, (2) welfare services for the aged and disabled and (3) other, which includes a range of targeted programs such as assistance to migrants and prisoner's aid (Australian Institute of Health and Welfare, 1997, p. 19). Family and child welfare includes the provision of childcare services.

3   In contrast to Queensland, South Australia, the other jurisdiction of particular focus in this chapter was a relatively high spending state: 1995/96, Total Welfare, $210; Family and Child Welfare, $53.

4   This section reports recorded crime rates for selected crimes in Australia over a 10-year period. However there is considerable variation in the definition of crimes and crime statistics systems between states. The data in this section have been collected by the Australian Institute of Criminology from reports by State Police Services. Thus this time series can only be regarded as indicative of crime trends, rather than definitive. A detailed table is available from the authors.

5   Much of the increase in malicious damage is accounted for by graffiti by "spray can artists."

6   The reporting rules for South Australia and Queensland differ substantially. In South Australia the counting unit for informal cautions is the "ancillary report." "There could be more than one offence per informal caution, but not more than one offender" (Juvenile Justice Advisory Committee, 1996, p. i.). The remaining matters are counted on the basis of apprehension reports. "If a police officer is aware that a young person has allegedly stole from 3 shops on the same day, one apprehension report containing 3 counts of theft will be submitted. Similarly, if a youth has allegedly committed three break and enters over three months, and the apprehending officer becomes aware of them on the same date, they will recorded in the one apprehension report" (Juvenile Justice Advisory Committee, 1996, p. i.). The Queensland figures are based on the Queensland Police Services offender count. (See Queensland Police Service, Statistical Review, for counting rules used in the collection and collation of crime statistics.) The offender count involves the number of offenders involved in a specific offence. One offence involving three juveniles would be counted as one cleared offence and three offenders; one juvenile apprehended for 10 break and enters would be counted as 10 offences and 10 offenders.

7   However, New South Wales has provided police with the power to enforce a juvenile curfew by removing children from the streets and returning them to their parents or a place of safety if they are out unsupervised at night.

8   Tasmania sets the lower age at seven years and the Australian Capital Territory has a minimum age of eight years.

9   This may be simply achieved by asking the child, for example, "Did you know it was wrong to steal the lollies from the shop?"

10 " 'Minor offence' means an offence to which this Act applies that should, in the opinion of the police officer in charge of the investigation of the offence, be dealt with as a minor offence because of the limited extent of the harm caused through the commission of the offence, the character and antecedents of the alleged offender, the improbability of the youth re-offending and, where relevant, the attitude of the youth's parents or guardians."

11 Two Australian jurisdictions have moved to mandatory custodial sentences. The Northern Territory and Western Australia has developed a variant of the American "three strikes and you're out" laws.

12 The outcome for 4% of cases was unknown.

13 51.1% involved 20 hours or less than.

14 Data supplied by the Queensland Police Service for this and previous papers (O'Connor, 1995) indicate a decreasing preference for diversion. In 1991/92, 46.5% of offenders were cautioned, in 1992/93, 46.3% were cautioned and in 1993/94, 55.1% of juvenile offenders were cautioned, rather than referred to court.

15 A final appearance refers to the occasion on which the outcome for the matter, or matters, is determined. An individual child's final appearance may involve one or more offence. A child who is charged on a number of separate occasions in a year for a number of separate matters that are determined on different dates will be recorded as making the relevant number of final appearances in that year. An offence refers to a separate offence.

16 There has been a considerable increase in the number of distinct children placed under detention orders (136 in 93/94).

CHAPTER 10

Conclusion: Trends in Juvenile Justice

Nicholas Bala, Joseph P. Hornick, and Howard N. Snyder

This book presents case studies of the juvenile justice systems of the world's major, predominately English-speaking countries. These case studies describe the relationship between the political, social, and economic context and the social and legal responses to youth crime.

Examining the experiences of the different jurisdictions allows for the identification of common problems and themes, as well as providing a better understanding of the strengths and weaknesses of the juvenile justice systems in each jurisdiction. This material can help policy makers, juvenile justice professionals, and members of the academic community consider a wider range of responses to youth offending and help them determine which strategies are likely to be an effective and efficient response to youth crime in their particular jurisdiction.

While there is great value in comparative study, making international comparisons poses considerable challenges. As many researchers engaging in cross-cultural study have found, concepts do not always translate well across national borders. Despite sharing a language and a common legal heritage, the countries in this study have legal systems that differ significantly, and they have adopted quite different policies for dealing with young offenders. There are major differences in the countries in this study in basic legal approaches and concepts. There is also wide variation in the types of statistical data available about juvenile offenders from police, juvenile courts, and youth corrections. In each country, criminologists, sociologists, psychologists, legal scholars, and policy analysts have undertaken research to better understand youth crime and the effectiveness of the responses to it in their country, but these researchers have often studied very different questions.

Nicholas Bala is a Professor of Law at Queen's University in Kingston, Ontario, Canada, who concentrates his research in the area of family and children's law.

Joseph P. Hornick is Executive Director of the Canadian Research Institute for Law and the Family, Alberta, Canada.

Howard N. Snyder is the Director of Systems Research for the National Center for Juvenile Justice in Pittsburgh, Pennsylvania, USA.

Despite the challenges involved in making international comparisons, this chapter identifies the major trends in youth crime and the development of societal responses to youth crime. Because of the incompatibility of concepts and data, the focus is more on the identification of broad themes and unique innovations rather than on detailed, direct comparisons.[1]

Profiles of Jurisdictions

The attitudes and approaches to juvenile justice in each of the jurisdictions can be properly understood only in the context of broader demographic, social, political, and economic conditions in each country. Accordingly, each chapter begins with a description of the conditions in that country, with a particular focus on policies and data concerning children and youth. There are some broad patterns of demographic and social change that are closely related to some important similarities and differences in approaches to the administration of youth justice.

Demographic Change

Each of the countries in this study has experienced significant demographic change in the past few decades. With the exception of Northern Ireland, in all of the countries populations are aging and, until recently, the number of adolescents was declining.

The most important demographic trend experienced in most of the countries in this study has been the changing age composition of the population. In the period following the Second World War, from 1946 to about 1965, most of the countries experienced a "Baby Boom" as returning servicemen married and started families. This was followed by the "Baby Bust" in the following period, from 1965 to 1980, with fewer children being born. Beginning in about 1980, the Baby Boomers began to have their own children. Demographers call these children the "Echo Generation." Although female fertility rates and average family size were substantially lower in the 1980s than after the Second World War, the number of births increased through the 1980s, peaking in about 1990. The increase in adolescent populations resulting from the Echo Generation has made youth justice a growing public policy concern in the 1990s, and the adolescent population will peak in the first decade of the millennium.

At the same time as experiencing the effects of demographic waves caused by the Depression and Second World War, all countries in this study experienced a general decline in birth rates over the past century due to a combination of improved birth control, urbanization, increased costs of child rearing, and changing social attitudes.

However, birth rates have remained relatively high among indigenous peoples and in some racial minority groups. In addition to high birth rates among some minority groups, most of the countries in this study have experienced significant increases in immigration by members of visible minority groups, compounding the growth of minority populations. This combination of immigration and high relative birth rates has meant that countries with populations that were formerly quite ethnically homogenous (with most people of European descent) are becoming increasingly racially diverse and that this diversity is represented disproportionately in their youth.

As the populations of these countries age, youth populations are increasingly racially different from the politically and economically powerful adults, and the typical alienation of youth, which arises from the biological and social changes associated with this stage of development, may be compounded by cultural and racial alienation. It is thus not surprising that there seems to be a significant increase in anti-youth sentiment and rhetoric.

These racial minority groups have tended to concentrate in urban areas and are of disproportionately lower income. Minority parents often have lower educational levels than the general population, and in the case of immigrant families, may be experiencing social, cultural, and economic dislocation. These factors are linked to the overrepresentation of minorities in the juvenile justice systems of most of these countries. There are relatively high rates of poverty and youth crime among racial minority adolescent populations in most of the countries in this study, including black and Hispanic youth in the United States of America; black youth in Canada; South Asian and Caribbean youth in England and Wales, and Polynesian youth in New Zealand.

Overrepresentation of indigenous, as well as minority, youth in the juvenile justice systems is also common to these countries. Important examples are the United States, Australia, Canada, and New Zealand, where indigenous groups such as Canadian Aboriginals and the Maori in New Zealand are overrepresented.

Although there is debate about the causes of higher representation of youths from certain ethnic and racial groups in the justice system, there are two basic explanations. First, the social, familial, and economic conditions faced by youths of different racial and ethnic backgrounds affect relative rates of offending behaviour. A second explanation for the overrepresentation of minority and indigenous youth in the justice system is that racism and discriminatory behaviour on the part of police, justice, and corrections officials may affect how youths of different races are dealt with by the justice system. Often the differential treatment in the juvenile system is subtle or unconscious, but it is clear from the countries in this study that overrepresentation of minority and indigenous youth in the juvenile justice systems of these countries is a pervasive and growing problem.

The combination of the changing age and racial composition of the populations of the countries in this study means that juvenile justice issues are likely to be more important and more divisive in the coming years.

Social Change

Over the past 20 years or so, changes in population, age, and ethnicity characteristics have been matched by dramatic social change. All countries report a decrease in family stability. Divorce rates have increased while lessened social stigma for unwed mothers has led many women to opt to raise their children as single parents, and as a result, the number of lone-parent families has increased substantially.

When historical disadvantages faced by women in the economy are considered, it is not surprising that lone-parent families, which are largely female-headed, are substantially more likely to live in poverty. Correspondingly, the countries studied show increases in the number of children living in poverty over the past 20 years. It is notable, however, that there was generally a slight decrease in child poverty rates in the late 1990s, which resulted from increases in employment levels and the booming global economy of that time.

The gradual increases in societal wealth have had positive effects on health and education levels of children and youth. While significant problems remain with respect to access to health care (especially in the United States), across these countries children are more educated and generally healthier than they were 20 years ago. While these trends are promising, there are growing concerns about those adolescents who are not completing their high school education. The employment prospects for those without a good education are shrinking. Most adolescents who are involved with the juvenile justice system also experience difficulty in school, or have dropped out of school, and will face difficulties in securing steady (let alone well-paid) employment as adults.

Further, as some contributors to this book caution, improvements in the general level of health and education of children do not necessarily imply improvement to the condition of disadvantaged groups. Indeed, higher general levels of education and health may serve to increase the social exclusion of some minority groups and make social upward mobility difficult. Increases in education and health levels of more advantaged groups may serve to increase the gap between the haves and have-nots.

Another important, though subtle, social change is the decline in respect for authority. While in certain political respects the countries in this study have become increasingly conservative, in some social respects these countries have become increasingly liberal. The development of a rights-based political environment is reflected in a fundamentally different set of social habits at the day-to-day level of interpersonal interaction. We live in a far less deferential time than the era in which senior citizens today, and even Baby Boomers, came of age. Professionals, high school teachers, and political leaders frequently appear in public in blue jeans and running shoes, clothes that, had they worn them as adolescents, would likely have resulted in their being sent home from school. Adult interactions take place increasingly on a first-name basis. Respect for authority is not displayed with the same deferential manner that it once was. There is greater social tolerance of profanity, and sexual matters are frequently a topic of media commentary.

This new informality has important repercussions for youth. A wider set of limits on the scope of acceptable behaviours means that, to test these limits, which is a normal step in attaining autonomy as one matures, adolescents have to go further. A generation ago, adolescent rebellion might be signaled by wearing blue jeans to school and, for males, by growing long hair. Today, this type of behaviour would be considered perfectly normal, and tattooing and body piercing are common forms of the adolescent (and early adult) search for distinctiveness.

Another social change is the increasing use and abuse of drugs by adolescents. Youth today are more likely to experiment with drugs than they were 20 years ago, and all jurisdictions studied in this book are facing drug abuse problems with their youth.

Adolescents today treat adults in a manner in which previous generations would never have considered behaving towards their elders. This behaviour can be shocking and is easy to perceive as disrespectful. However, less deferential adolescent behaviour simply mirrors a less deferential society.

Dissatisfaction of adults with the behaviour of young people often underpins calls for tougher measures to deal with youth offending. As is discussed below, such "get tough" rhetoric may in part be an unconscious scapegoating of youth in general, as well as reflecting apprehension and confusion about social change.

Trends in Offending Rates

Despite the fact that much public attention has been focused on the issue of youth crime, it is very difficult to get an accurate picture of the extent and nature of youth crime in the countries in this study. While most jurisdictions collect information on reported crime and the rate of charging, the scope and quality of data vary considerably. In Scotland, for example, the police do not record crime by age of the offender. Other countries, such as the United States, Canada, and England and Wales, systematically collect data on the type of offence by age of the alleged offender, but even these data are of limited use in capturing trends over time.

Within the limitations of the statistical information, some interesting trends emerged in this study.

- There was a significant increase in the rate of reported crime and charging of juvenile offenders from the mid-1980s to the mid-1990s in all of the jurisdictions except Scotland (no information) and Northern

Ireland. In New Zealand, while there were increases in the amount of cleared crime attributed to juveniles, there were significant decreases in the number and rate of those being charged since the new legislation came into effect.

- In three jurisdictions, Canada, the United States, and England and Wales, the rate of youth crime increased to the early 1990s and then dropped significantly during the 1990s.

- Although one must be very cautious in making direct comparisons of crime rates between countries due to the differences in the ways in which data are reported, juveniles in the United States are significantly more likely to commit serious violent offences, such as murder and weapons offences, and drug offences than youth in other countries.

- In all countries that collect data on youth crime rates, the reported rates are now significantly higher than they were 20 years ago.

- The use of custody as a sentence for juvenile offenders is more prevalent in the United States and Canada than in any of the other jurisdictions.

- Official data and adolescent self-report studies show that the preponderance of juvenile offending behaviour across all of the countries in this study is not violent. Rather, most of it is property crime, with most of that being minor property crime such as thefts, vandalism, and shoplifting. However, in countries where overall reported youth crime rates have decreased significantly, decreases in property crime have been larger than the decreases in crimes against persons.

- In terms of recent trends in youth offending, most countries (i.e., Canada, the United States, England and Wales, New Zealand, and Australia) reported increases in the proportion of offences committed by female adolescents, though in all countries males continue to commit substantially more offences.

- Countries with indigenous populations all reported significant overrepresentation of these groups in the juvenile justice system. In the United States, black youth are likewise overrepresented in the criminal justice system. The problem of gangs, on the other hand, has decreased significantly in recent years. In Canada, ethnic gangs appear to be an emerging problem.

It is important to be cautious when interpreting official statistics on youth offending behaviour that are based on charges or court files. Changes in these official statistics are affected by such factors as new school policies on reporting of minor offences to the police and changes in police charging practices. However, the public concern in several jurisdictions that youth crime, particularly youth violence, has increased at an alarming rate is not supported by statistics of charges and of reported crime.

All of the chapters in this book indicate that there are very significant discrepancies between self-report data and youth crime statistics. It is clear that most adolescent offending behavior is not reflected in official statistics. While there are significant variations in reporting practices, more serious offences are more likely to result in some type of police response that is likely to be reflected in official statistics.

While no single factor can explain increases or decreases in youth offending rates, there are social circumstances with which increases or decreases in offending behaviour often correlate. It is important to remember that the apparent decrease in youth crime in the latter part of the 1990s came at a time when the economies of these countries were booming and employment levels were increasing. It remains to be seen whether this downtrend in offending rates will continue, though there are some indications that there are unlikely to be further declines in rates of youth offending in the coming years.

Juvenile Justice Systems

Recognizing Adolescence

Modern legal regimes recognize at least three distinct stages of criminal accountability: childhood, juvenile justice, and adulthood.

The first years of life are a period of childhood, without criminal liability, though serious behavioural problems may result in child welfare intervention. The minimum age in the countries in this study for any form of criminal accountability varies from the ages of 7 to 12.

After childhood is a period of what is often referred to as juvenile justice jurisdiction (also called Youth or Children's Court jurisdiction). The minimum and maximum age limits of juvenile court vary substantially between countries, but in all countries in this study, the juvenile justice systems cover a significant portion of adolescence, from at least 12 to 15 years of age.

Even within countries there may be substantial variation in age jurisdiction for juvenile courts, and within one legal system, the age limits have often changed over time. While philosophies and legal regimes vary significantly, the hallmark of the juvenile justice response is that, in comparison to the adult system, it places greater emphasis on rehabilitation with less emphasis on accountability and punishment.

Adulthood provides full legal accountability as well as a full set of adult rights. For criminal law purposes, the minimum age of full adult accountability varies from 16 to 21 years of age.

In some jurisdictions there is, at least in legislative terms, a single juvenile justice regime, while other countries have two or three distinct criminal justice responses to children and youth differing in age from late childhood (from 10 to 13) to early adulthood. Every juvenile justice regime has some provision for treating the most serious youth offenders as adults, at least for some purposes. There is, however, enormous variation in the extent to which these types of provisions are used.

The rationale for this distinctive age-based approach can be found in the basic premises of criminal law and in the nature of childhood and adolescence as distinct periods of life. The fundamental criminal law concept of moral accountability and the policy objective of social protection through deterrence of crime and rehabilitation apply differently to children and youth than to adults, because children and youths are different from adults.

A central premise of criminal law is that individuals are to be held accountable for their acts only if they have a requisite degree of moral culpability or responsibility, often known as the *mens rea* or guilty mind. Adolescents, and even more so children, lack a fully developed adult sense of moral judgment. Adolescents also lack the intellectual and emotional capacity to appreciate fully the consequences of their acts. In many contexts youth will act without foresight or self-awareness, and may lack empathy for those who may be the victims of their wrongful acts. When youths are apprehended and asked why they committed a crime, a common response is: "I don't know."

Because of their lack of judgment and foresight, youths tend to be "poor" criminals as well and, at least in comparison to adults, are relatively easy to apprehend. Not infrequently youths who commit horrible murders will boast of their deeds to their peers, or even take their friends to see the body of the victim, making their arrest inevitable. This is not to argue that adolescent offenders should not be held morally or legally accountable for their criminal acts, but only that their accountability should, in general, be more limited than is the case for adults.

Juvenile Courts

An important function of the criminal justice system is the protection of society through deterrence of potential offenders. People may resist the impulse to commit crimes for fear of being caught and punished. However, because youth, especially those who are prone to committing offences, generally have less foresight and judgment than adults, as well as poorer impulse control, the deterrent effect of the juvenile justice system is much weaker than that of the criminal justice system for adults.

Although improved policing — increasing the chances of getting caught — can have some deterrent effect on some types of youth crime, increasing the severity of sanctions — that is, increasing the consequences of getting caught —

appears to have no impact on youth crime.[2] This is not to argue that there should be no consequences for youths who commit criminal offences, but rather that one should not expect that social protection can be increased by imposing more severe punishments on young offenders. This difference in response to sentencing is one of the rationales for having a juvenile justice system separate from the adult system.

Another rationale for having a separate juvenile court system is that adolescents generally lack the judgment and knowledge to effectively participate in the court process, and may be more vulnerable than adults. This justifies having a special process with special legal rules and procedures for adolescent offenders. Interestingly all of the jurisdictions in this study have youth or children's courts that are in some way separate from the adult courts, though it is not uncommon to have judges dealing with both youth and adult cases, albeit at different times.

Several characteristics of the juvenile justice systems presented in this book are the following:

- Special Training for Juvenile Court Judges — Only England and Wales (for magistrates) and New Zealand currently require special training for juvenile court judges. Other countries, such as Canada and the United States, provide training for judges, but it is not required.

- Adult Sanctions — Every jurisdiction in this study has some mechanism for dealing with youth in adult court or imposing adult-like sanctions. Usually only very serious offenders are transferred and most jurisdictions transfer very few cases. The United States transfers juveniles into adult court and places them in prison with adults at a rate that is many times higher than the rate in any other country.[3]

- Use of Juvenile Records — Half of the jurisdictions in this study (Canada, Scotland, Northern Ireland, and New Zealand) generally do not permit the use of juvenile records when the youth becomes an adult. The others (United States, England and Wales, Republic of Ireland, and Australia), under certain circumstances, permit the use of juvenile records when the youth becomes an adult.

- Legal Aid — All the jurisdictions in this study provide for some type of legal aid (e.g., staff lawyers in clinics or lawyers in private practice paid on a fee-for-service basis) for youths who are arrested. In some jurisdictions, such as England and Wales, access to this type of service is means tested on the basis of parents' income. In most jurisdictions, legal aid services are available only for those youths facing more serious charges, though Canada, the United States, and New Zealand provide for representation by government-paid lawyers for any type of case dealt with in youth court.

- Publication Restrictions — There are restrictions on the publication of identifying information on young offenders in all jurisdictions in this study, except the United States and England and Wales. In the U.S., some states allow for the publication of identifying pictures and information about juveniles, though other states restrict the publication of such material. In England and Wales, it is now up to the discretion of the magistrate as to whether there are reporting restrictions on juvenile trials.

- Parental Responsibilities — Parents of juveniles are required to attend all juvenile court proceedings in all jurisdictions except Canada and the United States. In England and Wales, parental attendance is required for juveniles aged 15 and younger. Most of the jurisdictions in this study do not have legislation that allows for the civil liability of parents of juvenile offenders. However, most American states, Northern Ireland, and the Canadian provinces of British Columbia, Manitoba, and Ontario have legislation providing for the civil liability of parents for damage caused by their children in the course of committing criminal acts. England and Wales are probably the most active in dealing with parental responsibility. In addition to requiring the attendance of parents at proceedings for juveniles aged 15 and younger, parenting orders may require a young offender's parents to attend counseling or guidance sessions. Further, parental "bind-overs" permit the court to order a parent to exercise proper control over a juvenile, including specific terms, and to fine a parent who fails to comply with such an order. Other jurisdictions such as the United States and New Zealand also allow courts to order parents to meet certain conditions for the supervision of juvenile offenders.

- Victim Involvement — In all jurisdictions, increasing the involvement of victims in the juvenile court process is a major current issue. Victim impact statements are commonly used, and in most jurisdictions agencies have been established to provide support for victims.

- Disposition/Range of Services — There is clearly a trend in most jurisdictions to make less use of dispositions involving incarceration and to make greater use of dispositions involving community-based alternatives. Canada, the United States, England and Wales, Scotland, Northern Ireland, Ireland and New Zealand are increasing access to community-based sentencing options, or have plans to do so. In Australia there appears to be a wide range of possible dispositions in urban areas, but in rural areas, there are severe limitations that substantially affect the range of plans available for indigenous offenders.

- Diversion — Diversion of youth who commit offences from the formal court process is increasing in most jurisdictions (see later discussion).

- Police Role — The role of police in dealing with youth varies considerably among the jurisdictions in this study. In the United States, police forces are most likely to take a traditional approach to dealing with youth crime, with the emphasis on enforcement and security. Even in that country, however, police are increasing efforts at "community policing," which may involve working more closely with schools or trying to deal more effectively with youth gangs. Perhaps the most comprehensive and innovative police responses to youth offending are in New Zealand. The Youth Aid Section is a national, specially trained unit; its officers make decisions about diverting young persons or referring them to family group conferences. This unit diverts approximately 60% of the young offenders who have contact with the police. The Australian jurisdictions also have specialized police units similar to the New Zealand model. Likewise, both Northern Ireland and the Republic of Ireland have specially trained Juvenile Liaison Officers and a national program. Most police agencies in England and Wales, Canada, and Scotland do not have specially trained units or officers for dealing with youth crime, but larger police agencies often have special youth bureau units or individual officers who have a special interest in youth issues.

Recent Developments in Juvenile Justice

Legislative Reform

In the late 1990s and the early years of the twenty-first century, a number of countries have enacted, or are on the brink of enacting, a new set of juvenile justice laws. The new legal regimes that these statutes have created or will create vary in how different they are from those they revise or replace. These new statutes include: Canada's new *Youth Criminal Justice Act* (enacted in 2002); the *Crime and Disorder Act 1998* of the United Kingdom; Northern Ireland's *Criminal Justice Order* (also enacted in 1998); Ireland's *Children Act 2001*; and Scotland's *Children Act* of 1995. The juvenile justice system in England and Wales has been radically altered by the new act. The system is now a purely justice-based model, with complete separation from welfare. In other countries, the new statutes are more evolutionary than revolutionary. They do not radically revamp but modify the juvenile justice systems in their respective countries, in some cases in an attempt to make legislation consistent with the United Nations *Convention on the Rights of the Child*.

At this time, it is too soon to be certain how these modified legal regimes will affect juvenile justice in their respective countries, or how they will affect international comparisons. It is apparent, however, that there are some similarities in the new approaches.

In most jurisdictions, public outcry over youth violence has led to an emphasis within new laws and policies on the protection of society and on a more punitive approach. Recently enacted laws in many American states and in England and Wales make adolescents liable to longer sentences at younger ages; these are obvious examples of an increased harshness in new juvenile justice laws. Similarly, Canada's proposed *Youth Criminal Justice Act*, likely to be in force in 2003, and South Australia's new *Juvenile Justice Act* are also intended to respond to the "get tough" political climate and make it easier for youths to receive adult sentences. Paradoxically, some of the new statutes that allow for longer sentences or make it easier to treat juveniles as adult offenders are also enacted with the stated purpose of ensuring better compliance with the international standards set out in the United Nations *Convention on the Rights of the Child*.

Prevention

While some of the rhetoric and policy change has been in the direction of more punitive responses to youth crime, there is also a growing recognition of the value of trying to prevent youth crime rather than merely responding to it. While England and Wales, Canada, the United States, and Australia are probably the leaders in crime prevention, virtually all jurisdictions have established a range of innovative programs with a focus on prevention.

Because there is no single cause of youth crime, prevention strategies have the difficult task of addressing a range of complex problems. Self-report data indicate that virtually all adolescents commit some crimes, but that a disproportionate number of offences can be attributed to a smaller group of persistent, or repeat, offenders. As a small group of persistent offenders are responsible for much youth crime, some prevention strategies focus on this high risk group and are interlinked with rehabilitation.

There are initiatives in a number of countries that are intended to aid early identification of children at high risk of offending, and to support these children and their families in their pre-school and pre-adolescent years. A number of these programs have long-term research components that demonstrate the long-term economic value of early intervention in terms of reducing later offending and reducing teen pregnancy and early school leaving. The recent Report of the U.S. Surgeon General on Youth Violence identifies 27 existing programs that have proven successful in preventing violence and diverting youth away from criminal behavior in the United States.[4]

Diverse school-based programs aimed at the prevention of youth crime have also been put into place. Examples include anti-bullying programs, anti-vandalism campaigns and peace-building initiatives. In some programs, peer-peer mediation is encouraged and facilitated by school staff.[5] Conflict resolution conferences and workshops are being held in schools in many countries.

Some educational programs focus on deterrence. For example, the D.A.R.E. (Drug Abuse Resistance Education) program, which is used in schools in the United States, Canada, the United Kingdom, and New Zealand presents a harsh look at what drugs can do with presentations made by uniformed police officers in classrooms.[6] This type of school-based program, and indeed all prevention and rehabilitation programs, needs to be rigorously studied. Research makes clear that some programs that may appeal to community leaders and adults in general may not actually be effective in preventing adolescent criminal behaviour or drug abuse.[7] Programs need to be developmentally appropriate and focused on the needs of high-risk youth in order to be effective.

Improved policing can have a role in deterring some types of youth crime and increasing community safety. While the prospect of harsher sentences is too remote to affect the behaviour of youths who are likely to offend, increasing the chances of apprehension can affect the behaviour of some youths. Hence community-based policing and increased police presence in schools with high offending rates may have an effect on youth crime. This police presence in schools is paralleled by community policing initiatives and other community-based programs that seek to integrate community resources to help prevent youth crime.

A range of community-based programs can also help prevent youth crime or rehabilitate juvenile offenders. Programs that are community based and work with adolescents and their families are often more effective than those that remove youth from their communities. Multi-agency partnerships for mentoring and employment programs for at-risk youth work to present youth with viable alternatives to crime. New sentencing options such as multi-systemic therapy in the U.S. and Canada bring together community resources to rehabilitate youth who have offended, and so prevent re-offending. Increased use of community resources to sanction youths for offending behaviour and greater emphasis on community reintegration upon release of young offenders from custody are innovations that seek to condition adolescent behaviour in their own community. These have promising prospects. Enhanced use of community-based sentencing alternatives is integral to Canada's new *Youth Criminal Justice Act* and is an important aspect of South Australia's cautioning system.

Certain custodial innovations, such as "boot camps" in the United States and Canada, are a more controversial sentencing option intended to prevent re-offending. Boot camps are intended to provide a "strict discipline" environment, training adolescents to respond to externally imposed discipline. The trouble is that the environment of a "boot camp" in which teens are responding differs fundamentally from that to which they return when released. While the best boot camp programs provide counseling, education, and good community follow-up, and have had some success in reducing recidivism, there is little evidence that merely exposing adolescent offenders to a regime of strict discipline in custody produces positive long-term effects on their behaviour after their release.

Diversion

Diversion is a set of processes based on the idea that most youths who have committed offences should not be dealt with by formal youth court processes but rather should be "diverted" from the system and dealt with informally. Proponents of diversion do not advocate the abolition of juvenile courts, as there are youth who require more intrusive responses that should be regulated by the court process. Rather the proponents of diversion argue for less use of court. Characteristic of most new juvenile justice regimes is an increased reliance on diversion, shifting from formal processes to a re-thinking of who should make decisions and how. Diversion includes both police screening and the use of various community-based programs. The community-based programs are often less intrusive and more informal, expeditious, and cost-effective. They may also permit greater involvement of members of the community, victims, and parents of juvenile offenders than is possible in the formal court system.

Many diversion programs incorporate a restorative justice philosophy, with an effort to leave victims feeling that offenders have apologized and accepted responsibility for their acts. Some form of restitution and compensation to victims is a common feature of diversion programs.

An innovative and influential new forum for juvenile justice in these countries is developing out of traditional practices of New Zealand's indigenous Maori. The juvenile justice regime in New Zealand now makes extensive use of "family group conferences," informal sessions in which the youth, his or her parents, other relatives, community members, and the victim of the crime come together to discuss what should be done. Just as the 1899 Juvenile Court of Illinois became the model for youth courts throughout these countries in diverting juveniles from the adult system, New Zealand's family group conferences are providing a model for legislation elsewhere, diverting many youths from the court process. In both Queensland and South Australia, as well as in the United States, Canada, and England and Wales, family group conferences are being instituted based on the New Zealand model.

An aspect of diversion is changing who will decide what consequences an adolescent must face. In South Australia, the formal caution system now allows a police officer to require a youth to make "undertakings" to carry out certain plans as an aspect of a formal police warning. There is also increased use by police of informal and restorative responses to minor crimes where the community and the family are involved in proceedings. In effect, the police are carrying out certain functions that in the past were done by courts. These informal processes, while at least in part modelled on Aboriginal practices, are also in some respects similar to the Scottish Children's Hearings, which for many years have been used as a means to deal with offending behaviour by 7- to 15-year-olds. These similarities reflect the fact that diversion has been a common theme of juvenile justice regimes from their inception.

Diversion, originally from the adult justice and corrections system, and now from formal juvenile courts, is a thread connecting the welfare model regimes characteristic of the juvenile justice systems of the first half of the twentieth century with the newer legislation. While diversion has an important role in youth justice, it should only be implemented in a way that respects the rights of youth, and should not be used as a means of denying innocent youth the opportunity for due process.

A More Nuanced Approach

New juvenile justice regimes, such as Canada's *Youth Criminal Justice Act,* have some provisions that are intended to increase use of police cautioning and community diversion, and other provisions that are likely to increase the number of youths receiving adult sentences. It may seem paradoxical that in several countries there are trends both towards greater harshness for the most serious offenders and a greater emphasis on prevention, restorative justice, and diversion. This type of legislative reform is difficult to analyze using the traditional concepts of "welfare" and "justice" models. What is similar about some of these new legal regimes, and what may help social scientists and lawyers make sense of their internal logic, is that they offer more nuanced responses to adolescent offending. Different youth have different types of problems, and the legal responses, programs, and facilities that may be appropriate for one youth may not be appropriate for another.

It seems that what is evolving out of this legislation may not be one new juvenile justice system, but a series of overlapping systems designed to deal with different types of offending behaviour. Given the diverse nature of the antisocial behaviours lumped together as youth crime, there is obvious wisdom in allowing for a greater range of responses.

For minor or first-time youth offending, various forms of diversion such as warnings or cautions are clearly likely to be the most cost-effective and humane response. It is clear that serious and persistent youth offenders require different responses from other youth. There is, however, a real concern that some responses to the more serious and persistent youth offenders may result in a society that has less protection in the long term rather than more. For a relatively small group of youth offenders in each country, there is a need for removal from the community. But responses that are merely punitive, or incarcerate youths without access to appropriate educational and rehabilitative services, or that treat adolescent offenders as adults, will only result in a society that has more crime in the long run.

Notes

1. This concluding chapter summarizes the material presented in the individual chapters. In addition, after the chapters had all been submitted, the editors of the book interviewed each of the contributors. The interviews focused on clarification and explanation of trends and components of the juvenile justice systems. Some of the information from the interviews is also incorporated into this concluding chapter.

   In May 1998, as the preparation of this book was beginning, the contributors of the individual chapters and editors of this volume met at a conference held in Ottawa, presenting some of the material that is in this volume and discussing trends in youth justice. Ideas from some of those discussions are also reflected in this chapter and in Chapter 1.

2. See, for example, A.N. Doob, V. Marinos, and K.N. Varma, *Youth Crime and the Youth Justice System in Canada: A Research Perspective* (Toronto: Centre of Criminology, University of Toronto, 1995).

3. There are significant difficulties in directly comparing the rates at which juveniles are treated as adults. Some of the difficulties arise because of differences in the age at which adult criminal responsibility begins. Further, comparative rates could be based on total, adolescent populations, populations of adolescent offenders, or could in some way be controlled by the offence mix. On any measure, far more juvenile offenders are treated as adults in the United States than in any of the other countries.

4. *Youth Violence, A Report of the Surgeon General* (2001). Website: www.surgeongeneral.gov/library/youth violence/sgsummary.htm.

5. For a Canadian example, see Paiement et al., *Resolve it! The National Youth Conference on Peacebuilding and Conflict Resolution.* YouCan 1999.

6. See website: www.dare.com.

7. *Youth Violence, A Report of the Surgeon General.* Website: www.surgeongeneral.gov/library/youthviolence/chapter 5.

Quebec, Canada
2002